THE IDEA OF ORDER

The Idea of Order

The Circular Archetype in Prehistoric Europe

RICHARD BRADLEY

OXFORD

UNIVERSITY PRESS

OXFORD
UNIVERSITY PRESS

Great Clarendon Street, Oxford, OX2 6DP,
United Kingdom

Oxford University Press is a department of the University of Oxford.
It furthers the University's objective of excellence in research, scholarship,
and education by publishing worldwide. Oxford is a registered trade mark of
Oxford University Press in the UK and in certain other countries

British Library Cataloguing in Publication Data
Data available

Library of Congress Cataloging in Publication Data
Data available

ISBN 978-0-19-960809-6

Printed in Great Britain by
MPG Books Group, Bodmin and King's Lynn

For my colleagues and students in Reading, 1971–2011

Preface

The title of the book comes from a poem by Wallace Stevens: 'The Idea of Order at Key West'. The subtitle is more prosaic but more exact. This is a study of prehistoric architecture and conceptions of space, which investigates the importance of the circle to people in the past.

I became interested in the subject as soon as I took up archaeology. As I describe in Chapter Two, one powerful stimulus was a conference held in London four decades ago. A more recent source of inspiration has been a series of excavations I have carried out since 1994 at stone circles and related monuments in Scotland, some of them conducted jointly with my colleague Amanda Clarke. I first wrote about circular monuments in the 1990s, but that discussion was limited to the evidence from Britain and Ireland and considered only a small part of a larger picture. I have been encouraged to broaden my horizons by presenting papers at conferences at University College Dublin and Kiel University, and, most recently, by giving the Albert Reckitt Lecture at the British Academy.

Another important stimulus was visiting prehistoric monuments with colleagues who have discussed many of these ideas. They include Lara Bacelar Alves, Ana Bettencourt, Charlotte Fabech, Ramón Fábregas, Joakim Goldhahn, Eoin Grogan, Mats Larsson, Ulf Näsman, Peter Skoglund, and Dag Widholm. I must also thank Lara Bacelar Alves, Chris Evans, and Antonio Carlos Valera for copies of publications which are currently in press, and Ruth Van Dyke for sending me her important book, *The Chaco Experience*.

I am especially grateful to Bob Chapman and Mike Fulford for reading and commenting on parts of the text, and to Hella Eckardt, Ramón Fábregas, Tony Mathews, and Evi Riikonen for their help with the bibliography. Elise Fraser helped prepare the final text for the press. The fine photograph of the Castro de Baroña was provided by Lara Bacelar Alves. Like my other work, this book could not have been written without Katherine's understanding and support.

The figure drawings are the work of Margaret Mathews who has prepared them with her customary efficiency and eye for detail. In a few cases they incorporate material provided by Aaron Watson. I am very grateful for her contribution. Where they draw on published material, the sources of the illustrations are noted on pp. xii–xv. Every attempt has been made to seek the permission of the copyright holders, but in a few cases this has not been possible. This omission will be rectified if more information becomes available.

I joined the staff of Reading University not long after I attended the conference on '*Man, Settlement and Urbanism*', and I have worked there ever since. It is a stimulating environment in which to do research and I am grateful to successive Vice Chancellors, Deans, and Heads of Department for allowing me the time to complete this, and other, projects. For that reason, I am dedicating the book to my colleagues and students at the university.

Table of Contents

List of Figures   xii

Part I: Times and Spaces

1 *The Circular Ruins*   3
  The middle land   3
  A circular archetype?   7
  The distribution of circular architecture in prehistoric Europe   10
    The organization of space and the adoption of farming   10
    An accommodation between circular and rectilinear forms   13
    Identities, exchange, and the persistence of circular architecture   17
    Circular monuments and rectangular dwellings   19
  The organization of the argument   20
    The four parts of the book   20
    The individual chapters   20
  The circular ruins   24

2 *Conceptions and Perceptions*   25
  Two ways of looking at houses   25
  Functional considerations in the study of houses   27
  Some caveats   32
  Symbolic considerations in the study of houses   33
  Modelling the cosmos   36
  Perceptions and preconceptions   39
  Summary: three relationships   41
  Another caveat   43

3 *Life and Art*   46
  Introduction: unearthing ancient art   46
  Cultural geometry   48
  Symbols in action   49
    The Nuba   50
    The Nankani   51
  Patterning in prehistory   52
    The Linear Pottery Culture   53
    Grooved Ware and megalithic art   53
    Bell Beaker artefacts, settlements, and monuments
    in the British Isles   56

Bronze Age settlements, pottery, and metalwork in
Northern Europe   57
Art styles and the domestic architecture of the
European Iron Age   59
The 'ultimate La Tène' in Ireland   62
Ideas of order   64
Sacred and secular   65
Female and male   67
Conclusion   68

Part II: Circular Structures in a Circular World

4 *Houses into Tombs*   71
Aillevans and Sant' Andrea Priu   71
The deaths of houses   74
Circular tombs, rectangular tombs   76
The connection between houses and tombs   79
Circular houses and circular monuments   79
Rectangular houses and rectangular monuments   81
Insights from ethnography   84
Chronological relationships between circular
and rectilinear tombs   86
The cemetery at Bougon   88
Summary and conclusions   89

5 *Turning to Stone*   93
Stone and wood   93
Statues and standing stones   95
Stone circles and stone alignments   98
Stone circles and passage graves   102
Stone circles and henge monuments   107
Summary   112

6 *The Enormous Room*   115
Sea and Sardinia   115
The growth of towers   115
The language of size   120
The round earth   125
Circles, ringworks, and royal centres   125
Neolithic monuments   126
Late Bronze Age and Iron Age monuments   130
Uisneach again   135

Part III: Circular Structures in a Rectilinear World

7 *Significant Forms* 139
Tells, roundels, and flat settlements 139
Barrows, sanctuaries, and shrines 146
Ismantorp and Eketorp 151
An overview 156
Coda 159

8 *The Attraction of Opposites* 161
Thorny Down and De Bogen 161
Stora Kalvö 164
Mortuary houses and cult houses 167
Mortuary houses and domestic dwellings 169
Juxtaposition, succession, and belief 169
Degrees of separation 173
Chronological patterns 175
Round barrows and roundhouses in the
Bronze Age of Britain and Ireland 177
Barrows and houses in Northern Europe:
a speculative model 180

9 *The New Order* 184
Observations in Africa 184
From huts to houses 186
Roundhouses in Britannia 189
Two examples 192
Silchester 192
Piercebridge 194
The end of an archetype: the Castro Culture
in Portugal and Spain 195
The end of an archetype: Early Medieval Ireland 199

Part IV: Summing Up

10 *From Centre to Circumference* 207
Dialogues between designs 207
Histories of the circle 209
Geographies of the circle 213
Epilogue: the view from Loughcrew 217

References 219
Index 239

List of Figures

1 The area visible from Uisneach. Information from Macalister and
Praeger (1928)　　4

2 The provinces of Early Medieval Ireland. Information from
Rees and Rees (1961)　　5

3 The sequence at Rathnew, Uisneach. Information from Macalister
and Praeger (1928) and Schot (2006)　　6

4 Map showing the principal forms of houses in prehistoric Europe　　10

5 Round and square house plans in Neolithic Cyprus. Information from
Dikaios and Stewart (1962) and Steel (2004)　　12

6 House plans at Serra Órrios-Dorgàli. Information from Liliu (1988)　　14

7 Bronze Age house plans at Monte Castellaccio di Imola and Rome.
Information from Bietti Sestieri (2010) and Carandini and Cappelli (2007)　　15

8 Excavation plan of the Rath of the Synods, Tara. Information from
Grogan (2008)　　18

9 The pattern of replacement of roundhouses and rectangular dwellings　　29

10 The sequence of replacement and extension of houses at Ein el-Hariri,
Weisweiler, and Elsloo. Information from Rowan and Golden (2009)
and Rück (2009)　　31

11 Perceptions of the landscape from settlements in open and closed
environments　　35

12 Simplified plan of a Pirá-paraná longhouse. Information from
Hugh-Jones (1979)　　36

13 The layout of a Navajo hogan. Information from Griffin-Pierce (1992)　　37

14 The *axis mundi* linking the planes of a three-tier cosmos　　39

15 Round and rectangular buildings as microcosms of the local
environment　　42

16 A circular public building at Jerf-al-Ahmad, Syria. Information from
Akkermans and Schwartz (2003)　　44

17 A building model from the Balkans, and two house urns from Italy.
Information from Naumov (2007 and 2009) and Sabatini (2007)　　47

18 Mesakin Qisar and Nankani settlement plans and house decoration.
Information from Hodder (1982) and Cole (2000)　　50

19 Sequence of Linear Pottery Culture longhouses and decorated vessels
in north-west Germany. Information from Stöckli (2005)　　54

20 Linear and curvilinear decoration in Late Neolithic Britain and Ireland. Information from Bradley (2009) 55

21 Outline plans of Bell Beaker houses in Europe. Information from Besse and Desideria (2005) with additions and modifications 57

22 An unprovenanced Early Bronze Age belt ornament from southern Sweden and the plan of a longhouse of the same date at Skydstrup, Denmark. Information from Randsborg (2006) 58

23 Curvilinear motifs employed in Celtic Art. Information from Jacobsthal (1944) 61

24 'Ultimate La Tène' motifs at Inishkea, Ireland. Information from Henry (1965) 63

25 The structural sequence at Aillevans, and a reconstruction of the timber building on the site. Information from Pétrequin and Pinigre (1976) 71

26 Plan and cross section of the subterranean tomb at Sant' Andrea Priu. Information from Lilliu (1988) 73

27 Regional patterns in the external appearance of chambered mounds and cairns in Europe. 77

28 Outline plans of the Maeshowe chambered tomb and an above-ground building at Barnhouse. Information from Bradley, Phillips, Richards and Webb (2001) 81

29 The megalithic tomb at Aveny and the decoration in its entrance. Information from Shee Twohig (1981) 85

30 Regional contrasts in the treatment of the houses and the dead in Neolithic England and Ireland 85

31 Chambered tombs overlying Neolithic houses at Damsbo. Information from Andersen (2009) 87

32 Outline sequence of mortuary monuments at Bougon. Information from Mohen and Scarre (2002) 88

33 The structural sequence at Lochill, illustrating the use of stone and timber. Information from Noble (2006) 94

34 The positions of the Carnac alignments in relation to the Neolithic coastline. Information from Cassen (2009) and Scarre (2011) 99

35 Megalithic enclosure, long barrow, and stone alignment at Kerlescan. Information from Bradley (2002) 100

36 Outline plan of the passage grave and stone circle at Newgrange. Information from O'Kelly (1982) 102

37 Plans of four chambered tombs associated with stone circles. Information from Henshall (1972), Burl (2000), Bradley (2000b), and Burrow (2010) 103

38 The chronological relationship between stone circles and passage graves   106

39 The spatial organization of Irish passage graves. Information from
     Robin (2009)   108

40 The structure of henges in relation to the rites of passage   110

41 Outline plans of Sardinian nuraghi and chambered tombs. Information
     from Lilliu (1988)   117

42 Plan of a Sardinian 'sacred well'. Information from Lilliu (1988)   119

43 The structure of a Majorcan talayot   122

44 Plans of Late Neolithic houses and timber circles in Britain and Ireland.
     Information from Bradley (2007)   127

45 Plan of the henge monument at Durrington Walls. Information from Parker
     Pearson (2007) and Thomas (2007)   129

46 Plans of the enclosures at Mucking and Thwing. Information from
     Manby (2007) and Evans and Lucy (in press)   131

47 Two successive structures at Navan Fort. Information from
     Waterman (1997)   133

48 Two schemes summarizing the subdivision of ancient Ireland with
     Midh at its centre.   136

49 Plan of the tell and surrounding earthworks at Uivar. Information from
     Schier (2008)   141

50 Plan of the tell and open settlmement at Polgár-Csöszhalom.
     Information from Raczky and Anders (2008)   142

51 Plans of the circular monuments at Goseck and Quenstedt. Information
     from Biehl (2007 and 2010) and Behrens (1981)   143

52 Outline plans of the temple complexes at Perigueux and Thetford.
     Information from Coupry (1977) and Gregory (1991)   148

53 The reused round barrows at Ursel-Rozenstraat and Haddenham.
     Information from Bourgeois (1998) and Evans and Hodder (2006)   150

54 Plans of the ringforts at Ismantorp and Eketorp. Information from
     Andrén (2006) and Borg, Näsman and Wegraeus (1976)   152

55 Plan of the cemetery at Gåtebo, Öland. Information from Beskow
     Sjöberg (1987)   153

56 The relationship between Pueblo Bonito and the Great Kiva of Casa
     Rinconada. Information from Van Dyke (2007)   157

57 Alternative reconstructions of the Bronze Age settlement of
     Thorny Down. Information from Piggott (1965) and
     Ellison (1987)   162

58 The sequence at De Bogen. Information from Bourgeois and Fontijn (2008) and Meijlink (2008) 163

59 The siting of monuments on the island of Stora Kalvö 165

60 Round barrows associated with rectilinear structures at three sites in Denmark. Information from Aner and Kersten (1973 and 1978) and Nielsen and Beck (2004) 167

61 The relationship between longhouses and round barrows at two sites in Germany and Denmark. Information from Bradley (2005b) 171

62 Bronze Age house urns in the form of a raised granary. Information from Bradley (2005b) 173

63 The relationship between houses and round barrows at Eigenblock-West and Itford Hill. Information from Bourgeois and Fontijn (2008) and Bradley (1998) 176

64 Timber avenues leading to round barrows at sites in Northern Europe. Information from Thörn (2007) and Fokkens and Jansen (2004) 182

65 The relationship between rectilinear and curvilinear compounds in Cameroon. Information from Lyons (1996) 186

66 The changing forms of stone buildings in Sicily. Information from Hodos (2006) 189

67 Circular and polygonal temples in Roman Britain. Information from Lewis (1966) 192

68 The relationship between a roundhouse and a range of rectangular buildings at Silchester. Information from Clarke, Fulford, Rains and Tootell (2007) 193

69 The structural sequence at Piercebridge. Information from Cool and Mason (2008) 194

70 Plan of the Castro at Cividade de Terroso. Information from Da Silva (1986) 197

71 Circular buildings and streets inside the Castro at Sanfins. Information from Da Silva (1986) 199

72 Plan of the excavated ringfort of Dressogagh Rath. Information from Collins (1966) 201

73 Neolithic carved design from the passage grave at Loughcrew, and details of the decoration on two Iron Age bone flakes. Information from Shee Twohig (1981) and Raftery (1984) 209

74 The dual character of prehistoric Europe during the Neolithic period and the Late Bronze Age. 216

Part I

Times and Spaces

1

The Circular Ruins

This is not a book about a period or a place; it is about an idea. Why did so many people in prehistoric Europe build circular monuments? Why did they choose to live in circular houses, when other communities rejected them? Why was it that those who preferred to inhabit a world of rectangular dwellings so often buried their dead in round mounds and worshipped their gods in circular temples? The best way of introducing such questions is through a specific example.

THE MIDDLE LAND

Certain monuments exert a special fascination.

Beside the road at Uisneach in the Irish Republic is a signboard which makes some remarkable claims. This was the 'site of the Celtic festival of Beltane' and 'an ancient place of assembly'. It was associated with 'the Druidic fire cult' and the 'seat of Irish kings'. The notice makes a still more intriguing assertion, for the Hill of Uisneach was also the 'sacred centre of Ireland in pagan times'.

The archaeology of the hill is hardly less remarkable, and it is easy to see how it has suggested such ideas. Some interpretations of the site are based on its distinctive topography, and others on literary evidence (Schot 2006, 2011).

The hill is an irregular plateau which rises out of an extensive plain. It is also at the junction of two different landscapes. To the east, there have been many discoveries dating from the prehistoric and early medieval periods. To the west, where the soil is less fertile, they are comparatively rare. Uisneach dominates the view from all directions. It also commands an extensive vista on every side. Indeed, Macalister and Praeger (1928) who studied its archaeology over eighty years ago published a map showing the land that can be seen from the hilltop. Although it is claimed that twenty Irish counties are represented, the area does not extend as far as the coast (Figure 1). Not all those regions can be observed from a single point. In order to appreciate the full extent of the view, it is necessary to move between a series of ancient

Figure 1 The area visible from the Irish royal centre at Uisneach.

monuments. In the 1928 map the area surveyed from Uisneach is notably irregular, but one receives an entirely different impression on the ground, for the hill seems to be located at the centre of an enormous circular landscape.

Uisneach has other distinctive features. There are a number of pools, which can appear or disappear as a result of local hydrology. It is also the source of several streams and rivers. Towards its western limit is an enormous glacial erratic known as the Cat Stone.

All these elements feature in early Irish literature. They also play an important part in folklore. As the notice board suggests, for a long time Uisneach has been identified as the centre of Ireland. In some accounts, it was associated with Midh—the 'middle land'—and in other schemes it was the meeting point of the ancient provinces of Ireland—Ulster, Leinster, Connaught, and Munster (Rees and Rees 1961: Chapter 5; Figure 2). It played an important role in the geography of the early Middle Ages and, for a time, it may have provided a neutral location for ceremonies taking place on the margins of these kingdoms. A new study suggests that Uisneach was originally a sacred site, quite different from royal capitals like Tara (Schot 2011). Only later did people live there.

There was a holy well and also a sacred tree on the site at Uisneach. The idea that the hill was at the middle of the island was expressed in several ways. It was thought that Uisneach was the source of all the Irish rivers. Similarly, the eroded appearance of the Cat Stone suggested the notion that different parts of the rock faced each of the provinces of Ireland. It was interpreted as 'umbilicus Hibernie'—the navel of the country.

Figure 2 A reconstruction of the provinces of Early Medieval Ireland.

At the same time, there has been a long-established belief that this was where the festival of Beltane was celebrated. It was one of the fixed points of the ritual calendar in Ireland and took place at the beginning of May, midway between the spring equinox and the summer solstice. This was when cattle were driven between two fires to protect them from disease. Given the prominent location of the hill, the flames would have been visible from far away. Indeed, early writers believed that great assemblies were held at Uisneach.

The hill contains at least twenty ancient monuments and more have been located by geophysical survey (Schot 2011). Perhaps the most prominent are the two conjoined circular enclosures at Rathnew, which may have been approached by a walled avenue or roadway (Macalister and Praeger 1928). There was also a megalithic tomb, whilst a round mound close to the most prominent monument was located at the centre of a circular ditched enclosure no less than 200 metres in diameter. Recent fieldwork has shown that the Hill of Uisneach also contained a considerable number of small circular barrows or ring ditches. They probably commemorated the dead, although none has been excavated.

The fieldwork undertaken by Macalister and Praeger focused on the two linked enclosures at Rathnew, each of which contained the remains of a stone house, as well as other features dating from the first millennium AD (Figure 3). Beneath one of these earthworks was the site of an older, circular enclosure associated with a deposit of animal bones and a considerable amount of burnt

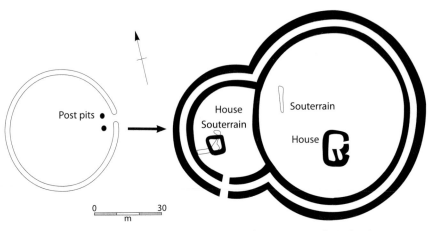

Figure 3 Outline of the structural sequence at Rathnew, Uisneach, Ireland.

material. All these features suggested links with the legendary history of the hill. The bones were interpreted as evidence of feasting, whilst the two earthworks, which formed a figure of eight, were strikingly similar to those at Navan Fort and Tara, which were among the royal capitals mentioned in early Irish literature (Newman 1997; Waddell et al. 2009). At the same time, the evidence for burning recalls the tradition that the Hill of Uisneach was associated with ceremonies involving fires. That is why the modern notice board refers to a 'Druidic fire cult'.

The archaeological evidence from the Cat Stone is even more striking. It is a massive rock and at one time was interpreted, quite implausibly, as a megalithic tomb. In fact, it was carried to Uisneach by melting ice and shows no sign of any modification by the people who used the hill. It is not located in a central position, nor is it an especially prominent feature of the terrain. That makes it all the more remarkable that it assumed such special connotations. It is associated with only one ancient monument. The surface around the base of the stone seems to have been quarried to create a platform, whilst the excavated material was used to build a bank. As a result, the navel of Ireland is located at the centre of another circular enclosure. That earthwork is not unlike the ring barrows elsewhere on the hill whose history is thought to extend from the Early Bronze Age to the Iron Age.

Schot (2011) has shown how the sacred associations of Uisneach have played a part in the political history of medieval Ireland. It happened because in later times people could draw on the legendary associations of the site. To a certain extent, that process involved what Hobsbawm and Ranger (1983) have termed 'the invention of tradition'. It has happened again in recent years. After a long period during which the significance of the hill was largely forgotten, the landowner has instituted an annual Fire Festival (www.festivalofthefires.com).

This is not the place to discuss contemporary use of Uisneach, but two details are important here. The modern festival involves the construction of a series of temporary wooden buildings which share a common characteristic: all of them are approximately circular in plan, just as nearly all the ancient monuments on the site conform to a similar outline. At the same time, some of the structures erected for the festival were embellished with curvilinear designs of the kind characterized as 'Celtic art'. In this respect, the festival may echo the concerns of those who originally assembled on the hilltop.

Of course it was a deliberate decision to reflect the configuration of the local monuments, but those structures form only part of a much wider pattern in Ireland, where many prehistoric settlements, houses, fortifications, and burial mounds conform to a circular outline. The evidence extends from Neolithic monuments like the megalithic tombs of the Boyne Valley to the royal centres of the Irish Iron Age. It even includes some of the earliest monasteries. By renewing this tradition for the Fire Festival, the owner was acknowledging a way of organizing space which was epitomized by many of the existing features on the hill: the ring forts and the ring barrows; a great enclosure discovered by geophysical survey; even the distinctive earthwork that surrounds the Cat Stone. But it was a pattern that extended further still, for the view from the hilltop is of a vast circular landscape, whilst, in local legend, the site itself is the exact centre of Ireland. Uisneach illustrates the importance of circular architecture in European archaeology, but why did that tradition develop in the first place and how can its persistence be explained?

A CIRCULAR ARCHETYPE?

For some scholars there is an easy answer to both questions. Circular structures, particularly roundhouses, are a special feature of the westernmost limits of Europe. In other areas, rectilinear buildings are the commonest, and usually the only, form. The presence of circular dwellings in Britain and Ireland has always been one of the features that distinguish the insular Iron Age from its counterpart in mainland Europe. In the same way, the persistence of circular monuments, including domestic buildings, has been considered as a special feature of those regions which remained outside the Roman world. To some extent, that argument has been applied to Scottish sites, but the idea has been much more influential in Ireland (Harding 2009). Recent research also emphasizes the importance of long distance connections along the Atlantic coastline. As a result, Iron Age settlements in Brittany have been drawn into the discussion and, occasionally, such studies have extended even further to the south to take account of circular dwellings of the same date in the Iberian Peninsula (Cunliffe 2001: Chapters 7–9; Henderson 2007: Chapters 6 and 7).

Such approaches have obvious limitations. Most accounts have been concerned with the distribution and chronology of roundhouses, but these buildings form only one component of a more general tradition of circular architecture. Uisneach illustrates this point, for here it is not the dwellings that assume a curvilinear outline but a variety of different structures, including enclosures and mounds. The same point is relevant in other areas where roundhouses have been identified. For example, it applies to walled enclosures whose circular outline echoes the configuration of the domestic buildings within them. That is as true in Portugal or Spain as it is in Ireland.

Another problem concerns the chronology of circular architecture. The difficulty arises because later prehistoric settlements are often easier to identify and excavate than their predecessors. It is true that in certain parts of Europe, of which the Atlantic coastline provides a good example, houses seem to have been rather more robust from the middle of the Bronze Age. Before that time there are areas in which they left little trace. However, that does not apply to other circular structures, such as passage tombs, henge monuments, round barrows, and cairns. They had an altogether longer history and that is why it is important to study a more extended sequence. It is not easy to do so when many prehistorians are period specialists.

The emphasis on Atlantic Europe has drawn attention away from other areas in which circular architecture played an important role. To some extent it happened because this style was superseded by a different structural tradition, but it means that the striking evidence from the Mediterranean is often overlooked or, even worse, is studied in different terms from the use of space in the west. This difficulty is particularly obvious where long sequences are available for study. Excavation suggests that, in most regions, the last hunter gatherers and the earliest farmers employed circular buildings. In many areas they were rapidly replaced by rectilinear dwellings, but that was not always true. There are other cases in which they retained their importance for a longer period of time. It follows that the unusually durable architecture of the Iron Age may be entirely exceptional. It cannot provide a satisfactory basis for a more ambitious study. It is necessary for researchers to range widely across space and time.

It seems possible that this emphasis on prehistoric architecture may also be too limited. It is concerned with the shapes and construction methods of different kinds of building, but it overlooks the important information provided by portable artefacts. One of the strongest arguments that the distinction between curvilinear and rectilinear forms possessed a wider significance is that it was not confined to the built environment. There are regions in which the contrast between these designs went even further. In some cases circular structures were used by people who employed curvilinear motifs on their pottery and metalwork; perhaps this idea is conveyed by the decorative motifs associated with the modern festival at Uisneach. In other cases the opposite was true and, in the past, settlements composed of circular buildings were associated with objects embellished with entirely linear decoration. Of course, there were communities in which it did not happen, but there are sufficient examples of this relationship to suggest that the distinction between these forms should be part of a broader enquiry.

That is why the title of this book refers to a circular 'archetype'. This word is employed in its definition of 'an original model or prototype' on which other examples are based; it can also be a 'recurrent symbol in art' (*The Concise Oxford Dictionary*). The term is not used in the more specialized sense found in Jung's account of the collective unconscious (Jung 1980), nor does it have the spiritual dimension invoked by Eliade (1954). In this discussion it is intended to suggest the ubiquity of circular forms in prehistoric architecture and the design of objects. It is also meant to imply that this form could persist for a long time. That is not to overlook the differences between the media in which it was expressed, from earthwork building to pottery decoration and from metalworking to house construction. However, it will be easier to identify the themes that need to be addressed by moving from the general to the particular. That is what this book attempts to do.

It would be possible to explore in detail the chronologies, forms, and distributions of different types of prehistoric architecture, but that would occupy a volume on its own. Moreover, such an account would be largely descriptive. Not only might it overlook exceptional cases, it could under-emphasize some significant points. The reason for studying the circular archetype is to relate this evidence to other characteristics of prehistoric society in Europe. For that reason, the main emphasis will be on detailed studies of periods, regions and sites whose archaeological evidence raises points of wider interest. This is why there is such an emphasis on case studies. They are organized thematically, but each example illustrates a wider point. In order to see these patterns in perspective it is necessary to sketch the extent of that phenomenon as a whole.

There are two ways of achieving this. The first would be a chronological review akin to studies of early agriculture or metalworking, but there is a risk of losing the reader amidst a mass of detail. A second method is adopted here. There are, perhaps, four different *strands* in the establishment of circular structures in prehistoric Europe and their relationship to an alternative tradition of rectilinear architecture. There is still more diversity in their relations with other aspects of visual culture, yet the broad outlines are clear enough to allow a brief summary of this evidence.

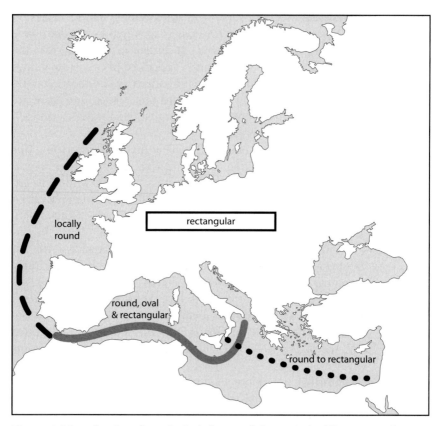

Figure 4 Map showing the principal forms of domestic buildings in prehistoric Europe.

THE DISTRIBUTION OF CIRCULAR ARCHITECTURE IN PREHISTORIC EUROPE (FIGURE 4)

The organization of space and the adoption of farming

The first strand is associated with the adoption of agriculture. In most cases it is characterized by the initial replacement of circular dwellings by rectilinear buildings. This chapter has already made the point that hunter gatherers throughout Europe tended to occupy circular structures. This way of organizing domestic space seems to have been practically universal, but that is not to deny that there are rare exceptions. There appear to have been rectilinear houses in the Mesolithic of Northern Europe where Grøn (1995) has explored the forms of living sites. Similarly, some of the best known structures dating from this period are those at Lepenski Vir, but this remarkable site is perhaps the exception that proves the rule (Borić 2003). The people who erected these trapezoidal buildings were already in contact with neighbouring farmers and it is by no means certain that all these constructions were dwellings.

The clearest sequence is found in Southwest Asia where there is the first evidence for the domestication of plants and animals. It took place during the Neolithic period. Here, there is a revealing problem of terminology. For Childe, the 'Neolithic revolution' could be characterized by a series of distinct elements: domesticated cereals and livestock; sedentary settlements with permanent dwellings; and a new material culture that included pottery and ground stone tools (1958: Chapter 3). Those features no longer appear to be associated with one another. Wild plants and animals may have been domesticated at different times in different regions; the first farmers did not necessarily live in permanent settlements and pottery was not used at the beginning of this period. That accounts for the use of the ungainly term 'Pre-pottery Neolithic'. It is directly relevant to the present account. Despite the evidence for economic change, Pre-Pottery Neolithic A (PPNA) dwellings were circular structures, whilst those of the next phase (PPNB) were generally rectilinear (Kuijt 2000; Kuijt and Goring-Morris 2002; Watkins 2004, 2008, 2010). The change has given rise to various interpretations that relate house form to social and economic factors. They will be considered in Chapter 2. For present purposes, it is enough to say that new developments in the organization of living space did not always happen at the *beginning* of the Neolithic period in this area.

Of course, there are exceptions to the trend. Some may arise from purely practical considerations, whilst others could have a more lasting significance. It is difficult to fit small structures into a dense concentration of circular houses, and there are settlements where small square buildings may have been inserted in between them (Figure 5). They need not have been dwellings. There are other examples in which settlements in peripheral areas—possibly ones that were occupied for only part of the year—still consisted of circular buildings when a rectilinear layout had been adopted elsewhere. In fact, there are instances in which the circular form came back into use as exploitation of the landscape changed. That occurred in Northern Syria (Akkermans and Schwartz 2003: 103–5), but such a sequence is unusual. There are many cases in which rectilinear architecture replaced a pattern of curvilinear dwellings, but very few changes in the opposite direction.

The contrast is even more apparent in regions where farming was introduced from outside. It seems possible that it happened as people colonized new land—it is certainly true that in these areas the wild prototypes of the domesticated animals and plants were not available. The best example is provided by the settlement of two large islands in the Mediterranean: Cyprus and Crete. Here, there is an interesting contrast. The oldest buildings at Knossos are rectangular (Evans 1971), but those in Cyprus are roundhouses

Khirokitia   Sotira-Teppes

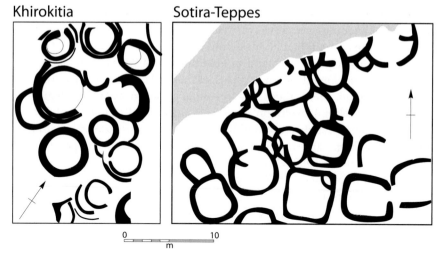

0 _____ 10
          m

Figure 5 Plans of Neolithic roundhouses at Khirokitia, and circular and square buildings at Sotira-Teppes, Cyprus.

which can be identified in considerable numbers (Steel 2004: Chapters 3 and 4). In this case, the change to rectangular dwellings came later. The inhabitants of both islands practiced an agricultural economy, but such contrasts in their use of space lasted for a long time. That is one reason for supposing that architectural forms were not necessarily dictated by the character of the subsistence economy.

The same point can be made in other parts of prehistoric Europe. From Anatolia to the Balkans, the first farmers are associated with rectangular dwellings, but there is evidence that these buildings replaced pit houses, some of which were circular (Bailey 2000: 153–5 and 264–5). The rectilinear buildings could be densely packed together and individual dwellings may have been burnt down and replaced every generation (Stepanovic 1997). Their inhabitants continued to occupy the same places, with the result that new structures were built over the remains of their predecessors until the settlement formed a conspicuous mound or *tell*. Even so, this is not the only evidence of occupation in these regions, for there are other places where these practices did not occur, with the result that living sites have been more difficult to find. In both cases, the builders favoured the same style of architecture.

That predilection for rectilinear dwellings became still more obvious as farming spread beyond the Mediterranean and the Danube into Central and Western Europe. It was here that settlements of enormous longhouses were first established. The largest dwellings were of a size that was rarely matched until the Middle Ages (Coudart 1998). Again, the buildings may have been replaced at regular intervals, but in this case it was uncommon for successive structures to occupy the same positions. As a result, the excavated settlements appear exceptionally large. Although these massive houses were eventually succeeded by other styles of building, the use of such big rectangular dwellings remained important until about 4500 BC when settlement became more dispersed. Once it happened, houses were less monumental. Nevertheless, Neolithic developments set the agenda for the remainder of the prehistoric period and, during the Bronze Age and Iron Age, virtually all the domestic structures in Central and Northern Europe adhered to a rectangular outline.

An accommodation between circular and rectilinear forms

Thus, one strand in the agricultural settlement of Europe connects Central Europe to Northern France and the Southern Netherlands. It was associated with the Linear Pottery Culture and its successors. A different axis connected Greece to the West Mediterranean and extended along the Atlantic coastline as far as Western France. In its initial phase it is associated with the ceramic styles known collectively as Impressed Wares. Little is known about the architecture associated with this tradition, but it is certainly true that from Spain and Portugal, and as far as Scotland and Ireland, there were circular tombs. There is more limited evidence of circular dwellings of the same date. The complex relationship between monuments and houses is considered in Part Two.

There was an accommodation between different architectural traditions in the West Mediterranean. The available evidence is unevenly distributed, but it is clear that from the first agricultural settlement in the Neolithic period to the end of the Bronze Age there were domestic sites that contained both circular and rectilinear buildings. Another form was an apsidal or oval house which combined elements of both designs. No doubt such structures assumed local forms from one region to another, but the persistence of this building type is remarkable. Examples of this distinctive mixture of forms are documented over a very wide area and are particularly well represented in parts of the West Mediterranean, including Sicily, Sardinia, Corsica, the Aeolian Islands, and the Balearics (Figure 6). All these places were connected by sea, but the same variety of architectural forms can be found on the mainland of Southern Europe. It can be identified at individual sites in Italy, France, and Spain, although it may not represent a general pattern in any of these cases. The evidence from Central Italy is especially striking for excavation in Rome has shown that oval and circular houses existed on the site before the city was built (Figure 7; Carandini and Cappelli 2007).

Serra Órrios-Dorgàli

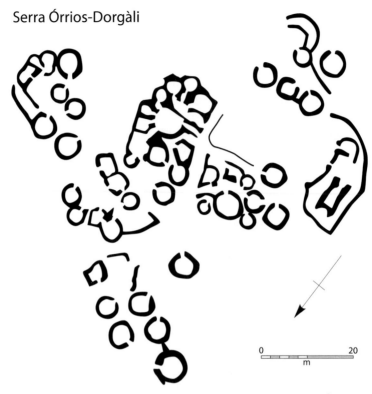

Figure 6 Plans of stone roundhouses and related features at Serra Órrios-Dorgàli, Sardinia.

In some regions, domestic architecture offered a source of inspiration for more monumental structures. In Southern Italy, for instance, there is a series of Neolithic settlements. They are usually defined by a curvilinear ditched enclosure, within which there were a large number of roughly circular compounds. They are interpreted as the sites of domestic buildings, although few house plans have been identified (Malone 2003: 252–7). In the same way, Chalcolithic oval dwellings in Languedoc are associated with massive walled enclosures, some of them augmented by bastions (Coularou 2008).

The same developments have been identified in other areas, although there is little to suggest that they represent a unitary phenomenon. In the Iberian Peninsula, for instance, stone-built roundhouses are, again, associated with walled enclosures, the largest of which were built on such a scale that they could have been defended against attack. They can be associated with a specialized material culture and may have been high status settlements. Individual examples seem to be equipped with round towers. Los Millares in south-east Spain is associated with a cemetery of megalithic tombs, although

Monte Castellaccio di Imola

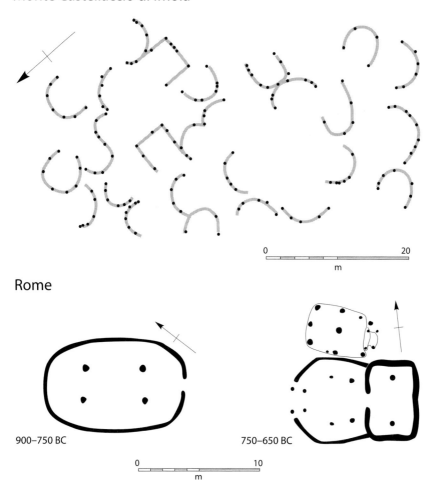

Figure 7 Outline plans of Bronze Age wooden circular, oval, and rectangular houses at Monte Castellaccio di Imola and Rome, Italy.

their chronological relationship is uncertain (Almagro and Arribas 1963; Chapman 2008: 203–5). There is also a series of stone forts in the surrounding area, some of them circular in plan. Other defended sites may be connected with decorated cave sanctuaries and rock shelters, and span the period between the Chalcolithic and the Early Bronze Age. A different tradition of architecture is found in La Mancha where walled enclosures are built around a conspicuous tower; the central structure may be either rectangular or round. Some of these *motillas* monumentalize the traditional form of the roundhouse (Fernández-Posse et al. 2000).

A similar, but rather later, transformation of oval and circular architecture can be recognized on most of the islands in the West Mediterranean during the Bronze Age. Thus, the oval and circular dwellings in Sardinia are sometimes grouped into villages with a massive tower at their centre. Similar structures (*nuraghi*) have also been found in isolation. It is clear that some of these buildings enjoyed a special status. Not only would they have taken a considerable effort to erect, their characteristic forms are represented by models made of stone or bronze (Pirovano 1985). Although they are less well known, monumental structures were also built on Corsica, where they are known as *torres* (Costa 2004: 114–18), and on Majorca, where both round and square buildings are described as *talayots* (Waldren 1982: Chapter 8) The special importance of the Corsican site at Filitosa was emphasized by reusing statues of armed warriors in the fabric of the central monument. These developments obviously took local forms and none was based exclusively on a circular design, despite the important role it played in domestic architecture. Rectilinear structures were also significant.

The situation was very different along the Atlantic coastline and here both major currents in the archaeology of Neolithic Europe came together. The earliest architecture in Britain and Ireland was largely rectangular, but, unusually, houses of this form were succeeded by circular dwellings. The result was a complex sequence in which the first Neolithic buildings were in a style associated with the agricultural colonization of Central and Northern Europe. After a period of no more than five hundred years, this tradition was supplanted, or even replaced, by a series of curvilinear structures more directly related to the Atlantic axis. A similar change may have taken place among the stone and earthwork monuments of both islands where the circular archetype assumed a growing importance (Bradley 2007: Chapters 2 and 3; Darvill 2010, Chapter 5). Much the same process can be recognized in the Neolithic of north-west France where megalithic tombs illustrate an interplay between round and rectangular forms (Scarre 2004a). In some cases, monuments changed their shapes in the course of their construction. On other sites, the finished building combined both curvilinear and rectilinear elements.

After the Neolithic period, parts of Atlantic Europe were characterized by circular buildings to the virtual exclusion of other forms, but the distribution of roundhouses was discontinuous and structures of this type went out of favour at different times from the Bronze Age to the Early Medieval period. Like their counterparts in the Mediterranean, they provided a source of inspiration for new kinds of monuments, including circular hillforts and the extraordinary Iron Age towers or *brochs* in the west and north of Scotland (Armit 2003).

Identities, exchange, and the persistence of circular architecture

The main reason why it was difficult to compare the architectural traditions considered in the previous section is that they lasted for different lengths of time. They may have had distant roots in the Neolithic period when domesticated animals and plants were first exploited in Southern and Western Europe, but by the Chalcolithic phase, and even the Bronze Age, these traditions had diverged from one another. On the West Mediterranean islands they took distinctive forms. There were contacts between these areas, but the local sequences were truncated at different points as communities were drawn into patterns of long-distance exchange. Sometimes it may have involved settlement from overseas, whilst in other cases the integration of the native people into larger networks had an equally drastic impact. At times, it resulted in the assimilation of foreign practices and even the adoption of an exotic material culture. That remained the case whether those contacts were with Mycenaeans, with Greek colonists, or with Phoenician traders (Cunliffe 2001: Chapters 7–9). Similar developments happened with the growth of Etruscan and Roman power. In many regions, the forms of the built environment changed radically, and, as part of this process, curvilinear buildings were largely abandoned. That happened at different times in different areas, and the entire development was played out over a millennium or more.

If the adoption of new architectural forms had a role in the political process, so, in another way, did local resistance to change. There were areas where curvilinear architecture was well established, whether or not it coexisted with rectangular buildings, and here the established traditions continued and were occasionally expressed in a more conspicuous form. This had nothing to do with social or geographical isolation and must have been a deliberate decision. To take one obvious example, the Atlantic Bronze Age integrated a series of local exchange networks extending from Ireland to Iberia and continuing into the West Mediterranean. It witnessed the movement of artefacts, raw materials, ideas, and social practices, but, apart from the construction of hillforts, it had little impact on the built environment (Ruiz-Gálvez Priego 1998). Whilst building forms changed rapidly in Southern Spain, circular structures—both houses and monuments—came to play a more prominent part along the Atlantic seaboard and continued to do so until at least the Roman period. Yet that did not happen everywhere; it was confined to certain regions, so that curvilinear architecture retained, or even increased, its importance in Northern Spain and Portugal, just as it did in the British Isles. At the same time, it played little, or no, part in Western France during the same period.

The same point can be made in other ways. In 1964, Hodson used the evidence of circular buildings to show how different the inhabitants of Iron Age Britain were from contemporary societies on the Continent. Because rectilinear architecture was largely absent, he emphasized the distinctiveness of insular culture and criticized the prevailing model which supposed that the island had been colonized by sea at the beginning of this period. There have been many excavations in the fifty years that followed, but his original observation is still accepted. At the same time, close connections have been postulated between the late prehistoric inhabitants of Britain and their neighbours across the English Channel and the North Sea. They extend to the use of similar artefacts, the discovery of similar settlements, and a growing body of evidence that people engaged in the same ritual practices. There was obviously a close relationship between these regions, and yet, with few exceptions, the contrast between their buildings remains as Hodson described it. In the same way, circular architecture persisted to varying extents in Scotland, Wales, and Ireland—even when the island of Britain was incorporated into the Roman Empire. Again, there is evidence of interaction and yet its impact must have been limited. A good example is provided by the Rath of the Synods at the Irish royal site of Tara (Grogan 2008). It contained a distinctive range of Roman imports, some of them used for serving food and drink. There was a wooden building of the site, which was approximately square in plan. It was built using Roman nails and even secured by a Roman padlock, and yet it was located in the middle of a *circular* enclosure bounded by concentric rings of banks and ditches (Figure 8). Again, there were close contacts between

Rath of the Synods

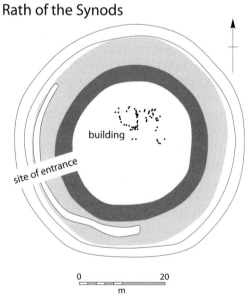

Figure 8 Simplified plan of the Rath of the Synods, Tara, Ireland, showing the position of the rectilinear structure associated with imported Roman artefacts.

different communities, but a conscious decision was made to maintain traditional norms.

Circular monuments and rectangular dwellings

Even when a different decision was taken, the circular archetype might remain important. In this case, the emphasis was not on regional self-consciousness or on maintaining a traditional form, as the main factor is the ubiquity of rectilinear structures. They might have been adopted for all the reasons mentioned earlier and, in this case, it is the striking contrast with circular buildings that is most significant. Whilst broad regional developments are considered, more specific relationships are commonly overlooked. That is because they were expressed in many different ways.

It is comparatively easy to discuss the chronology and construction of roundhouses; it is a little harder to consider the relationships between circular domestic dwellings and the public buildings that took them as their prototypes. But how are archaeologists to explain the choice of circular enclosures to delimit settlements of rectangular houses of the kind that have been recorded in the Neolithic of south-east Europe? Why were Central European longhouses associated with circular ditched and palisaded enclosures? If the construction of passage tombs referred to the configuration of roundhouses, why are circular burial mounds so common in areas where all the domestic buildings have square or rectilinear plans? Similar questions arise in the archaeology of later periods. Why, for instance, were circular temples erected in Roman towns? In such cases, it is perhaps the contrast between these forms that is significant. Could it be that the circular plan assumed a special power precisely because it was so different from the structures encountered in daily life? Indeed, it even seems possible that linear and curvilinear architectures give rise to distinctive perceptions of the world: a point that will be discussed in Chapter 2.

Such contrasts are not the prerogative of one region or one period of prehistory. They are widely distributed and there may have been no direct connections between the people who made use of them. But they do occur in most parts of Europe and, for that reason, they require an explanation. The same applies to the contrast between rectilinear and curvilinear forms found in other media. Again, they may have assumed a local importance precisely because they were different, but, if that distinction was exploited, it was used for local reasons and in local ways. What is significant in both cases is that they suggest that curvilinear and rectilinear forms stand for particular ideas of order and that those concepts cannot be reduced to a purely functional scheme. Even if rectangular houses were more efficient containers than circular buildings, there is no reason to suppose that circular burial mounds made better memorials than square ones, or that circular designs on prehistoric pottery made those vessels more suitable for use than ceramics with linear decoration. Close attention to contrasts of these kinds, whether they apply to domestic buildings, monuments or artefacts, could draw attention to the reality, and perhaps the importance, of the circular archetype for people in the past. There are patterns that do not follow regional lines and for that reason they pose a special problem for archaeologists.

THE ORGANIZATION OF THE ARGUMENT

The four parts of the book

Like Medieval Ireland, this book is divided into four parts. Part One introduces the problems posed by circular houses and surveys their distribution in ancient Europe. It reviews the ways in which they have been studied by archaeologists and compares their ideas with what is known from the ethnographic record. It also comments on the striking contrasts between curvilinear and linear art styles in relation to the dwellings of the same periods.

Part Two is devoted to those parts of ancient Europe in which a 'circular' perception of space was longest lived. In particular, it considers both the architecture of ancient dwellings and their relationship to the forms of larger monuments. Part Three complements this analysis by studying the distinctive roles of circular structures in societies where rectilinear architecture was the norm. It also investigates the circumstances in which the circular archetype was abandoned. Lastly, Part Four summarizes the main findings of this research.

The texts of Parts Two and Three are structured around three chapters. In each case, the first introduces a topic on a broad geographical scale and considers how it is related to wider themes in contemporary archaeology. The other two provide more detailed studies from particular phases or regions. Those examples extend from the Neolithic period to the Middle Ages and consider evidence from Germany and Austria, Portugal and Spain, Hungary and Romania, the Netherlands and South Scandinavia, Britain, Ireland, and north-west France.

The individual chapters

If this chapter has offered an overview of circular structures in ancient Europe, Chapter 2 considers how the contrasts between round and rectilinear dwellings have been interpreted by archaeologists and social anthropologists. It begins by reviewing purely functional explanations for the differences between these kinds of architecture. They have usually focused on the distinction between mobility and sedentism, and the significance of changing forms of social organization in the past. Such approaches were a major feature of archaeology in the 1970s and 1980s, but have been less discussed since then. Another approach is to consider the interpretation of circular structures in terms of systems of belief. The two interpretations are not necessarily incompatible and can complement one another. Chapter 2 draws on ethnographic evidence to illuminate these issues. It also considers how the uses of these different kinds of buildings are related to more general perceptions of space in prehistoric societies.

One reason for supposing that the contrast between circular and rectilinear structures was related to fundamental ideas about the ordering of space is that the same duality can be found in ancient art. It is studied in Chapter 3. Although there are many exceptions, some of the societies that occupied circular dwellings employed linear decoration to embellish their portable artefacts. Similarly, prehistoric communities who occupied rectangular houses could show a predilection for curvilinear motifs on their ceramics and metalwork. The chapter explores the significance of this pattern using ethnographic examples, as well as those from well-studied regions of prehistoric Europe. It also investigates two further issues. Firstly, it suggests that in a number of different societies artefacts embellished with curvilinear designs played a particular role in ritual and ceremonial. Secondly, it emphasizes the importance of ceramic models of houses, as their decoration and wider associations shed light on the special significance of domestic buildings.

Much of the discussion of circular architecture has been concerned with roundhouses and the practicalities of using them. This work has been important and original, but it overlooks the crucial problem that the same principles of order were employed on a larger scale in the construction of stone and earthwork monuments. This applies particularly to tombs, which provide the subject of Chapter 4. The relationship between longhouses and long mounds has been debated for many years, but a similar approach to the evidence may be relevant to the first appearance of round cairns in Neolithic Europe, and to their relationship with circular houses and related structures. Chapter 4 considers the extent to which domestic buildings provided a source of inspiration for more monumental constructions. On an even broader scale it reconsiders the relationship between private and public architecture among the first farmers.

Chapter 5 expands on some of the themes introduced in Chapter 4, with a detailed study of the relationship between domestic buildings, circular cairns, and the settings of standing stones on either side of the English Channel and the Irish Sea. Their history extends between about 4500 BC and 1500 BC. It draws on the results of recent fieldwork and investigates the argument that stone circles were associated with the dead and asks whether individual monoliths might have been regarded as statues. If they represented particular people in the past, the circular configuration of those monuments could have provided an image of the community as a whole. In that case, it might shed light on changes in social organization from the Neolithic period to the Bronze Age. Those ideas are compared with the results of new investigations of anthropomorphic images in Continental Europe.

There have been valuable discussions of prehistoric roundhouses and the ways in which their interiors were organized and used. Those structures could also provide the source of inspiration for stone-built tombs, but less has been said about the ways in which their characteristic forms were copied by public buildings—some of which may never have been roofed. Chapter 6 draws on the concept of the Great House developed in American archaeology and considers the part played by large curvilinear structures in prehistoric Europe. It considers monumental architecture in the Bronze Age of the West Mediterranean and develops some of the same ideas by discussing three groups of circular timber or earthwork enclosures which are frequently compared with one another: the Neolithic henge monuments of Southern England, the Late Bronze Age ringforts of lowland Britain, and the royal sites of the Irish Iron Age. It is true that they share common features, but in this case it is worth paying more attention to their placing in the landscape, and even to their relationship with the sky and the movements of the sun. The British and Irish enclosures have the same circular ground plan as the buildings inside them. It may be important to consider these structures as microcosms of the wider world.

Part Three introduces another theme. What is the significance of circular monuments in regions dominated by rectilinear architecture? Although some of them are roofed buildings like those discussed already, more are enclosures or mounds. The distinction between these different forms seems to have been significant. Chapter 7 begins with Neolithic tells and the circular 'roundels' of Central Europe. They are sometimes discussed in relation to the British monuments considered in Part Two, but they are not of the same date and can be associated with settlements of longhouses. In fact, with few exceptions, the circular constructions found in periods characterized by rectangular buildings seem to have played a role in public ceremonies. In the south-west USA, the contrast is exemplified by the 'Great Kivas' associated with rectilinear architecture. Something different happened during the Roman period in England and France, but again the contrast between squares and circles was significant. In this case, it extends to a series of shrines or sanctuaries. The chapter concludes with an account of the Late Iron Age ringforts on the Baltic island of Öland, where there is still more striking evidence for relationships of this kind.

Similar contrasts are explored in detail in Chapter 8, which considers the houses and burial mounds of the Bronze Age in the Netherlands and South Scandinavia. Here, the interplay between circular and rectilinear structures takes several different forms. In some regions both are found together and the positions of older longhouses can be marked by the construction of round barrows. In other cases, they were located in different parts of the landscape. The burial mounds can even be associated with specialized wooden or stone enclosures whose proportions are the same as those of domestic buildings, but these 'cult houses' were never roofed and adopted a separate alignment from the dwellings of the same period. In the Netherlands, the relationship between longhouses and round barrows is different again. In this case, burial mounds appear to be paired with dwellings, but their dates are not the same. The round barrows were constructed during a period with little evidence of domestic architecture. By contrast, the houses belong to a later phase. Their positions are closely related to those of the older mounds, but barrows of that kind were no longer built. In this case, the contrast between rectilinear and circular structures seems to have been played out over time. Chapter 8 concludes with a short discussion of the relationship between circular monuments and Bronze Age cosmology in Northern Europe.

Circular architecture was supplanted by rectilinear structures during two main phases. The first was towards the beginning of the Neolithic and is considered in Part One. The second phase extended over a longer period of time. In this case, buildings changed their forms as social organization became more complex. This process is considered in Chapter 9. It was often influenced by the adoption of foreign prototypes which were treated as a source of prestige. Where circular constructions had been especially long lived they were gradually replaced by new kinds of domestic and public buildings. That development happened with the expansion of long distance contacts along the shores of the Mediterranean and the Atlantic, and is best exemplified by the influence of Greek and Roman architecture in Southern and Western Europe. Chapter 9 traces these processes and the ways in which conceptions of space were transformed.

One of the clearest illustrations of these processes is provided by the Castro Culture of north-west Spain and Northern Portugal, which is studied in more detail. In their original form, *castros* were circular fortified enclosures. Most examples contain a dense distribution of round houses, some of them organized into compounds. Certain of these places were first occupied during the Atlantic Bronze Age, but their history extends into the Late Iron Age and Roman periods, and it was then that their character changed. Rectangular buildings began to replace circular structures, and on some of the larger sites existing roundhouses or groups of roundhouses were incorporated into a rudimentary street grid. The result was an uneasy accommodation between two architectural styles, one of them long-established and the other new. The discussion shows how the organization of space on the western margin of Europe sheds light on wider social and political changes. The same process is illustrated by the adoption of Viking and Anglo-Norman styles of building in Ireland. Again, it was a protracted process and, in this case, the last circular houses date from the Middle Ages—a time when round mounds were still used for inaugurating kings.

The final chapter returns to the ideas discussed in Part One of the book and considers how far they account for the observations presented in Chapters 4–9.

THE CIRCULAR RUINS

Finally, a word about the title of this chapter. It is taken from a story by Jorge Luis Borges, published in his collection *Fictions* (1965). In his account, a traveller arrives at a circular temple which has been 'devoured by an ancient conflagration'. The 'anonymous grey man', as Borges describes him, has come there with an extraordinary objective. His aim is *'to dream a man'*. He provides offerings for the spirits of the earth and water, but it is only when he prostrates himself before the effigy of an animal ('perhaps a tiger or perhaps a colt') that his plan is fulfilled. His dreams bring another person to life. It takes him many years, but, having completed his task, he sends his creature away to 'practice identical rites in other circular ruins'. Like Uisneach, all these places are associated with a cult of fire.

The hero of Borges's story dispatches his son to visit circular temples like the one in which he was created. The reader of this book will follow a similar course, as my account explores a series of structures which share the same geometric form. It considers houses and enclosures, sanctuaries and mounds, but not all of them will have had the same significance. It is a problem that needs to be investigated using the methods of archaeology. That process begins in Chapter 2.

2

Conceptions and Perceptions

TWO WAYS OF LOOKING AT HOUSES

The first academic conference I attended was held in 1970. Its proceedings were published two years later with the title *Man, Settlement and Urbanism.* The book was notable for including contributions from both archaeologists and anthropologists. The meeting itself had an unusual format—part of the audience was hidden from view. Instead of participating in the discussion, we gathered in another room and watched the proceedings on closed circuit television. Only at the final reception was the barrier removed so that we were able to see the protagonists in the flesh. As this chapter will suggest, obstacles to communication still remain.

At the time, one paper had a special impact—Kent Flannery's discussion of 'The origins of the village as a settlement type in Mesoamerica and the Near East' (Flannery 1972). Four decades after it appeared in print it is still being quoted. Other contributors to the meeting covered some of the same themes, but, true to the spirit of the conference, the distinguished social anthropologist Mary Douglas considered the perils of archaeological interpretation. Her paper 'Symbolic orders in the use of domestic space' presented a series of cautionary tales which compared the approaches of prehistorians with those of contemporary ethnographers (Douglas 1972).

If Flannery's paper had an immediate impact, Douglas's was rarely cited, perhaps because it dismayed so many of those at the conference. There could have been other reasons why it was overlooked. The article was short and lacked much direct reference to archaeological research. That is ironic, for a decade later her work was to exert a major influence on theorists in archaeology. Indeed, it played a growing role in their thinking through to her death in 2007 (Gosden 2004). Although she appreciated the attention, it was a role that she was reluctant to assume.

The differences between Flannery's paper and Douglas's are not those between the disciplines of archaeology and anthropology. Flannery was well aware of ethnographic accounts of settlements in traditional societies. Rather, their articles reflect two different strands in twentieth-century thought. Flannery's approach was influenced by functionalist anthropology and Douglas's by structuralism. That is why her work provided a source of inspiration for those who became disenchanted with processual archaeology. Her thoughts on settlements, houses, boundaries, and notions of pollution became increasingly influential through the work of Ian Hodder (1982) and Henrietta Moore (1986).

On one level, the distinction between Flannery's paper and Douglas's contribution reflects their different interests. Flannery was concerned with the way in which settlements changed over time and with the various reasons why that happened. He discussed general principles, as he intended his research to have an impact outside his study areas. Douglas, on the other hand, offered no general theory and emphasized the sheer diversity of settlements in traditional societies. Her concern was with the meanings and significance of domestic space. She exposed the fragility of functional interpretations but went no further, although in her other writings she did engage in cross-cultural analysis.

It is all too easy to suggest that one kind of research has replaced another way of thinking, for that is how the history of archaeology is written. Flannery's paper was conceived at a time when archaeologists were particularly concerned with subsistence, ecology, and the political economy. Those themes run through many of the chapters in *Man, Settlement and Urbanism*, and it would be wrong to reject such studies because they were a product of their time. It is better to recognize their ambitions than to castigate their limitations. They were contributions to an emerging discipline which was looking for general principles in the workings of ancient society and, for that reason, it is irrelevant to criticize them for a lack of concern with specific cases. Different research projects work at different scales and, over the last three decades, there has been a growing interest in local particulars at the expense of larger patterns. The only conflict between these different approaches is where such detailed studies show that a wider framework is misconceived. Otherwise, the scale of any analysis is partly a matter of taste, and in theoretical archaeology tastes are all too often determined by what is fashionable at the time.

For that reason, the discussion that follows does not set Flannery's approach in opposition to that of Douglas, nor does it suggest that one kind of analysis is right and the other wrong. Instead, this account will begin by describing research that has been conducted on an extensive geographical scale. It does have limitations and these cannot be overlooked, but it has virtues, too. This chapter will go on to consider approaches which complement, and even modify, those findings at the local level. They are more akin to the ideas put forward by Douglas. But one way of thinking about the past does not cancel out the other. It is far more helpful to consider those methods as complementary and to look for the connections between them. Houses are three-dimensional structures that are meant to be inhabited over longer or shorter periods. For that reason they must have certain physical characteristics. At the same time, they play a central role in the beliefs of the people who live there, and those ideas should also be studied in detail. The relationship between the two approaches is subtle and sometimes confusing, but it cannot be investigated unless both elements are treated on equal terms. In what follows, functional arguments of the kind employed by Flannery are considered first. A separate section develops the insights of anthropologists like Douglas.

FUNCTIONAL CONSIDERATIONS IN THE STUDY OF HOUSES

Flannery's study was based on a detailed knowledge of the archaeological sequences in two different parts of the world and deployed that information to good effect. That is why his article had an immediate impact; it was closely related to the kind of comparative analysis that was favoured at the time. In many cases, such work was based on the evidence codified in the Human Relations Area Files which summarized the available information on 415 separate cultures. The Ethnographic Atlas, which drew on this material, allowed scholars to search for relationships between such features as climate and methods of food production, or social structures and the treatment of the dead. Although Binford employed rather different sources of information in his book *Constructing Frames of Reference*, it takes much the same approach. In his words, it describes 'an analytical method for archaeological theory building, using ethnographic and environmental data sets' (Binford 2001). A similar strategy was adopted by Kent (1990) and by Blanton (1994) in their cross-cultural studies of settlements and households, respectively.

When Flannery published his conference paper in 1972, the importance of circular architecture had been investigated by the same method using the information contained in the Human Relations Area Files. Researchers had already come to several conclusions. Both Robbins (1966) and Whiting and Ayres (1968) had investigated the relationship between domestic architecture and the pattern of settlement. Dwellings were classified as rectilinear or curvilinear, and the populations who used them were identified as sedentary, nomadic, or semi-nomadic. The results of these studies did not agree in detail, but showed that roundhouses tended to be associated with small communities and with relatively impermanent settlements. They were found mainly with hunter gatherers and pastoralists. Agriculture played little part in their lives. Rectangular buildings, on the other hand, were occupied by larger groups. They were associated with sedentary settlements and with intensive mixed farming. There were significant exceptions to both trends, but social

relationships appeared to be more stable among those who occupied rectilinear dwellings, and more volatile among the occupants of roundhouses. Here,
polygyny was an important institution, with different wives living in separate
dwellings.

As Hunter-Anderson observed some years later, these were tentative
correlations; they were not *explanations* of the patterns that were identified
(Hunter-Anderson 1977). Flannery's paper made more progress by suggesting
why the distinction between round and rectangular houses would have been
significant. He also considered why one kind of building replaced the other in
both his study areas. Subsequent papers provided further insights into this
process.

One of the main issues is the physical fabric of these buildings. Are certain
houses more durable than others and how easy is it to replace them? When a
house is built, is it intended to last for more than a generation? Will that
building be replaced as the people who live there change, and will the
settlement of which it forms a part be inhabited over a long period of time?
If not, there are advantages in building insubstantial structures whose elements can be recycled when the population moves. For example, there are the
settlements of farmers who practise shifting agriculture. In that case, new areas
will be exploited on a predictable basis. Again, there are the shelters built by
hunter gatherers who can occupy many different camp sites in the course of a
year. An important consideration is that their dwellings are easy to erect and
just as easy to dismantle.

The same questions can be framed in another way. Are successive generations expected to live together in the same dwelling or the same group of
buildings, or is the 'developmental cycle' (Goody 1958) played out across a
series of separate locations? This is an important question for studies of social
organization, but it has consequences for the architecture of settlements. If the
size of a single house is expected to increase over time, there has to be some
way of finding the necessary space. As Flannery recognized in 1972, this is
easier to achieve with a rectilinear building than a circular one (Figure 9).
Additional rooms can be tacked on to a rectangular house but it is much more
difficult to extend a circular structure. Instead, it is likely that additional roundhouses will be built, perhaps in an adjacent area. That could be why such
structures are often grouped in compounds. It can easily happen as the size of
the domestic group increases and may explain why circular dwellings were
supposedly associated with polygyny, with different wives occupying different
buildings. It is important to emphasize that this is only one possible model.

Of course, some of these problems can be circumvented by careful planning
for the future, but even then there are problems. Whilst sufficient space can be
left vacant for a rectangular building to be enlarged, a roundhouse is a unitary
structure and any decisions about its intended size have to be made at the
outset. That involves some simple practical considerations. In principle, a

Round

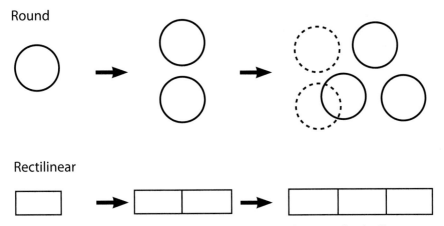

Rectilinear

Figure 9 The pattern of replacement of roundhouses and rectangular dwellings.

longhouse can be extended to any length. The only limitation is its width, for a building of this kind must not be too broad to support a roof. Otherwise, the main decision to be made is where to locate the entrances. In the case of a roundhouse, however, there is a practical limit to the size of a building that can be roofed. Beyond that point there is no possibility of making the dwelling any larger.

To some extent, these issues influence the final form of the dwelling. Other features are important, too: the choice of raw materials and its stability in strong winds.

Studies that depend on the shapes of buildings do not pay sufficient attention to the materials out of which they are made. Hunter gatherers may be associated with insubstantial circular shelters, but roundhouses may also be made of stone. They share the same geometric form, but the choice of material would affect the lifespan of the dwelling. The same applies to the construction of rectangular houses. A second question concerns their structural stability. Circular buildings provide more resistance to gales than their rectangular counterparts which need to be carefully aligned. Ideally, their narrow ends should face into the wind, although much depends on their siting in relation to the local topography and vegetation.

There are other practical problems to consider. Rectilinear buildings can be extended at either end or even by adding annexes to the side walls. Parts of the structure can be allowed to go out of use without jeopardizing its stability. Thus, one end of a longhouse can be abandoned whilst new spaces are created elsewhere. This lengthens the overall lifespan of the dwelling. Piecemeal repairs can also be made to a roundhouse, but it is hard to replace large parts of the structure in quite the same way; it is more vulnerable than its rectangular counterpart. Either it must be demolished and rebuilt on the same site, or another will be erected nearby. In the circumstances, it is hardly surprising that cross-cultural surveys should show that circular buildings are occupied over shorter periods than longhouses. Again, the question arises why one kind of dwelling was favoured in some areas but not in others.

All these considerations can be illustrated by archaeological evidence. There are excavated longhouses in which the sequence of construction is quite clear. Additional compartments may have been built onto one or both ends of the building during its period of use. There are signs of piecemeal repairs which will not have threatened the stability of the structure as a whole and there are sometimes indications that individual parts of a longhouse changed their functions over time. Particular rooms may have been given up as living areas and used for storage or for penning animals. Such evidence is widely distributed and can take similar forms in different areas. Thus, the 'chains' of rectangular houses identified on Neolithic settlements in Israel illustrate the same process as the extension of Linear Pottery Culture dwellings in Central or Northern Europe (Rowan and Golden 2009: 30–1; Rück 2009; Figure 10). In contrast, there are settlements in Southern and Western Europe which illustrate the regular replacement of roundhouses. Some were rebuilt in exactly the same positions so that their plans are superimposed or overlap, whilst others were replaced on adjacent plots of land.

Flannery's paper introduced another issue (Flannery 1972; see also Rapaport 1969 and Saidel 1993). The development of rectilinear buildings can have implications for the storage of wealth. On one level it provides more closed spaces in which produce can be kept, whilst, on another, it allows more privacy for the inhabitants of the building. Although the importance attached to privacy differs from one society to another, the possibility of concealment has major implications. Many hunter gatherer communities are characterized by an ethic of sharing—that is one reason why they show few signs of status divisions. The adoption of agriculture involved the ownership of particular resources and it also allowed the accumulation of a surplus which could play a part in the political economy. By accumulating agricultural produce and sponsoring a feast, groups or individuals might have attempted to raise their status in the community. That is probably what happened in Flannery's study areas. The social changes that followed the adoption of farming encouraged the development of villages of rectangular houses.

A later review by Kent (1990) investigated the ways in which settlement space was subdivided. She considered five different kinds of society in the ethnographic record, but only her Categories 1–3 are relevant to this discussion. Nomads and hunter gatherers who lack major social distinctions form her Category 1 and those 'with limited socio-political stratification and a recognised formal chief' make up Category 2. Again, they include hunter gatherers, but they also incorporate some pastoralists and horticulturalists. Category 3 consists of communities with greater social divisions. They practice

a) Ein el-Hariri

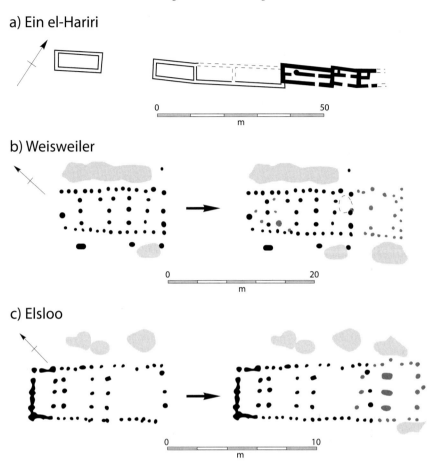

b) Weisweiler

c) Elsloo

Figure 10 The sequence of replacement and extension of rectangular houses at Ein el-Hariri (Israel), Weisweiler (Germany), and Elsloo (the Netherlands).

agriculture and, in many cases, live in villages like those discussed by Flannery. Distinctions of wealth are more important in this group, whose members may engage in craft specialization, exchange, and warfare.

Again, these distinctions appear to be matched by differences in the use of architecture and the organization of space. The communities in Kent's Category 1 occupy multipurpose buildings with few internal subdivisions, whilst the structures occupied by people in her second group are sometimes partitioned, and sometimes not; there is considerable diversity. On the other hand, the architecture of Category 3 societies 'is a little more segmented in terms of interior partitions, exterior separate buildings, and functionally restricted activity areas'. Her analysis shows that the buildings of the settlements become more diverse as social differences increase. The variety of distinct 'activity areas' increases, too. Kent is less concerned with the shapes of domestic buildings, but her choice of illustrations is revealing. Category 1 is represented by a 'grass hut' and a windbreak employed by hunter gatherers. Category 2 is epitomized by two Navajo dwellings, one circular and the other rectangular, whilst her examples of Category 3 are two rectilinear buildings, each of which is divided into a series of separate rooms.

SOME CAVEATS

Some of the practical arguments discussed in the previous section have obvious limitations. Much of the problem arises from the use of cross-cultural comparison. Many different societies are classed together as 'mobile', but, as Binford's study recognized, there are numerous variations among recorded hunter gatherers and they cannot be treated as an ideal type. The same applies to pastoralists. There are differences in the ways in which these communities are organized, just as there are many contrasts among their patterns of settlement. In any case, pastoralists should not be grouped together with hunter gatherers as their methods of food production are not the same, nor are the ways in which they occupy the land. Neither group needs to be entirely nomadic. In some cases, only part of a pastoral community moves with its animals, whilst others occupy the same location year round. All these points were raised by a critique by Hunter-Anderson (1977).

Cross-cultural comparisons have other limitations, for they take too little account of regional differences, so that structures made out of mud, or even branches and grass, can be placed in the same category as houses built of stone. To a large extent that is because the present day distribution of circular buildings bears little resemblance to the situation in the past, so that examples from African and Native American communities play a disproportionate role in the ethnographic present. In regions where similar buildings lost their importance in the past they cannot be included in this kind of research.

The societies that feature in these studies provide a misleading impression in yet another way. Many of them live in temperate climates where shelter from the sun is the main requirement and there is no need to insulate the structures against cold. For that reason the sample is dominated by what are described as 'mud huts'. It is also biased towards contemporary groups of hunter gatherers who occupy arid regions which are poorly suited to agriculture. Indeed, some of those groups may originally have been farmers who had been forced to change their way of life. A potential weakness of Flannery's argument is that he was studying two areas with a warm climate. Here, it is understandable that roundhouses would be relatively insubstantial.

There are other problems of a more theoretical kind. There is no reason for archaeologists to assume that the societies that have been documented by contemporary ethnographers show the same range of variation as peoples in the past; that is, to treat living communities as 'survivals' of more ancient traditions (Trigger 1981). It does not consider the possibility that prehistoric populations may have lived in other ways from those documented by social anthropologists over the last hundred years. Moreover, by averaging so many important differences between individual societies, even in the present, a large amount of information has been lost.

Another criticism is directly related to the archaeological record in Europe. It does not share some of the characteristics that are claimed by this kind of analysis. This is not to deny that hunter gatherers lived in small groups of circular dwellings but, in the field record, pastoralists seem to be rare. Where ancient people moved with their animals, it seems likely that they formed only part of a larger community and travelled to more distant grazing land on a seasonal basis. The nomadic pastoralists that feature prominently in the ethnographic record were better represented in Asia, which is outside the region studied in this book. Where circular houses are recorded in Europe, from the Neolithic period to the early Middle Ages, they were generally associated with sedentary farmers. It is true that in many cases roundhouses were eventually replaced by rectangular buildings—the evidence for this sequence was summarized in Chapter One—but there is nothing to suggest a simple relationship between circular architecture and a mobile pattern of settlement.

Nor were groups of curvilinear buildings necessarily ephemeral. In fact, they varied considerably in their size and elaboration—just as the frequency of these structures changed from site to site. Many locations were occupied continuously over a long period of time and individual houses could have been built to last. They consumed large quantities of timber, stone, and thatch, and there is little reason to suppose that rectangular dwellings built out of the same materials would have been any longer lived. A comparison with Anglo-Saxon houses in lowland England supports this assertion (Hamerow 2010: 5–10). They seem to have been abandoned and replaced with much the same frequency as the pre-Roman Iron Age roundhouses in the same region.

SYMBOLIC CONSIDERATIONS IN THE STUDY OF HOUSES

The practical issues discussed in the first part of this chapter were considered by McGuire and Schiffer (1983) in their 'Theory of architectural design'. They studied many of the variations among domestic buildings and the influences that contributed to their final forms. For them, the key elements were the projected lifespan of the dwellings, the difficulty or ease of repairing them, and the selection of raw materials. The optimum solution was likely to be based on a kind of cost benefit analysis. Although their study considered almost all the features discussed so far, it had one additional element. It also referred to the symbolic significance of ancient structures. This is the very area emphasized by Douglas in her contribution to *Man, Settlement and Urbanism*. Just as studies of prehistoric exchange systems should not be based on contemporary economic models, the interpretation of ancient architecture does not depend entirely on quantity surveying.

Perhaps there are two ways of approaching the problems posed by ancient buildings. One asks how the human experience of space was reflected in the components of the built environment, whilst the other starts from the opposite direction by asking how the construction and use of domestic dwellings would have influenced perceptions of the world. Both approaches have an important contribution to make, but they are based on different observations.

Perceptions of space are as varied as other parts of human culture. Although all human beings share the same senses, the values that they assign to them differ from one society to another. So do the ways in which particular phenomena are interpreted. Some communities will place a special emphasis on vision, whilst hearing may be at least as important among other groups (Gell 1995; Ingold 2000). Those contrasts are not entirely arbitrary, nor are they necessarily learned responses. Thus, groups who live in closed forest may be more aware of sounds and smells than those in an open terrain where it is possible to see long distances (Figure 11). By extension, people who travel by sea share a different awareness of space from communities on land. Some groups live in a closed environment where they must move along paths, rivers, and streams. Their experience of space is of points linked together by lines (Ingold 2007: Chapter 3).

Sailors in open water have a clear view of the sky. The positions of the sun, moon, and stars play a fundamental part in navigation, but it is easy to forget that the same features can be observed by people in open country. That also applies to those who live on the coast and to the occupants of small islands, most of whom can observe a distant horizon. Particular directions play an important part in their thinking, but, in this case, they can decide which ones to imbue with significance. Many groups are able to view the entire dome of the sky. They can also identify the places where the earth meets the heavens and where both touch the sea. As part of that process they become especially aware of the movements of the sun and moon.

By contrast, people who live in woodland will be less aware of the sky overhead, although they should be able to identify a few of the heavenly bodies. They may not be able to recognize distant landmarks, and even neighbouring settlements may be hidden from view. For that reason, their notions of space can be dominated by the importance of certain *directions*,

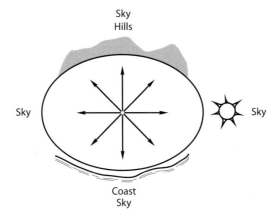

Open Environment

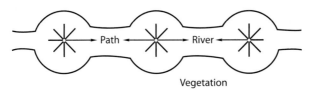

Closed Environment

Figure 11 Perceptions of the landscape from settlements in open and closed environments.

often the trails they follow in the course of their daily lives and the paths that lead between different communities.

These arguments suggest that in the past there would have been two very different ways of perceiving space: ways which are intimately related to the environments in which people lived. Although those environments would have changed as trees were cleared and scrub was replaced by grassland, those processes would have taken a long time. By then, people might have developed their own ideas. For some communities space would have seemed essentially linear: a world of paths and trails. For others, it was curvilinear and extended as far as the horizon. This circular configuration was mirrored by the dome of the sky.

Such contrasts need not have been expressed explicitly, although they sometimes were. They also affected the ways in which places were seen. It is possible that the experience of living in these different settings could have influenced the depth of view registered by the senses and the ways in which distance was perceived (Segall et al. 1966; Lawrence and Low 1990; Gregory 1998). The argument is difficult to evaluate as so much depends on anecdotal evidence.

MODELLING THE COSMOS

It is likely that these experiences also affected the perception of space at a local level. They may even be related to the forms chosen for domestic buildings. It is not a new idea to suggest that houses can be constructed in the image of the cosmos (Sharples 2010: Chapter 4). As Chapter 1 has shown, they can be either rectilinear or curvilinear. The contrasts between these models are illustrated by two examples from the Americas.

One of the most explicit discussions of the relationship between a longhouse and the wider world is Hugh-Jones's book *From the Milk River* which studies traditional cosmology in the north-west Amazon (Hugh-Jones 1979; Figure 12). Two features are significant here. One is the forest in which the Pirá-paraná live and the other is the presence of the river which gives the book its title. It is no accident that these people should live in longhouses, as the alignment of the building is very important. It is located near the river and is considered to share its orientation. At the same time, it is situated in between the water and the forest. The movement of the current provides a metaphor which informs the understanding of the house. The ancestors are believed to have travelled up the river in the past and this history is reflected in the structure of the dwelling. One end of the building indicates the direction from which the first settlers arrived, but at its other end, towards the source of the river, is the forest which is inhabited by evil spirits. Different sections of the building are associated with different groups of people. The distinctions are based on status and gender. Thus, there are chiefs and servants, warriors, and dancers. Shamans occupy the end of the building connected with the forest. Hugh-Jones summarizes the situation in this way:

> The universe is treated as a conceptual construction which contains the activity and power associated with ancestral creation...[People]...construct their houses to represent the universe (Hugh-Jones 1979: 235).

Although the symbolism of these dwellings is specific to the Pirá-paraná, the idea that such a building provides a model of the cosmos can be found in other places.

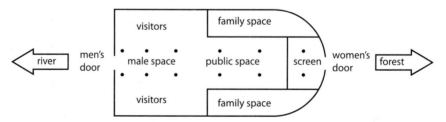

Figure 12 Simplified plan of a Pirá-paraná longhouse.

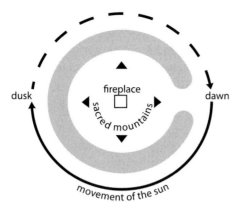

Figure 13 The layout of a Navajo hogan and the symbolism of its component parts.

Roundhouses show the same principle at work. For example, it is well documented among the Navajo in the south-west USA, where a similar scheme epitomizes a wider pattern in the New World. In this case, the principal domestic buildings (*hogans*) are approximately circular in plan (Griffin-Pierce 1992; Figure 13). Three components of these structures are particularly relevant here: the four upright posts that support the roof, the dome that spans the building, and the position of the entrance.

The hogan is the main family dwelling. It is constructed out of logs, earth, and bark according to procedures laid down in the Navajo origin myth, for each of these structural elements has a wider significance. The posts that hold up the roof represent four sacred mountains. Other parts of the building refer to fundamental elements in the cosmology of the occupants. Thus, the floor is thought of as Mother Earth and the domed roof stands for Father Sky. The house is where both these elements are combined. The entire landscape is considered to be sacred so that the hogan is both a domestic dwelling and a place where rituals are conducted. Indeed, the history of the building is linked to life itself as the umbilical cord of a newborn baby must be buried nearby. The structure is abandoned and destroyed when one of the inhabitants has died.

Just as the posts of the hogan are related to features of the wider terrain, the circular outline of the building refers to the sky overhead. The entrance is always positioned to the east to admit the morning light, but it is important that the sun should travel around the exterior of the building every day. Its progress is reflected in the internal organization of the house, which is divided into four notional parts. It is also reflected by the way in which the hogan is built, for the logs that make up its outer wall must be arranged in sun-wise fashion around the perimeter of the dwelling. In turn, that wall is related to the wider topography and is considered to represent the vista of mountains, hills, and trees beyond the settlement. Thus, the North and South American examples share certain features in common, even though they are associated with quite different beliefs. In each example, a domestic dwelling—a rectilinear longhouse in one case, a roundhouse in the other—provides a model of the wider world, although the elements that contribute to this interpretation are entirely different. Among the Pirá-paraná, they are the river and the forest; among the Navajo, their equivalents are the mountains, sun, and the sky.

Orientations are equally important in the longhouse studied by Hugh-Jones (1979). In one sense, the building is closely related to its surroundings but, at the same time, it summarizes the history of the community and celebrates its origin in a distant area. In theory, it also extends from east to west, reflecting the path of the sun across the sky. In the course of the day it passes from the men's door towards the river to the women's door at the opposite end of the building. Then it travels beneath the earth to return to its point of departure.

In this case, the axis of the house lacks much practical significance, but in the Navajo example both functional and symbolic elements are combined. The eastern entrance of the hogan faces the rising sun which lights the interior (Griffin-Pierce 1992). That is not its only significance, for the domed roof of the building is conceived in the image of the sky. At the same time, the four posts supporting that roof mark the cardinal points. Each is illuminated in turn. In other societies the significance of cardinal points depends on an abstract model of the world, for, unlike the solstices, those directions do not correspond to a conspicuous change in the position of the sun.

It is obvious that the horizontal axis is important in the layout of these buildings, but the vertical dimension is significant too. The four posts inside the hogan represent mountains that extend into the sky. In the same way, the outer wall refers to hills and trees. A similar observation applies to the longhouse of the Pirá-paraná, for it is spanned by an enormous roof that is difficult to reach from the floor. These people think of the universe as a series of superimposed layers. Above the earth there are five levels: trees and mountains; birds; rain, thunder, and wind; the heavenly bodies; and, finally, the circuit of the sun. Beneath the surface are three more, represented by underground worms, ants and termites, and the passage of the sun during the hours of darkness. The covering of the longhouse is equated with the sky and the ornaments that are displayed between the floor and the rafters represent mountains and trees. In contrast, the graves beneath the dwellings make a literal reference to the underworld. Again, there are features in common between the dwellings of the Pirá-paraná and the structure of the hogans occupied by the Navajo. Although there are no connections between these two societies, both share the same idea that the universe is composed of several layers and that the architecture of domestic buildings should refer to the connections between them. The same idea of an *axis mundi* which links the earth to the sky (and sometimes to an underworld) is found in other places (Eliade 1954; Figure 14).

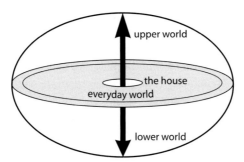

Figure 14 The *axis mundi* linking a house and its surroundings to the layers of a three-tier cosmos.

The Amazonian and Navajo examples share a further feature. The Pirá-paraná longhouse is conceptualized not only as a river, but also as a human body, and even a womb (Hugh-Jones 1979: 249–51). In the same way, the Navajo dwelling shares some of the attributes of the inhabitants and can be thought of as a living creature. It is associated with an umbilical cord and must be destroyed when an occupant dies (Griffin-Pierce 1992). In that sense every house will have a biography of its own. Similar beliefs are found in other communities, some of whom provide special offerings when a new structure is erected (Herva 2009). Perhaps they do this in order to bring it to life.

In short, the houses studied by social anthropologists often share common characteristics. They can provide microcosms of the environment around them, but are not intended as *copies* of the features observed in daily life. Rather, they offer *interpretations* of the ideas on which the natural order depends.

PERCEPTIONS AND PRECONCEPTIONS

These are public and widely shared beliefs. The organization of ancient houses would also have affected the behaviour of people in a less direct manner. Like the Navajo hogan, circular buildings have a distinctive layout. Most have only one entrance and can be divided between a central zone and a peripheral area under the eaves. On entering the building, visitors may have approached the centre directly. Otherwise, they could have been obliged to take a more circuitous route, turning either left or right once they had reached the interior. The focal point was probably located towards the rear wall where it faced the doorway. Less often, a circular dwelling had two different entrances, one opposite the other. They might have been used by different groups or individuals.

The area around the hearth provided the central focus of the dwelling. It might have been considered as a public space where food was prepared and consumed by the inhabitants. In the hogan, the central area with its fireplace is described as the 'sky centre' of the dwelling (Griffin-Pierce 1992). Of course that is not the only possibility and, in some cases, it seems more likely that food was prepared in a separate structure. At all events the communal consumption of food would have been an important event. Although social distinctions could have been reinforced by serving different portions to different people, the circular plan of the roundhouse would have made it hard to express such distinctions though the grading of space. By contrast, that would have been easier to achieve inside a rectangular dwelling.

Longhouses would have offered a much wider range of options. They might contain a series of self-contained rooms, each communicating with its neighbour, or they could enclose a single continuous space. There could be a door in the end wall, providing access to a sequence of different compartments, or the entrances could be located on the long axis, leading into different rooms or groups of rooms. Again, there was also the option of entering the structure from both sides of the building. Particular doorways could be used by different groups of people—young and old, men and women, hosts and visitors—and might be associated with different routes into the dwelling. Access to some spaces could have been restricted, whilst others were considered to be more public and were used on appropriate occasions by the wider community. The Pirá-paraná longhouse illustrates some of these distinctions. Specific spaces are considered appropriate for men or women who are provided with separate doors at either end of the building (Hugh-Jones 1979: 246–9).

Of course, it is no longer possible to work out exactly how houses were organized in the past, but that is not the important issue. The point is that the division of space inside these different structures—in prehistory and in the ethnographic present—could express some fundamental distinctions among the occupants of the building. It could also influence the ways in which they interacted with one another, for it was on such conventions that social organization depended. Even more importantly, these may not have been explicit rules, requiring some things to happen and proscribing others. Rather, they were habits that developed almost unconsciously through the process of living alongside other people, observing their conduct, and responding to it in the appropriate manner. In that sense, the layout of a dwelling, like the layout of the settlement of which it formed a part, expressed some of the fundamental concerns of the community and helped to develop an awareness of the correct forms of behaviour among its members (Bourdieu 1990). That was not a deliberate strategy on the part of the builders, but it must have been through conventions that people took for granted from childhood that the house exerted an influence over its occupants. The layout of the domestic dwellings reflected some of these concerns.

If the perception of domestic space is never neutral, certain influences may be experienced much more directly than others. For example, it has been claimed that people who occupy circular buildings have a different sense of space from those who live in a 'carpentered environment' of rectilinear structures (Segall et al 1966; Lawrence and Low 1990; Gregory 1998). Such arguments are difficult to evaluate as they depend on laboratory experiments rather than first-hand observation, but one indication of the importance of such ideas comes from the research of Fletcher (1977). It is unusual because it is based on fieldwork. He accepts the view that human perceptions are governed by an acute awareness of distance. Thus, the sizes of buildings may be in proportion to the amount of space in between them, and the dimensions of their doorways, the organization of individual rooms, and even the sizes of furniture may be directly related to one another. All these measurement conform to a single scheme, albeit an unconscious one. That is fascinating, but of even greater interest is Fletcher's discovery that these systems of intuitive measurement differ between human groups, even in the same area. The clearest demonstration of this point is his account of the organization of a Hopi pueblo in Arizona and that of a nearby Franciscan mission. He could identify a distinct set of dimensions in each context but they were entirely separate from one another, suggesting that perceptions of distance may vary between communities. That is true even when they occupy the same environment.

SUMMARY: THREE RELATIONSHIPS

This discussion has considered three kinds of relationship in the past and in the ethnographic present. The final section of the chapter considers how they are connected with one another.

It is a truism that houses are adapted to their environments. They must provide shelter from the elements, they should be insulated from extremes of heat and cold, and they should be able to maintain their stability, even in the strongest winds. Unless they do so, they cannot perform their primary function. Some of the contrasts observed between prehistoric buildings reflect these considerations and, to that extent, their characteristic architecture will differ from one region to another. It will also change its nature according to the length of time over which a dwelling is occupied. As Flannery observed forty years ago, those relationships play a fundamental part in any analysis, but they do not determine the precise forms taken by ancient houses. Nor do they shed much light on the symbolic significance of these buildings. Although the meanings ascribed to particular elements may not be unique, they cannot be inferred on the basis of cross-cultural comparison. It was one of the points made by Douglas in her contribution to *Man, Settlement and Urbanism*.

That is because two other relationships must be considered (Figure 15). The first extends from the regional scale to the local. The forms taken by domestic buildings are influenced by the ways in which the people who construct them perceive the wider world. On one level there are some straightforward contrasts; for instance, an open landscape appears completely different from a forested environment. These factors influence people's conceptions of space, so that their contrasting experiences may affect the ways in which they design their buildings. At the same time, the forms of domestic structures are not the direct outcome of the inhabitants' lived experience, for their houses also provide a commentary on the world and their place within it. That is why Hugh-Jones says that the Pirá-paraná 'construct their houses to represent the universe' (1979: 235).

The experience of living in houses also affects the attitudes of different communities and reinforces the unspoken conventions on which social life depends. It influences the perception of space on a much more local scale. That can easily extend to other aspects of the built environment. For this reason, it is claimed that the inhabitants of rectilinear buildings and settlements see the world in a different way from those who live in roundhouses. If that argument has any merit, it would mean that similar conceptions of space might have been important at two completely different scales. The forms of the familiar landscape might have coloured the ways in which domestic houses were organized, whilst the plans of those buildings also influenced how their occupants viewed the world. Both perspectives reinforced one another and the importance of these issues perhaps increased over time.

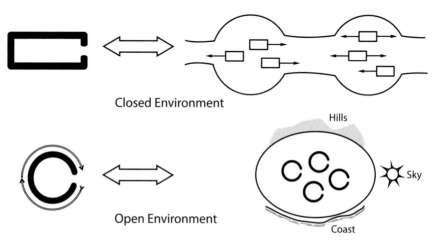

Figure 15 Round and rectangular buildings as microcosms of the local environment.

ANOTHER CAVEAT

Here, there is a danger of adopting a purely functional model. As Chapter 1 has indicated, circular houses were widely distributed before the adoption of agriculture. It is tempting to suppose that it happened for entirely practical reasons—such structures are easy to build and often easy to dismantle—but that is no reason to suppose that they lacked any further significance. Did the symbolic importance of the house begin with the change from hunting and gathering to farming? Current research in the Near East does not support that view.

In fact, it seems likely that the organization of houses and settlements became more complex well before the first changes from circular to rectilinear buildings (Kuijt 2000; Kuijt and Goring-Morris 2002; Watkins 2010). A number of separate features seem to be represented over the entire sequence from the last hunter gatherers to the development of villages of sedentary farmers. None has an obvious 'functional' explanation. They include: arrangements of animal bones laid out in anthropomorphic or zoomorphic patterns; the erection of monoliths inside the dwellings; and the deposition of human remains, particularly skulls. All these practices intensified as buildings became larger and more frequent, and settlements increased in size. For the most part, they retained their significance after roundhouses were replaced by rectangular buildings.

If the organization of the house helped to shape the conventions on which society was based, might these ideas have gained more influence where large numbers of people lived together? That might be true where they occupied the same dwellings for a longer period of time. As their relationships with one another became more intense, it seems possible that the spatial organization of these structures took on additional connotations.

Developments of this kind are suggested by two observations which arise out of recent fieldwork. The first is that space inside the settlement became increasingly segmented (Kuijt 2000). Certain areas may have been set aside for use in communal events and it seems likely that a small number of subterranean structures were used as public buildings (Figure 16). They are circular in plan and in Western Asia they can be associated with human remains (Goring-Morris and Belfer-Cohen 2010). It seems possible that their development set in train a process of architectural elaboration which was to lead to the creation of other monuments.

Göbekli Tepe in modern Turkey is the best example of this process. Work at the site is still in progress, but it is clear that it contains a series of monumental circular structures whose floors were excavated into the bedrock. They may originally have been roofed and in the centre of each structure were two massive pillars which could have been anthropomorphic. Others were arranged around the periphery of the building. The monoliths were decorated

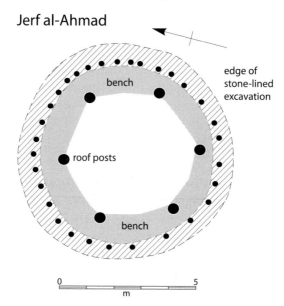

Figure 16 Outline plan of a circular public building at Jerf-al-Ahmad, Syria.

with a series of images, most of which depicted wild animals, and it may be significant that the bones found in the excavation also belong to wild species. Although these monuments date from a period which provides the first evidence of domesticated resources, the excavator believes that these monuments could have been the work of hunters. It is not surprising that he considers this site to be the world's oldest temple (Schmidt 2006).

This view has recently been challenged by Banning (2011), who suggests the alternative interpretation that the structures were monumental houses located within a larger settlement. They might well have played a specialized role, but they should not necessarily be consigned to a distinct category of sacred architecture. Nor need they be considered the work of mobile communities rather than early farmers. Banning receives considerable support from commentators on his article, although it is clear that the problem will not be solved until excavation on the site is further advanced. At the moment, the most significant point is that the subterranean structures at Göbekli Tepe resemble those found in early villages in Anatolia and the Near East and could have been exceptionally elaborate versions of a domestic prototype. Like many other examples of circular architecture, they were replaced in a subsequent phase by rectilinear buildings.

Such dwellings provide one other kind of information. So far, they have been studied in terms of their plans and elevations, as if they existed only as architects' drawings, and yet they formed just part of a more elaborate visual culture. It is known that the interiors of roundhouses and more specialized buildings in the Near East were carefully plastered. Recent fieldwork shows that a few of them were also embellished with painted and incised designs (Watkins 2004, 2010). One feature that has still to be discussed is the fact that circular structures could be decorated with rectilinear motifs. The significance of this observation is not clear, but very similar relationships can be identified in Europe where the contrasts between rectangles and circles, angles, and curves extend from the footprints of ancient buildings to the patterns on their walls. The same applies to the portable artefacts made and used by the inhabitants. This provides an entirely different perspective on ancient perceptions of space. The evidence is elusive and often difficult to interpret, but, for all its problems, it provides the subject matter of Chapter 3.

3

Life and Art

INTRODUCTION: UNEARTHING ANCIENT ART

Not many prehistoric houses survive above their foundations. The three dimensions of the buildings are collapsed (sometimes literally) into the two dimensions of the site plan. That may be all that can be discovered by archaeology, and yet the missing component could have been all-important. The change of perspective is revealing, for the treatment of the walls and roof may be just as significant as the layout of the floor. Few excavated houses are as well preserved as those in the Near East, and there are many parts of Europe in which the question cannot be investigated directly. Here, the existence of ceramic models suggests an alternative approach.

During 2010, two exhibitions featuring the arts of the first farmers took place in Britain. They ran simultaneously, one in Oxford and the other in Norwich. They also complemented one another geographically and thematically. *The Lost World of Old Europe* was organized by The Institute for the Study of the Ancient World at New York University (Anthony 2010), and *Unearthed* by the Sainsbury Centre for Visual Arts of the University of East Anglia (Bailey et al 2010). The display at the Ashmolean Museum in Oxford featured artefacts from Romania, Moldova, and Bulgaria, whilst that in Norwich was restricted to finds of figurines from Romania, Albania, and Macedonia, although they were compared with others from the Jomon Culture of Japan. Not surprisingly, the Neolithic and Chalcolithic objects spanned a long period of time and were associated with several regional groups. Some were elaborately decorated, while others were entirely plain.

The artefacts shown in Norwich were all depictions of the human form, but those in Oxford also included pottery vessels, stone artefacts, and early metalwork. One small group of objects was especially striking, for it consisted of ceramic models of domestic buildings. In one case, from the Cucuteni Culture of Romania, a group of figurines had been discovered inside a miniature house of this kind.

The evidence of such models is revealing. There were examples in which the outer wall was highlighted by angular designs, as if to emphasize the rectilinear outline of the building, but there was also a model in the Oxford exhibition which showed a structure with a similar ground plan whose exterior was covered by curvilinear motifs. It seems that more than one kind of image might have been used concurrently, so that angular motifs reinforced the traditional form of the dwellings, whilst curved designs created a link with other media. In certain cases, both occurred together, but it is difficult to say how frequently this happened because few of these miniature dwellings come from well-documented contexts.

Fortunately, there is another region in which such relationships can be studied in more detail. Between the tenth and eighth centuries BC a group of miniature buildings was made in Central Italy (Bartoloni et al. 1987; Sabatini 2007; Figure 17). Again, they were ceramic vessels whose appearance was modelled on the forms of domestic dwellings. In this case, the artefacts depicted roundhouses, although some of the excavated structures of the same period have, in fact, oval plans. Not all these vessels were decorated, but, where this did occur, the outer wall was embellished with complex linear designs. In contrast to the houses in south-east Europe, the plan of the building conformed to a circular archetype, but its exterior was characterized by angular motifs.

It was not the only way in which Italian house urns were treated. Two vessels from the cemetery at Vulci are unusual because they are made of

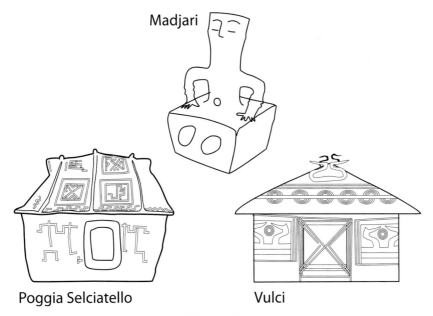

Figure 17 An anthropomorphic building model from Macedonia and two house urns from Italy.

bronze (Sabatini 2007: 153–5). Their decoration is also informative. It recalls the metalwork of the Urnfield period in Central Europe and features a series of concentric circles, as well as naturalistic images of birds (Kossack 1954). Their presence raises an important issue, for similar depictions of birds occur on top of some of the ceramic models. It suggests that these buildings might have played a special role, and this idea is supported by the fact that such urns are found in cemeteries and contain human bones. It may be no accident that birds play such an important part in a period when cremation was the mortuary rite. Their presence might have symbolized the dissolution of the body as smoke rose into the sky (Gräslund 1994).

If the Italian hut urns combined model buildings with depictions of birds, the Neolithic models found in Southern Europe also had a composite character. Decoration is found on ceramic stamps and figurines. Moreover, there are vessels with similar designs that feature images of the human body, including faces, eyes, legs, and genitals. They were obviously intended to portray women. Still more striking are a number of artefacts which combine the human form with that of a domestic building. Naumov (2007) has suggested that the female images represent the household and that the dwelling was associated with nurture and fertility. Like the Amazonian longhouses discussed in Chapter Two, they could be compared with the womb. This idea recalls the evidence that houses can be regarded as living creatures (Herva 2009). Again, the study of prehistoric buildings cannot be restricted to practical concerns.

CULTURAL GEOMETRY

One of the most original studies of the Neolithic period is a book by Jacques Cauvin, first published in French in 1994 and translated into English six years later. Its title is intriguing: *The Birth of the Gods and the Origins of Agriculture.* Long before it was fashionable to do so, Cauvin argued that it was vital to investigate the first farmers through their beliefs about the world.

One part of his research concerned the forms of domestic buildings, but instead of confining himself to the kinds of functional argument considered already, he emphasized the wider connotations of the circle and the rectangle:

> In the universal language of simple forms, the circle (or the sphere) signifies both that which transcends man and remains beyond his reach (the sun, the cosmic totality, 'God'), and also that which, at its own sub-lunar level, relates to germination, to the maternal, to the intimate. On the contrary, the rectangle, examples of which are rare in our everyday observations of nature, requires human initiative for its existence; the stone is not cubic or rectangular unless so fashioned. The square and the rectangle denote, then, the manifest, the concrete, that which has been realised (Cauvin 2000: 132)

The quotation is taken from a discussion of Neolithic house plans, but, in principle, it could have even wider implications. Was the same distinction between the circular and the rectangular expressed in other media? That would mean that the argument could apply not only to architecture but also to decorated artefacts.

Cauvin advanced a second, more provocative idea. It is difficult to discuss, but is considered here because it is so closely linked to his other suggestions on the significance of rectangles and circles:

> We also know that at the level of the still very elemental imagination, the curve is feminine while the straight line and the angular are masculine (Cauvin 2000: 132)

In this case, ethnographic sources may be more informative than the results of archaeological fieldwork.

SYMBOLS IN ACTION

If the exhibition in Oxford allowed the viewer to compare different aspects of Neolithic visual culture, its counterpart in Norwich had a different remit, for it was limited to depictions of the human body and its aim was to compare examples from south-east Europe with others from Japan.

The comparative perspective is important, but can be misunderstood. Its purpose is to consider the visual environment in which ancient people lived and the attention they devoted to particular kinds of decoration. It is not to make cross-cultural generalizations of the kind suggested by Cauvin. This approach does not allow researchers to discover the meaning of any particular design. At best, it helps them to consider the *contexts* in which it might have been *meaningful*. That method is especially relevant to accounts of ancient buildings.

An important source of comparison is provided by ethnoarchaeology. Here, a good starting point is Hodder's book *Symbols in Action* (Hodder 1982). Its aim was to assess some of the ways in which material culture had been studied by comparing the approaches taken by archaeologists with the results of research among contemporary communities in Africa. Hodder's main concern was with spatial patterning, from settlements and artefacts to houses and cemeteries. His work suggested that the patterns observed by prehistorians might be the result of factors they had overlooked. The archaeological record was not a simple reflection of communications or identities in the past.

If house decoration supplies one source of information, what can be said of the designs in other media? Did similar conventions extend to the decoration of artefacts and human bodies? That is certainly suggested by African ethnography.

The Nuba

One of Hodder's most detailed studies was concerned with the Nuba of Sudan (1982: chapter 8). It compared the use of material culture in three tribal groups: the Moro, Mesakin Tiwal, and Mesakin Qisar. He placed a particular emphasis on the decoration applied to their dwellings, their bodies, and their portable artefacts. That is why his work is relevant to this study.

The Nuba live in roundhouses, grouped together to form small circular compounds (Figure 18). Each has a single entrance. Individual buildings played different roles, and there was an important distinction between the structures occupied by men and those inhabited by women. The compounds included space for domestic animals, and they also contained raised platforms and grain storage pits. The separate groups organized their activities in different ways, and it is clear from Hodder's account that fears about pollution were particularly important for the Mesakin.

That concern is reflected in several ways: by the patterns of movement around the occupied area; by distinctive attitudes to the disposal of refuse; by

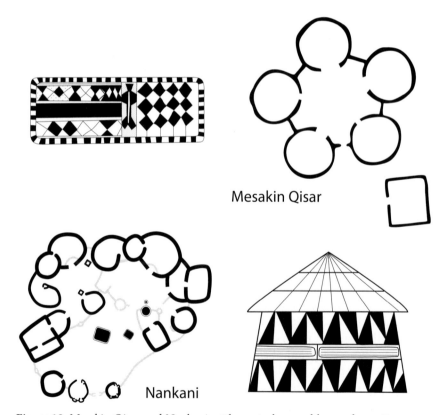

Mesakin Qisar

Nankani

Figure 18 Mesakin Qisar and Nankani settlement plans and house decoration.

the treatment of the dead; and by the elaboration of boundaries within the settlements themselves. Often those boundaries are decorated, but the forms that this decoration takes have even wider connotations, for the designs are closely related to those in other media. They include the motifs applied to human bodies and those on artefacts like pots and calabashes. Some of the most obvious decoration occurs on the walls of houses, especially the interior.

Hodder studies the distributions of these striking designs in an attempt to understand their significance. He investigates the ways in which they were composed, and their associations among the Nuba. Female breasts are depicted at the entrance to the huts, but, he says:

> The symbolism in the panels which surround this central female area is explicitly male. The designs are those which are painted and scarred on male bodies only . . . Symbolically, then, male symbols enclose the female area around the entrance to the hut (1982: 141).

At no point does he comment on one of their most striking characteristics. Curvilinear elements are comparatively rare, and Hodder's analysis of the visual culture of the Nuba focuses almost entirely on their use of angular motifs. It is these designs that are shared so widely between different media, yet nowhere in his book does he discuss the fact that the people who make them live in circular buildings. Indeed, those angular designs are sometimes applied to the walls of their dwellings, which recalls the evidence of Italian house urns.

The Nankani

A second African example illustrates some of the same points, but this time it has been studied as a contribution to social anthropology rather than archaeological theory. Like the Nuba, the Nankani, who straddle the border between Ghana and Burkina Faso, live in scattered compounds which are composed mainly of circular buildings (Cole 2000: 162–5). There are important contrasts with those just described. The domestic units are larger than their counterparts in Sudan and contain more separate structures. The layout of these enclosures also makes allowance for defence, as there are low barriers across the only opening to the compound, and others in the doorways of the individual houses. The dwellings are carefully located so that they command an uninterrupted view of the entrance. The domestic buildings are more varied than those of the Nuba. The main public space is in the centre of the compound, and it is where most tasks are undertaken. Here, there is a corral for cattle which is regarded as a masculine domain, but the area further from the entrance is thought of as increasingly private and is usually a female preserve. Granaries are also located within the enclosure, while just outside the entrance there is commonly a shrine. Other shrines are associated with individual dwellings.

The buildings of the settlement are lavishly decorated on both the interior and exterior, and the same applies to the furniture and portable objects within them. The structures are erected by the men, but it is the women who provide the decoration. There are a few curvilinear motifs which are usually three-dimensional and formed by moulding wet plaster while the designs are being made. They occupy inconspicuous locations; otherwise, the decorative schemes are predominantly linear and horizontal. To Western eyes they appear abstract, but for the Nankani they represent calabashes and nets. The same designs are rendered in other media, including ceramics and basketry. There is also a link with the human body, as the faces of men and women carry similar motifs, and Nankani masks are embellished in the same style. The quality of the decoration on the buildings is a particular source of prestige and it is renewed every few years.

Among the Nankani, roundhouses are associated with women. These buildings are compared to wombs, for they are where children are born and nurtured—a feature that recalls Naumov's interpretation of Neolithic houses in Southern Europe. Other buildings are associated with the preparation of food and, in this case, the link between human fertility and sustenance is enhanced because the different structures, their contents, and even the bodies of the occupants, carry the same decoration. If 'female' houses are compared with the womb, the same idea cannot apply to the rectangular buildings in which the men live. Thus, the contrasts between their architecture have wider implications.

Both these examples have been taken from African ethnography. They contrast in several ways, but both cases illustrate the same point: circular buildings can be the dominant, even the only, form of dwelling in societies in which the visual culture is predominantly linear. The contrast is so striking that it must have been intentional. It recalls the archaeological evidence from Bronze Age Italy where circular models of buildings were decorated with angular designs.

PATTERNING IN PREHISTORY

Similarities of this kind are striking, but are they relevant to prehistoric Europe? Is there sufficient evidence that the distinction between angles and curves emphasized by Cauvin really was important, and, if so, was it significant outside the built environment? The best starting point is to return to the Neolithic period and to consider two more examples, associated with each of the geographical axes discussed in Chapter 1. Further cases are taken from the Bronze Age, the Iron Age, and the Early Medieval period.

The Linear Pottery Culture

The ideal staring point is the Linear Pottery Culture because it characterizes the agricultural colonization of Central and Northern Europe. It is associated with longhouses of exceptional proportions. They show some variations from one region to another, and their forms changed in minor ways over the course of time. Even so, they were monumental buildings, and were first used in regions where there was little, or no, sign of circular constructions (Coudart 1998). The situation did not change significantly where their shapes were modified and they adopted a trapezoidal plan.

The houses of the Linear Pottery Culture altered their positions within the settled area. This may have happened at regular intervals, and it is tempting to suggest that such structures were replaced quite rapidly, as seems to have happened in the tells of south-east Europe. Over longer periods, entire settlements were abandoned as the inhabitants moved to new locations. These complex sequences provide the basis for sophisticated analyses of the associated pottery. Seriation of these vessels creates an overall chronology and it is only recently that radiocarbon has been used on a sufficient scale to offer another method of dating. The two approaches are in broad agreement with one another.

As the name suggests, the Linear Pottery Culture is as easily characterized by its ceramics as it is by domestic buildings (Figure 19). Recent research has shown that decorated pottery changed its form more rapidly than the houses with which it is found, but it happened in a distinctive way. In north-west Germany, where many settlements have been investigated, the earlier longhouses are associated with pottery with predominantly curvilinear decoration (Stöckli 2005). Thus, the elongated outline of the buildings contrasts sharply with the appearance of the ceramics used by the people who lived there. The situation gradually changed, so that around 5000 BC such motifs became less frequent and angular designs were more apparent. Still later in the sequence, the amount of decoration on the vessels diminished. It did not happen everywhere, but, in this particular case, it seems as if two different ways of dividing space—one monumental and the other one extremely small scale— gradually coalesced, with the result that what began as a striking contrast gradually disappeared.

Grooved Ware and megalithic art

A similar interplay between different forms is found in the Neolithic period in Britain and Ireland, and, again, its ramifications extend from the decoration of small objects to the forms of massive buildings. Chapter 1 made the point that

House plans   Main pottery
decoration

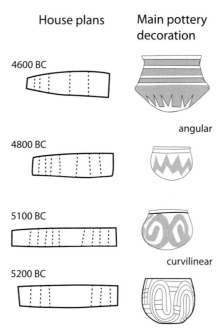

Figure 19 An outline of the sequence of Linear Pottery Culture longhouses and decorated vessels in north-west Germany.

this was one of the few regions to experience a change from rectangular to circular architecture over the course of time. It happened because of the growing influence of communities on the Atlantic seaboard and it had three results. The first was the construction of a series of megalithic tombs which were embellished by non-figurative incised and pecked motifs. The second was a growing emphasis on circular monuments that extended from the closed spaces of the passage grave to open arenas bounded by palisades, rings of upright stones, and earthworks. The oldest roundhouses may date from this phase. The last development was the emergence of a new tradition of deco-rated pottery—Grooved Ware—which probably originated in Orkney and, perhaps, in Ireland (Bradley 2007: 116–17; Darvill 2010: 139).

Each of these developments had implications for the perception of space. Passage graves were predominantly circular, as were the monuments like *henges* which probably succeeded them. These enclosures could also be asso-ciated with stone and timber circles, whose ground plans resemble those of some Late Neolithic domestic buildings. Many of the carved motifs associated with the chambered tombs were also circular, and similar motifs were made on rock outcrops in the open air. Angular designs occur in certain Irish passage tombs and most of those in Orkney, but similar motifs were much more common on the pottery that developed during this period. That observation is

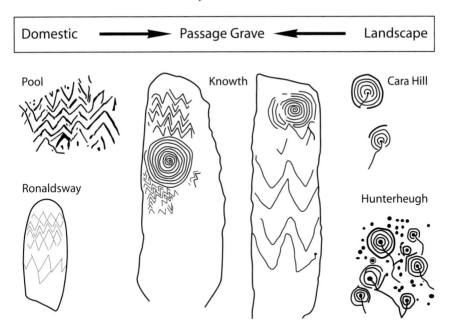

Figure 20 Linear and curvilinear decoration in Late Neolithic Britain and Ireland based on examples from domestic sites, open air rock carvings, and passage graves.

important, as Grooved Ware is the main ceramic tradition associated with henges, timber circles, and settlements. Similar geometric designs were incised on the walls of Orcadian houses.

As a result of these changes, there seem to have been two very different relationships between circular and angular forms during the Late Neolithic period. The first concerned timber settings and henge monuments, both of which adhered to a circular ground plan. Some domestic buildings did the same. All these structures were associated with pottery decorated with predominantly angular designs. It follows that there was a contrast between the forms employed in different contexts (Bradley 2007: 98–122). A second point concerns prehistoric rock art. The decoration pecked into natural outcrops features curvilinear forms and, in this case, angular designs are most unusual. Some of those decorated surfaces are found near groups of circular monuments.

There is only one context in which both strands come together: the decorated passage graves on either side of the Irish Sea and particularly those in the Boyne Valley (Figure 20). Perhaps they drew on different sources of inspiration. The first were the angular designs associated with decorated pottery and with the stone houses of Orkney. The second were the circular motifs found at natural places in the landscape. In megalithic art, both these groups were combined to form decorated panels that have no equivalents in other media. Again, it seems as if angular and curved designs had different connotations (Bradley 2009: 112–22). As happened in the African examples, people who constructed circular buildings used pottery and other artefacts with linear decoration.

Bell Beaker artefacts, settlements, and monuments in the British Isles

The Atlantic axis that was associated with passage graves was also a source of early metallurgy and the distinctive style of pottery known as the Bell Beaker. Over the course of time, the people who used these vessels exchanged artefacts and raw materials with other groups in Northern and Central Europe whose own ceramic tradition is known as Corded Ware. Elements of their local practices were gradually combined, and both traditions came to influence the archaeological sequence in the British Isles (Needham 2005). It is not clear how far this process involved the movement of people, but it is certainly true that Bell Beakers and their associations replaced the Grooved Ware tradition. Their relevance to this discussion is easy to explain. The pots and most of the metalwork associated with them have entirely linear decoration, whilst some of the burials in which they are found were deposited inside *circular* enclosures or beneath *round* barrows.

The importance of circular architecture was even greater than this summary suggests (Figure 21). The people who made Bell Beakers continued to employ henge monuments and may have constructed new ones (Bradley 2007: 152–3; Darvill 2010: 179–85). The same applies to stone circles and roundhouses. In fact, there are very few signs of rectilinear structures of any kind. To some extent that may be because the Beaker tradition first emerged in the fortified settlements of Iberia, which themselves included curvilinear enclosures, roundhouses, bastions, and towers (Kunst 2001). The idea remains controversial, but it is certainly true that from the first introduction of Beakers and metallurgy there was a continuous tradition of circular monuments and dwellings in Britain and Ireland. That remained the case throughout the Bronze Age. What is especially striking is that the predilection for curvilinear forms is completely absent from the pottery used at the same time and from nearly all the metalwork of the period. Indeed, there are certain kinds of artefact—gold collars (*lunulae*) and axeheads—which were decorated with the same designs as ceramics. The striking distinction between the embellishment of portable objects and the circular forms that characterized the built environment remained unchanged until the end of the insular Bronze Age (Bradley 2007: Chapter 4).

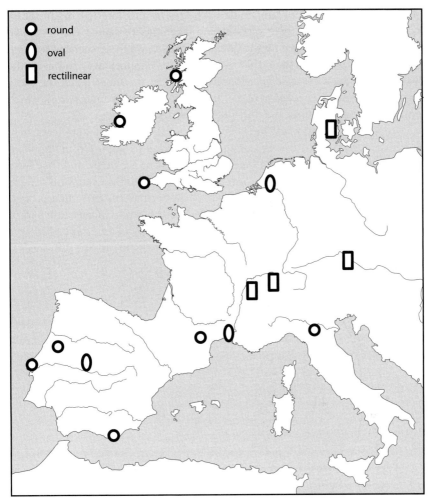

Figure 21 Outline plans of Bell Beaker houses based on excavated examples in different regions of Europe.

Bronze Age settlements, pottery, and metalwork in Northern Europe

Corded Ware and Bell Beakers are not associated with roundhouses in Northern or Central Europe, nor were any constructed after these styles of pottery had gone out of use. Instead, the houses associated with Bell Beakers take the traditional local forms and they are generally oval or rectangular in these regions (Besse and Desideria 2005). Just as roundhouses continued to be built throughout the British and Irish Bronze Ages, in South Scandinavia there was an unbroken tradition of longhouses. Their size and internal organization changed, but the basic form of domestic dwellings remained the same. To some extent, it was echoed by the linear decoration on the associated pottery, but, over the course of time, this lost its original importance, and after the Beaker phase most ceramic vessels were plain. On the other hand, the Early Bronze Age saw the development of a tradition of decorated metalwork which remained significant until the mid-first millennium BC (Figure 22).

Two points are important here. The first is that these metal artefacts were obviously special. Whether or not they were made of imported materials, it would have taken considerable time and skill to produce them, and they were deposited in distinctive contexts. Some were buried with the dead, while others were committed to the ground or placed in watery environments, such as bogs. They are rarely found inside settlements and need not have played any part in

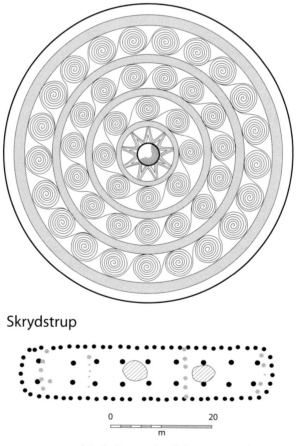

Skrydstrup

0   20
                m

Figure 22 An unprovenanced Early Bronze Age belt ornament from southern Sweden and the plan of a longhouse of the same date at Skrydstrup, Denmark.

daily life. Quite possibly they were displayed or worn only on rare occasions. The second point is more straightforward. With few exceptions, the decoration on these items was curvilinear, with an emphasis on circles and spirals.

Some of these designs have been studied by Randsborg (2006), who concludes that they represent the sun. It is possible, as comparable designs feature in South Scandinavian rock art, which has similar associations. That is certainly the contention of Kaul (2004) who has used the decorated metalwork of Bronze Age Denmark to reconstruct an ancient cosmology. Randsborg's account goes even further, for he suggests that the details of the circular designs carry information about the ancient calendar, but, while his analysis is ingenious, it may be too complicated. It is enough to say that much of the decorated metalwork had a restricted currency and a special meaning. It is certainly true that its imagery employs very different forms from the rectilinear buildings of the same period.

This relationship is the exact opposite of the situation in Britain and Ireland where people who lived in roundhouses embellished their artefacts with angular designs. In that case, it applied not only to specialized objects, but also to the pottery used in settlements. During the same period in Northern Europe, domestic ceramics were mostly undecorated. On the other hand, a series of metal items carried complex circular designs. There was a striking contrast within both areas, but also a contrast between them.

Art styles and the domestic architecture of the European Iron Age

So far, this account has identified some striking patterns. There were rectangular houses occupied by people whose artefacts were decorated with curvilinear motifs. That could be seen in the Neolithic period in parts of south-east Europe. It was also illustrated by the Bronze Age in Northern Europe. There were other examples in which the opposite relationship is found, so that during the Late Neolithic period in Britain and Ireland communities who built circular monuments used a style of pottery that, with only rare exceptions, was embellished with angular motifs. It was also true in the insular Early Bronze Age when roundhouses were the only form of domestic architecture.

There was another case in which pottery decoration changed whilst the shapes of the domestic houses remained largely unaltered. This happened in the Linear Pottery Culture in north-west Germany where curvilinear motifs became less frequent with the passage of time. A very similar pattern has been identified in the Iron Age of north-west Europe, but, in this case, the evidence extends from houses to both pottery and metal artefacts.

This is the period in which the contrast between rectilinear and circular architecture is most apparent. The important differences between the buildings found on either side of the English Channel and the North Sea were mentioned in Chapter 1. Now it is time to look at this evidence in more detail. Like the example from the Linear Pottery Culture, the relationship between the forms of houses and those of portable objects seems to have changed over time.

Certain points are generally accepted. In the early years of the Iron Age, domestic architecture was divided between three structural traditions. Round-houses were important in Britain, Ireland, and parts of the Iberian Peninsula. Further examples have been identified in Northern France, but so far they have been in areas close to the sea (Jahier et al. 2000). With that exception, the prevailing model was the rectangular dwelling. In South Scandinavia, there were longhouses similar to those occupied in the Late Bronze Age, but in other regions the buildings might be significantly smaller, with the result that it is difficult for excavators to distinguish between houses and ancillary structures. Only the raised granaries shared the same ground plan in all these traditions of architecture.

There are more sources of variation. Some of the Iron Age settlements were open sites, whilst others were enclosed. Those enclosures might be independent units, or they could be linked to one another to form a more extensive complex. They adopted a variety of ground plans, so that certain examples favoured a circular layout whilst others were approximately square or rectangular. At that level, there is little to distinguish the pattern on either side of the English Channel (Bastide 2000). The same applies to the defended sites described as hillforts. They could adopt similar plans, but the houses inside them were very different from one another.

The classic sequence in the European Iron Age extends from the Hallstatt period, characterized by the contents of a cemetery in Austria, to the La Tène phase. The latter is defined by the kinds of metalwork deposited in a Swiss river. Each tradition can be subdivided along chronological and regional lines, but, for the most part, their material culture changes in a striking manner (Megaw and Megaw 2001; Harding 2007). The pottery and metalwork of the Hallstatt tradition may be embellished with geometric patterns. The same is true of the textiles associated with the rich burial at Hochdorf (Banck-Burgess 1999). During the La Tène period, however, craft workers became aware of other styles of visual imagery. These influenced the appearance of decorated artefacts which underwent a complete transformation (Figure 23). The geometric patterns favoured during the Hallstatt phase were replaced by a growing abundance of curvilinear designs inspired by Classical prototypes. The new style is described as 'La Tène' or 'Celtic' art. As well as apparently abstract motifs, it incorporated vibrant images of people and animals (Megaw and Megaw 2001).

Whilst styles of metalwork and pottery decoration changed, domestic architecture remained virtually the same. As a result, Iron Age communities

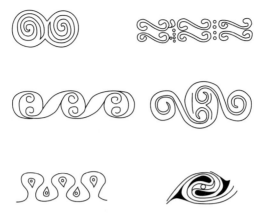

Figure 23 Examples of typical curvilinear motifs in Celtic Art identified by Paul Jacobsthal (1944).

on the continent continued living in rectangular houses, whilst the artefacts of the same period could be decorated with flowing curvilinear designs. By contrast, the inhabitants of Britain and Ireland made objects which had been elaborated in the same style, but, in this case, they lived in roundhouses (Jope 2000).

The contexts of these 'art objects' are worth considering in more detail, for they are seldom found in the excavation of settlements. Rather, they are frequently discovered in graves, in rivers, and also in a series of specialized sites which are interpreted as sanctuaries (Brunaux et al. 1985; Wells 2007). Like the decorated metalwork of the Nordic Bronze Age, these items may have played a restricted role. So much time and effort went into their creation that it is clear that they were not available to everyone. For a long time they were studied using the methods of art history, but now there is a greater willingness to integrate them with broader studies of Iron Age society. The Megaws, who have done more than most scholars to investigate 'Celtic art', have come to the conclusion that it possessed a sacred character and that the elaborately decorated artefacts were different from those employed in daily life (Megaw and Megaw 2001: 16–22).

Support for this contention comes from a paper by Christopher Evans (1989) who considers a large assemblage of well-preserved artefacts from the Glastonbury lake village in south-west England. Although the settlement lends its name to a ceramic style decorated with La Tène motifs, he observes how few of the objects carried any kind of embellishment; the great majority were plain. As many of them were made of wood which rarely survives on other sites, this is a striking conclusion. It reinforces the argument that this style of imagery could have played a specialized role.

The 'ultimate La Tène' in Ireland

Further light on some of these issues comes from studies of the latest phase in the development of 'Celtic' art in Ireland and Britain. This is a controversial subject. Either La Tène ornamentation persisted without a break into the later first millennium AD, or there were two distinct styles of imagery which resembled one another in certain respects but were largely independent phenomena. Much of the difficulty arises from the different histories of these islands. Large parts of Britain were incorporated into the Roman Empire, whilst Ireland remained outside the frontier altogether. Even this oversimplifies the issue, for the outer limit of Roman rule fluctuated over time so that areas of Northern Britain maintained their independence. For some scholars it was in those areas that Celtic art had a continuous history, re-emerging as a major element after the departure of the Roman army (Henry 1965; Megaw and Megaw 2001: Chapter 7). For other researchers, there is little, or no, evidence of continuity (Laing 2005). It seems possible that the traditional elements that were maintained in the art of Early Medieval Ireland were those that had already been assimilated into Late Roman visual culture. At all events, few of the artefact types found in Ireland date from the earlier first millennium AD.

There have been two important developments during recent years. The first is the direct dating of a number of decorated artefacts which belong to the corpus of Celtic art in Britain. This has been achieved by the study of small samples taken from the objects, or from the bones associated with them in graves. This work has had a drastic effect on the traditional chronology, for it has shown that decorated La Tène metalwork originated in the fourth century BC and that its main period of importance ended in the first century BC (Garrow et al. 2009). This was a radical revision as it had been supposed that this style was adopted later, and had remained in use for longer, in Britain than in continental Europe. The same chronology should apply to at least some of the Irish material, although it was not included in this programme. Barry Raftery (1984, 1994) has shown that there are striking similarities between the decorated metalwork of both islands. The radiocarbon dates call into question the results of previous research.

At the same time, it is clear that a smaller quantity of decorated metalwork was used after the Roman Conquest, but it was made in a distinctive style and was most common outside the urban landscape of lowland Britain (Hunter 2008). The curvilinear aspect remained important, as it may have done in Ireland, but, in its classic manifestation, the La Tène style lost much of its significance. This may be evidenced by a small group of radiocarbon dates obtained during the recent project. They are separated from the others by an interval of about a hundred years.

These arguments converge in suggesting that there was little direct connection between the visual arts of the pre- and post-Roman periods. Indeed, it was not until two centuries after the collapse of Roman rule in Britain that what Henry (1965) called the 'ultimate La Tène' style became important in Ireland (Figure 24). By that time, the inhabitants of large parts of England had adopted a quite different visual culture which had been introduced by settlers from Northern Europe. Where Irish art was essentially curvilinear, its Anglo-Saxon counterpart employed a mixture of curving and angular designs, together with complex interlacing patterns and depictions of humans and animals.

Two further contrasts are important. Whether or not 'Roman Celtic art' forms a link between the pre-Conquest phase and the early medieval period, it is clear that it was most common in regions near, or beyond, the frontier where a tradition of circular architecture retained its importance. That is as true of Scotland and Wales as it is of Ireland (Laing 2005; Hunter 2008). It is

Inishkea North

Figure 24 'Ultimate La Tène' motifs on a decorated slab from Inishkea, Ireland.

even more significant that in areas of Anglo-Saxon settlement, rectangular buildings became the norm.

Among the circular structures in Ireland there were early monasteries. Not all of them took this form, but it happened sufficiently widely to call for comment. Indeed, the persistence of the circular archetype can make it difficult to distinguish between sacred and secular structures during this period. Some insight is provided by literary evidence, but other information comes from the distinctive material culture of the ecclesiastical sites which includes fine metalwork embellished with curvilinear designs. Some of the most impressive carry Christian symbols. Where the earlier decorated metal-work was characterized by weapons, torcs, cauldrons, and horse gear, in the first millennium AD the most elaborate artefacts were used in the liturgy. Even the lavishly decorated brooches need not have been personal ornaments, for a few examples appear to have been attached to reliquaries (Nieke 1993). The last phase of 'Celtic art' took place after the conversion to Christianity and it is not surprising that it is also exemplified among Irish high crosses and illuminated manuscripts.

There were close contacts between Ireland and Britain, and metalwork in both styles was made at major centres like Dunadd (Lane and Campbell 2000) and the Mote of Mark in the west of Scotland (Laing and Longley 2006), just as they are represented together among the contents of the English cemetery at Sutton Hoo (Carver 2005). Even so, they retained their separate identities. The same contrast is apparent among traditions of domestic and public architecture, although it would be wrong to imagine that all these distinctions observed the contrast between curvilinear and rectilinear forms described by Cauvin. On the other hand, it may have been because the inhabitants of Ireland were accustomed to a world of circular architecture that the artistic vocabulary of the 'ultimate La Tène' was adopted with such enthusiasm and deployed to such spectacular effect. Chapter 10 will return to this topic.

IDEAS OF ORDER

Was Cauvin right to place so much emphasis on the differences between circular and rectangular forms? Is the distinction between angles and curves useful in prehistoric and early historical archaeology? The previous chapter considered the interplay between functional and ideological factors that went into the creation of houses. It was clearly impossible to dispense with either, for both could make an important contribution to research. On the other hand, the contrast between these two sets of decorative designs introduces quite different issues, even when those designs are directly related to ancient architecture. There is no reason why rectilinear decoration makes a house more habitable than the use of a circular design. In the same way, there is no practical advantage in reflecting the shapes of these buildings in the embellishment of portable objects. Indeed, there are cases in which the opposite relationship occurs in both archaeology and the ethnographic record. This chapter has considered a few examples which may typify a wider pattern.

The argument should not be over-stated. This account has described situations in which the forms of ancient buildings were reflected—or not reflected—by the decoration of the artefacts associated with them. In some cases, similarities or differences extend to designs in other media—deposits of fine metalwork, rock carvings, and megalithic art—which were not so clearly represented in the domestic domain. But there are other instances in which no patterning of either kind can be recognized. Many artefacts were never decorated, or were enhanced by decoration that has not survived. The shapes of ancient buildings can often be determined by excavation, yet their internal fittings, their contents, and their wall decoration (if any) have left no trace. The only source of information is provided by ceramic models whose original purpose is largely unknown. It follows that, whilst a few striking patterns can be identified, considerable uncertainty remains.

Even so, one idea links nearly all the cases considered here. It is the deceptively simple point that particular societies, both ancient and modern, have made a clear distinction between rectilinear and curvilinear forms. That contrast is rarely observed and still more rarely discussed, and yet it is found very widely. It applies to the ground plans of individual houses, to the ways in which they were decorated, and even to the artefacts associated with them. On that level, Cauvin's observation seems to be valid; however, it is less obvious whether he interpreted it correctly.

Sacred and secular

An important point is suggested by these styles of visual images. It may have been quite common for separate kinds of imagery to coexist in the same societies. This possibility was considered by Layton in his book on the anthropology of art. Quite different designs can be found in the same society; they simply play different roles. Thus, in Aboriginal Australia large figurative panels have the greatest visual impact, but it is the simple geometric forms that may be the most specialized of all (Layton 1991: 191). It is because it is impossible to interpret them without a guide. Can prehistorians recognize a similar distinction between the sacred and the secular, the private and public?

That is suggested by the interpretation of Celtic Art, but exactly the same point can be made about Neolithic and Bronze Age designs. The Megaws conclude that the most elaborate Iron Age metalwork had a religious character (Megaw and Megaw 2001: 16–22). It is partly because of its characteristic imagery, but their interpretation is also informed by the contexts in which these artefacts are found. In most cases they were buried with the dead, placed in votive deposits, or exhibited at sanctuaries. Much the same can be said about the decorated metalwork of the Nordic Bronze Age in which circular designs play a prominent role (Randsborg 2006). A comparable approach can be taken to the images created in other media. Thus, the special significance of circular motifs in Neolithic Britain depends on the observation that they are shared between distinctive places, like passage tombs, decorated outcrops, and stone circles. Angular motifs, however, occur on domestic pottery and occasionally on the walls of houses. In each case, the most specialized designs were formed out of arcs, circles, and spirals, but they are identified as special because of the contexts in which they were used and not because the circle has the same significance in every society. These contrasts between angular and circular designs need to be studied in their local contexts, as Hodder (1982) did when he wrote *Symbols in Action*.

In fact, this chapter has considered only one case in which archaeological interpretations can be assessed in relation to other sources of information—it is in Early Medieval Ireland. This account has already considered the arguments for and against a continuous tradition of 'Celtic art' extending from the pre-Roman Iron Age into the later first millennium AD. The discussion emphasized the continuing significance of a circular archetype in the visual culture of the Early Middle Ages. It also identified the contexts in which the most elaborate artefacts were made and used. Although similar designs can be found on personal ornaments, they are equally apparent on artefacts such as chalices, which were associated with the Christian church. They take their most elaborate form in the illuminated manuscripts created in the monasteries. Even the Irish high cross—perhaps the most public expression of the new religion—was surmounted by a distinctive circular device (Henry 1965). Whether or not a continuous tradition links the decorated artefacts of the prehistoric and early historical periods, there can be no doubt that in its latest manifestation the curvilinear art of ancient Ireland was deployed in a religious context.

To sum up, there are certain cases in which curvilinear motifs did play a specialized role, but are they sufficient to support Cauvin's striking assertion that 'the circle (or the sphere) signifies . . . that which transcends man and remains beyond his reach (the sun, the cosmic totality, "God")' (Cauvin 2000: 132)? This is an exaggeration, but it contains an element of truth. A few examples of this equation have been mentioned here and more will be discussed in Chapters 7 and 8 which consider the distinctive roles played by circular constructions in a world of rectangular buildings.

Female and male

Archaeological sources shed less light on Cauvin's second assertion that 'at the level of the still very elemental imagination, the curve is feminine while the straight line and the angular are masculine' (2000: 132).

It is true that Naumov's analysis of Neolithic pots with human features suggests that they represented women. Moreover, they combined such images with models of domestic dwellings so that these objects could have been associated with beliefs about nurture and fertility (Naumov 2007; cf. Naumov 2009). That is entirely plausible, but it does not involve the exclusive use of curvilinear forms in the way that Cauvin describes. In the same way, the ethnographic examples quoted in this chapter do suggest that certain houses might be a female domain and can even be thought of in the same terms as the womb. That idea was found in the South American example discussed in Chapter Two, and the same idea featured in discussion of the Nankani. But there is an important contrast. In the Amazon, the Pirá-paraná occupy longhouses, but in the West African example women live in the roundhouses and the men occupy rectangular buildings.

In principle, Cauvin's argument should extend to house decoration, but it does not always do so. Although the Nankani occupy rectangular and circular dwellings, the decorative devices found in their settlements are predominantly linear. The same observation was made in Hodder's study of the visual culture of the Nuba. In this case, he claims that male imagery is used to enclose the areas associated with women, but here it is just as hard to move between different scales of analysis. If the decoration applied to human bodies, pots, and calabashes was similar to that on the houses, Cauvin's hypothesis does nothing to explain why all the buildings in the settlements should be circular. Thus, there are cases where the distinctions between these geometric forms are used to highlight divisions in the living space, but there is no reason to suppose that all those differences are associated with gender.

In fact, Cauvin's hypothesis owes more to Leroi-Gourhan's analysis of Palaeolithic cave paintings than it does to any ethnographic evidence. He makes this clear when he states that:

> The Palaeolithic system in particular expressed itself through a purely symbolic classification of . . . species into two complementary sets, one 'masculine' the other 'feminine', always expressed with reciprocal exclusiveness in the pictorial space (Cauvin 2000: 68).

His approach is obviously indebted to structuralism, but this is an interpretation and not a statement of fact. It is significant that Leroi-Gourhan, who had originally proposed the idea, rejected this approach in later life (Leroi-Gourhan 1982). He had already done so *twelve years before* the French edition of Cauvin's book appeared.

CONCLUSION

Cauvin's hypothesis may have been too ambitious, but it has suggested a line of enquiry that extends beyond the spatial organization of houses and monuments. It seems possible that the contrast between curvilinear and rectilinear forms possessed a wider significance for some people in the past—but not for all. On one hand, this discussion shows that the circle may have been especially important in a number of different contexts, but, again, that must not be elevated into a general rule. On the other hand, the problems discussed in this chapter arise in other parts of ancient Europe, where they take a very different form. Part Three will discuss some striking evidence that people who lived in rectangular buildings from the Neolithic period to the Early Middle Ages erected circular structures for special purposes. Some were burial mounds and others temples. In these cases, the contrast between angles and curves that preoccupied Jacques Cauvin reasserts itself on a monumental scale.

Part II

Circular Structures in a Circular World

4

Houses into Tombs

AILLEVANS AND SANT' ANDREA PRIU

At the French site of Aillevans, not far from the border with Switzerland, there is a group of megalithic tombs (Pétrequin and Pinigre 1976). At first sight, these monuments conform to a wider tradition which is best represented at Sion on the Swiss side of the frontier, and at Aosta in Italy. In each case they feature massive stone cists associated with unburnt human bones (Mezzena 1998). These structures were sometimes located at one end of a low rubble platform or cairn, which could be either triangular or trapezoidal in plan. At Aosta and Sion they incorporated the remains of a series of anthropomorphic sculptures and, for that reason, the excavated evidence has played an important role in studies of statue menhirs.

Dolmen 1 at Aillevans is equally remarkable but, in this case, the results of excavation have not attracted the attention they deserve (Pétrequin and Pinigre 1976: 325–49; Figure 25). In its original form, this structure consisted

Aillevans

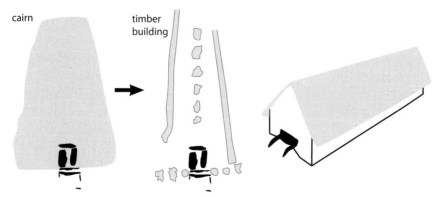

Figure 25 A simplified version of the structural sequence at Aillevans, France, and a reconstruction of the timber building on the site. The stone chamber and antechamber are indicated in black.

of a round mound six metres in diameter with a stone chamber and an antechamber. Again, it was associated with a quantity of disarticulated human bones. In a subsequent phase that construction was encased within a much larger trapezoidal cairn, seventeen metres in length. Although the circular monument was no longer a freestanding element, both its chamber and antechamber were retained. This was one of the latest megaliths in Europe, but sequences of this kind can be recognized at older tombs distributed across a much larger area.

In its final phase, Dolmen 1 changed its character again. The chambered tomb was enclosed within a large wooden structure which had a similar outline to the cairn. The excavators concluded that it had been a roofed building. The stone chamber was located inside its eastern end, but the antechamber was left uncovered and acted as a kind of porch. Seen from a distance, the monument might have looked like a domestic dwelling. Indeed, Pétrequin and Pinigre (1976) specifically compare it with the well preserved buildings in the waterlogged Late Neolithic settlement at Clairvaux. According to their account, a megalithic tomb at Aillevans was almost completely concealed inside what appeared to be a house.

The opposite relationship has been documented in Sardinia where the remains of early houses can be poorly preserved. Settlement sites have been excavated but, in some cases, irregular pits were the only features that were found. Although artefacts occur in some numbers, it can be difficult to identify convincing house plans. Indeed, Hayden (1999) has suggested that the pits were dug to obtain building material and that traces of the dwellings themselves have not always survived. He makes a further point which is of direct relevance to this account. In order to understand the nature of these structures it is necessary to turn to a quite different source of information: the Chalcolithic rock-cut tombs known as *Domus de janas* (the houses of the fairies).

They are associated mainly with the Ozieri Culture and date from the fourth millennium BC (Lilliu 1988: 229–54; Dettori Campus ed. 1989). Outside Mediterranean archaeology, they are best known for their characteristic decoration. These structures take many different forms, but their common characteristic is that they represent the interiors of domestic buildings (Figure 26). Some are found singly and others in small groups where the subterranean 'houses' are connected together by passages, as they would be in an actual village. The link is even closer for, whilst human remains have been found in the rock-cut tombs, the other artefacts associated with them have much in common with those from settlement excavations. Sites of both kinds are associated with arrowheads, scrapers, blades, querns, awls, and figurines. The only types peculiar to the occupation sites are weaving equipment. Polished axes are more frequent in the settlements, but beads are the one kind of artefact restricted to the tombs (Hayden 1999: 114–15). The fact that the collections overlap emphasizes the extent of cross reference between these contexts.

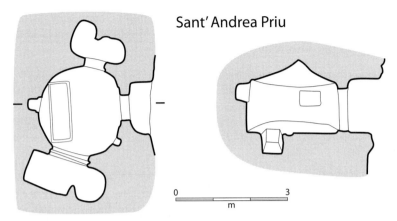

Sant' Andrea Priu

Figure 26 Plan and cross section of the subterranean tomb at Sant' Andrea Priu, Sardinia. Note the domed roof typical of a roundhouse.

The layout of the tombs makes the same point. Not only were they of the right size to represent domestic dwellings, important architectural details are clearly represented. They include porches, doorways, windows, niches, and roof supports. One distinctive feature may even represent a hearth. The structures seem to be based on two rather different prototypes among the houses of the living. Most are approximately rectangular, although they have rounded corners, but others depict the interior of a circular building. The connection even extends to the provision of a domed roof and rafters. Tombs of this kind belong to Demartis's Type VI and are most clearly represented at Sant' Andrea Priu (Demartis 1984).

A further point of comparison is that the tombs are painted and carved, as if to evoke the decoration inside an actual house. The designs include a pair of cattle horns (*bucrania*), as well as people and animals. More often there are spirals and arcs. In some ways they recall the evidence discussed in Chapter 3.

Dolmen 1 at Aillevans is unusual because the megalithic tomb was inside a building that looked like a house. In contrast, the houses occupied by the living at Sant' Andrea Priu provided the source of inspiration for a series of subterranean structures. In this case there is the added complication that the remains of ordinary dwellings have been difficult to identify at ground level so that the forms of Chalcolithic domestic architecture are inferred from the versions preserved in the tombs.

Although these examples have some unusual elements, both make a point that has already been intimated in Part 1 of this book. They provide a reminder, if reminder is needed, that a house is not just a building. Through the history of its occupants it can also be an institution. That is why the same term applies to an Oxford college, the audience in a theatre, and to a dynasty such as the House of Bourbon. In some cases, the building is considered as a living being (Herva 2009). Whilst the word 'house' may refer to both a physical structure and its occupants, the term 'dwelling' embraces both the building and the process of living there:

> Buildings themselves are not static ... Houses must be built and maintained, get modified to fit the needs of their occupants, are extended and rebuilt, and ultimately decay and fall down ... Such architectural processes are made to coincide, in various ways, with important events and processes in the lives of their occupants and are thought of in terms of them (Carsten and Hugh-Jones 1995: 39)

Sometimes such relationships can go even further, for houses have their own biographies. Like their occupants, they can be born, for a while they are alive, and, eventually, they die. For Carsten and Hugh-Jones this process can extend from the living house to the houses of the dead:

> On the one hand, people and groups are objectified in buildings; on the other hand, houses as buildings are personified and animated in thought and in life. *At one extreme are the lifeless ancestral houses, mountains or tombs, frozen in time but vividly permanent*; at the other extreme are those highly animated houses, in a constant state of changing but ultimately ephemeral (Carsten and Hugh-Jones 1995: 46; my emphasis).

That is an apt description of the contrasts illustrated by the archaeology of Sardinia.

THE DEATHS OF HOUSES

In the light of these suggestions it is worth considering what happened when houses 'died'.

There were two main processes in Neolithic Europe. The first was to replace domestic buildings every generation, perhaps on the death of one of the occupants. The clearest examples are in Central and south-east Europe where domestic buildings were commonly destroyed by fire (Stepanovic 1997). In many cases they were replaced in exactly the same positions, so that eventually the settlement developed into a conspicuous mound. As a result, the domestic cycle took on a monumental aspect.

A further version of the same process is found from Central Europe to the Southern Netherlands and Northern France and is associated with the Linear Pottery Culture. Again, houses were abandoned on a regular basis. It seems to have happened even though they were structurally sound and there is some evidence that their remains were allowed to decay whilst new buildings of the same kind were erected nearby. As a result, the settlements consisted of both the dwellings occupied by the living and the collapsed remains of longhouses that had once been inhabited (Bradley 1998: Chapter 3; Midgley 2005: 126–33). There are regions in which the positions of these two kinds of structure did not overlap, although they would do so during subsequent phases. Instead, they were spaced at equal intervals across the site as a whole.

Another process is clearly evidenced in Northern and Western Europe. Here, there is less uniformity in the treatment of abandoned houses. Some may have been set on fire, but others were left intact or even demolished. Rather than replacing one domestic building by another, it seems possible that their characteristic forms were copied in a more durable medium. The new constructions might be designed in the image of the house, but they are normally interpreted as tombs. That is not always easy to establish, but it is certainly true that many examples were associated with human remains.

A number of important issues still remain unresolved. Was the idea of constructing earthen mounds suggested by the remains of houses that had been left to collapse (Bradley 1998: Chapter 3; Midgley 2005: Fig. 38)? Did the monuments refer to the forms of buildings occupied in the present, or did their architecture recall the dwellings inhabited in a distant past? Were the mounds and cairns superimposed on the positions of individual houses, or were they placed over the sites of older settlements? It is unlikely that any one model will account for all the evidence.

There is another complication. The monuments interpreted as tombs take many different forms: forms that seem to have varied across space and time. Some have internal chambers which obviously remained accessible over a long period, whilst there are other structures where the building of a mound or cairn prevented access to the interior. Indeed there are even mounds with no internal features at all.

There have been two ways of studying such variations. The first is to consider how the architecture of particular monuments influenced the behaviour of the people allowed inside them (Thomas 1990). The other approach is to study these structures according to the same procedures as analyses of portable artefacts. The tombs are divided into 'types' and assigned to different phases and regional groups (Daniel 1958; Joussaume 1985; Joussaume et al. 2006). The separate approaches are rarely brought into alignment. In the case of megalithic architecture such studies are either very general, in which case the buildings are cut off from their immediate contexts, or they are excessively specific. In the latter case it can be hard to remember that developments at a regional level were related to wider processes in Neolithic Europe.

Traditional classifications of these structures do not take into account the very different audiences to whom the monuments were addressed. They depend on sophisticated analysis of their ground plans, but do not recognize that in the past more people will have been aware of the outward appearance of the mounds and cairns than might been allowed to go inside them. To some extent this argument is based on practical considerations—the entrance passages can be low and narrow, the chambers may be small—but it is also suggested by the placing of obstacles that prevent easy access to the interior. Most typological schemes are based on the forms taken by the chambers and less attention is paid to the outside of the monument. That is unfortunate, for, in many cases, it is the shape of the mound or cairn that has suggested a connection with domestic buildings.

Here there is yet another problem. Long mounds and long cairns have been compared with the plans of houses for over sixty years (Childe 1949), so there is already a large literature concerned with the subject, but it is only recently that similar arguments have been applied to the significance of circular monuments (Laporte and Tinévez 2004). It is a topic that deserves greater attention.

CIRCULAR TOMBS, RECTANGULAR TOMBS

It is easy to forget that monumental tombs are not found in every part of Neolithic Europe. They are confined to certain areas and are especially common in particular phases. Moreover, there are important differences between the chronological and geographical distributions of rectangular and circular monuments.

There are certain regions in which both types are largely absent. To the south, their distribution skirts that of caves containing Neolithic burials. They avoid the Rhine–Danube corridor which played an important part in the introduction of farming to Europe. Nor are they found throughout the Central Mediterranean where rock-cut tombs or hypogea sometimes take their place (Whitehouse 1981: 106–10; Cámara Serrano et al. 2010).

There are two major concentrations, one of them to the west and the other to the north (Daniel 1958; Joussaume 1985; Joussaume et al. 2006; Midgley 2008; Figure 27). For the most part, the first group is distributed along the sea routes leading from the West Mediterranean into the Atlantic, and from the Atlantic northwards between the Iberian Peninsula, France, and the British Isles. A second chain of connections links Northern Germany, Poland, and South Scandinavia to the coasts of the English Channel and the North Sea from the Netherlands to Brittany. That is not to suggest that monumental tombs are absent from inland areas, but they are not distributed continuously from Central Europe to the north in the way that is well documented for the settlements of the Linear Pottery Culture. Instead, the regions where these monuments are most abundant avoid the areas characterized by tells and by all but the last groups of Neolithic longhouses. Some of the places where monumental tombs are recorded may have had long-established contacts with

Figure 27 Regional patterns in the external appearance of chambered mounds and cairns in Europe.

one another, such as those between North Germany, the Netherlands and Denmark (Midgley 2005). In other cases, notably Britain and Ireland, there is little evidence of similar connections before the introduction of farming. If the distribution of these monuments avoids the areas with conspicuous settlements in Central and south-east Europe, the same is true of the northernmost extension of early farming in Scandinavia. Here, the distribution of these structures runs out, although there is some evidence for rectilinear houses and the exploitation of domesticates (Artursson et al. 2003).

Since the 1940s, it has been accepted that there were two distinct strands in the adoption of megalithic tombs (Daniel 1941). One involved the construction of elongated mounds or cairns whose distribution extends from Poland through Northern Germany, to Denmark and southern Sweden, and through the Netherlands, Belgium, and the north and west of France as far as the British Isles. Although there were many local variations among these monuments, the fact that they followed a rectilinear ground plan is the common element. It overrides local differences in the materials of which they were built, their dimensions, and the forms of any chambers.

The second tradition is represented in the Iberian Peninsula and the West Mediterranean, in one direction, and along the Atlantic coastline in the other. It also takes in Ireland and Britain, and, at its fullest extent, it reached Northern Europe. It was associated with a variety of circular monuments which, like the long cairns and long mounds, employed a wide range of forms and methods of construction. The distributions of these two styles of architecture overlap in certain regions so that both rectilinear and circular monuments can be found from western France to south Scandinavia. Still more confusing, some individual monuments incorporated both linear and curvilinear elements in the course of their histories. Even so, the distinction remains a real one. Composite monuments of this kind are a feature of the north of France, the British Isles, Germany and Scandinavia, but chambered tombs in Spain and Portugal are associated with circular cairns, just as the first monumental structures in Northern Europe are generally rectilinear. The overlap between these different forms is largely the result of an extended chronology in which the geographical limits of these building styles did not remain constant over time.

When the distinction between long mounds and circular monuments was first discussed, it was in terms of colonization by farmers along two geograph- ical axes, one of them associated with the Linear Pottery Culture, and the other with coastal communities on the Atlantic seaboard. Otherwise, prehistorians placed a greater emphasis on the spread of ideas and even on a process of religious conversion. In the case of circular structures, both approaches were based on a similar idea that passage graves spread gradually from south to north from an origin in the Mediterranean (Daniel 1958).

That approach has been abandoned as radiocarbon dating suggests another chronological model. It applies to rectilinear monuments, as well as round ones (Joussaume et al. 2006). There are three main issues to consider, although they are closely related. The first is that the earliest tombs may have been in north-west France rather than the Iberian Peninsula (Scarre 2011: 281–2). Second, the sequences in different areas share a surprising amount in com- mon. Thus, tombs which had always resembled one another on the ground prove to have been constructed at about the same times, suggesting that, in certain cases, long distance contacts were important. Third, there are local concentrations of structures with a narrow age range; within the limits of resolution of radiocarbon dating they could have been created simultaneously (Scarre 2010). Such peaks in the construction of chambered tombs have something of the character of events. That could have happened more than once. How do these changes of chronology affect the relationship between circular and rectilinear tombs?

THE CONNECTION BETWEEN HOUSES AND TOMBS

Most discussions of this topic have been concerned with rectangular houses—specifically with the domestic buildings of the Linear Pottery Culture. This account has a different point of departure. True to the theme of the book, it begins by considering the relationship between roundhouses and round cairns. More particularly, it investigates the connections between circular dwellings and passage tombs.

Circular houses and circular monuments

There is a fundamental distinction between the outward appearance of a mound or cairn and that of the structures concealed inside it. Schemes which combine these elements run the risk of adopting a perspective that was not available to everyone whilst the buildings were in use. The point is especially important as some of the earliest circular monuments in Atlantic Europe had chambers that were completely inaccessible. There was no entrance passage and any features beneath the mounds were cut off from the outside world. It makes it more difficult to compare them with the forms of domestic dwellings.

Other problems arise where the interior was accessible. The internal structures might be more irregular than the geometric outline of the perimeter would suggest; in certain instances it is appropriate to compare the architecture of the chamber with a cave rather than a house. It is certainly plausible, as caves were often employed for burial. Even when the building had a more regular appearance there are other contrasts to discuss. There is a considerable difference between a chamber with a domed roof and one covered by flat slabs. Sometimes that would be apparent from the height of the building, but even those structures that were spanned by corbelling can show significant variations from one monument to another. Those chambers could have been very high and the walls could have tapered towards a point so that the building would have looked rather like an industrial kiln. That arrangement characterizes a number of the earliest passage graves in north-west France, and it is unlikely that such towering structures resembled the internal arrangement of a house (Scarre 2011: chapter 6). Alternatively, the chamber walls could have tapered more gradually to create a rounded dome. Such structures were significantly lower than those just described. That would be an apt description of some of the passage tombs in southern Spain, including monuments in the cemetery of Los Millares (Almagro et al. 1963). They date from a later period and would have looked more like the interior of a roundhouse.

Los Millares is one place where both kinds of structure occur together, for traces of circular dwellings have been identified inside the fortified settlement associated with these tombs. Their chronological relationship has still to be established and the walled enclosure also includes a rectangular building (Chapman 2008: 203–5). In other cases, the links between circular cairns and roundhouses are more difficult to establish, although dwellings of this type have been recognized during recent excavations (Gianotti et al. 2011). The problem is that such links are not very common, as Neolithic domestic buildings in Atlantic Europe have left little trace behind. However, it is known that passage graves in the Iberian Peninsula were built over settlement sites (Senna-Martinez and Ventura 2008) and, even where roundhouses have not been identified, there is little evidence of rectangular dwellings. Otherwise, the most convincing evidence comes from the Boyne Valley where the passage tomb cemetery at Knowth was built on the site of a series of roundhouses. Elsewhere in Ireland there were groups of circular buildings outside the megalithic cemeteries at Carrowkeel and Knocknarea (Bradley 2007: 94–5). In Orkney there may have been a similar connection between passage graves and stone houses of the same date (Bradley et al. 2001).

The British and Irish examples illustrate another point. Again, the most plausible comparisons between circular monuments and circular dwellings come *at a late stage* in the history of chambered tombs. In this case it was around the end of the fourth millennium BC. That is not to suggest that the links between earlier monuments and circular buildings are illusory, but they are vague and poorly documented and depend almost entirely on the external appearance of the monuments. By contrast, the corbelled tombs found in south-east Spain are more like the domestic buildings recorded inside walled settlements of the same date, just as the latest chambered tombs in Orkney and Ireland have similar ground plans to houses (Figure 28). In this case, they were decorated and the placing of the images inside Orcadian passage tombs recalls their distribution within the dwellings (Bradley et al. 2001).

Subterranean monuments raise similar issues. The Sardinian *domus de janas* appear to be accurate copies of domestic buildings, but were carved out of the living rock. Again, they belong to a developed stage of the local sequence; whether they were round or rectangular, they were not among the earliest monuments (Lilliu 1988: Chapter 3). Thus, it seems as if two related developments can be identified in Neolithic and Chalcolithic Europe, although each of them took an essentially local form. The earlier circular tombs copied the *outward appearance* of the roundhouse, whilst it is in the *later structures* that the comparison extends to details of their internal organization and even their decoration. The connection between the houses of the living and those of the dead is strengthened by evidence from Britain, Ireland, and the Iberian Peninsula that both kinds of structure could have been located near to one another.

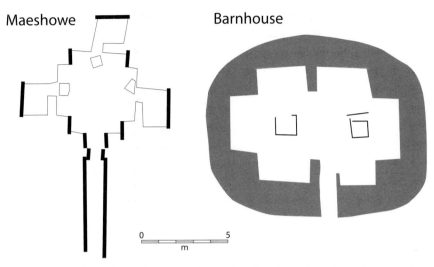

Figure 28 Outline plans of the Maeshowe chambered tomb and an above-ground building in the nearby settlement at Barnhouse, Orkney.

Rectangular houses and rectangular monuments

If the closest links between circular tombs and roundhouses come at the end of the sequence, the opposite claim has been made in the case of Neolithic longhouses. For more than half a century archaeologists have discussed the striking similarities between the dwellings of the Linear Pottery Culture and the forms of long mounds and long cairns (Childe 1949). Although the resemblance is striking, it has been difficult to explain and the models put forward in recent years remain extremely controversial.

Formal comparisons between these structures have been productive but difficult to interpret because of problems of chronology that do not arise in the case of circular buildings. Long mounds have similar plans to longhouses and both kinds of structure were approximately the same size as one another. In some cases the comparison extends to their orientations, although the details vary between different parts of Europe (Hodder 1984). Just as the longhouses of the Linear Pottery Culture were flanked by borrow pits which provided material for the walls, the mounds were bounded by ditches. Longhouses were usually entered through a doorway at one end—in most cases it was towards the south—whilst one end of a long mound could feature a monumental façade or even a burial chamber.

There are problems with comparisons of this kind. At present, there are only two areas where longhouses of the classic type are found in the same places as long mounds and these two regions are a considerable distance apart. One is in Poland and the other is in Northern France (Midgley 2005). With these important exceptions, there was a significant interval between the period when the last monumental dwellings went out of use (around 4500 BC), and the general currency of long barrows and long cairns which followed several centuries later. Even the Polish examples raise difficulties, for it is not agreed whether both kinds of structure were built and used during exactly the same phase. A recent study suggests that there was a limited overlap between their periods of use (Midgley 2005: 86). There is no doubt that the first local long barrows were constructed over the remains of settlements, but the houses that echo their characteristic form are found on different sites. That is not a problem in the French example, for the long mounds or enclosures at Balloy in the Yonne valley were superimposed on the sites of earlier longhouses, but in this case the two groups of structures were separated by about fifty years (Mordant 1998).

That raises a fundamental problem. If long mounds were built in the image of a house that had been inhabited in the past, how long could its configuration have been remembered? Half a century is a reasonable estimate, but in other areas of Europe the interval must have been much longer. That suggests a striking contrast with the relationship between passage graves and roundhouses. Although little is known about domestic buildings in Atlantic Europe, circular dwellings seem to have been preferred in many areas until at least the Copper Age. The houses of the Linear Pottery Culture and its immediate successors seem to share features in common with the layout of long barrows; however, the two traditions did not run in parallel. After the very first mounds had been built, smaller domestic buildings became the norm. That even applies to those structures buried beneath the famous barrow cemetery at Sarnowo in Poland (Pospieszny 2010). Throughout Northern Europe such buildings were generally rectangular, but they were much slighter than their predecessors and some of them had rounded ends (Artursson et al. 2003; Jensen 2006a: 284–90). If there was a significant relationship between domestic and funerary architecture it was by no means straightforward. Either the people who constructed long barrows retained a traditional format long after its prototypes had disappeared or the mounds were conceived as enormously enlarged copies of the dwellings that were actually inhabited by the living. There is some reason for preferring the latter view, as excavations in Northern and north-west Europe are starting to identify small rectangular houses buried beneath some of these monuments (Midgley 2005: Chapters 4 and 5). Long barrows and long cairns may have been conceived as the houses of the dead, but it seems unlikely that the majority were intended as precise copies of buildings which had gone out of use many years before.

Whichever model is preferred, it is clear that long barrows could only copy the external appearance of rectangular houses. The chambers buried beneath them rarely resembled the internal organization of a dwelling. The only exception is a group of rectilinear monuments in Orkney (Davidson and

Henshall 1989). Some of these cairns are straight-sided and are associated with a series of chambers which resemble the rooms inside a house; others were underneath round mounds. In either case, these structures are exceptional and were replaced by circular passage graves.

Often the long mounds or cairns were the last structures to be built on any site. Not only might they be built over older houses or settlements, there are cases in which the construction of the earthwork closed off access to the dead and to any features that held their remains. Here, it is important to distinguish between monuments associated with stone chambers, many of which could remain open for a long period, and those where their equivalents were made of wood. On the one hand, it is possible that some of the stone chambers were originally freestanding monuments, but this is difficult to prove. On the other hand, there are sites in Britain and Denmark where the corpse was placed inside an ephemeral timber structure (Madsen 1979). In some instances there is evidence that the wood had rotted or had been consumed by fire *before* any mound was built. In that case, the covering monument closed these structures to the living. Sometimes the process continued when the mounds or cairns were enlarged in a secondary phase.

There is another important distinction between these monuments and a number of the circular tombs which were considered earlier. The stone chambers associated with long mounds may, or may not, have been conceived as freestanding monuments, but that could not apply to a corbelled chamber. From early passage graves, such as those in north-west France, to the later monuments in south-east Spain, it would have been impossible to build the chamber unless the structure of the dome was supported by a 'core cairn'. Although their outward appearance could be modified during subsequent phases, corbelled passage tombs had to be unitary constructions.

If circular passage graves became more like houses with time, the opposite was the case with long mounds and long cairns. Although the idea of building them may have been suggested by the monumental dwellings of the past, the great majority were constructed long after such buildings had gone out of use. They are found in regions and periods where rectangular houses were the norm, but there is little to suggest a straightforward relationship between them. If anything, the link between domestic and funerary architecture be-came less direct, until the process culminated with the latest megalithic tombs of all, where part of the structure could be concealed beneath the ground. These monuments, which have been described as gallery graves or *allées couvertes*, had elongated rectangular chambers (Masset and Soulier 1995).

There is one striking exception to the general trend. Large timber structures with similar ground plans to allées couvertes have recently been identified in the west and centre of France, but these buildings are unusual and may not have been normal dwellings. The most extensive excavation has produced few finds of artefacts—it is possible that the biggest of these constructions was set on fire. It is difficult to work out how these massive buildings are related to the tombs, but a recent study by Scarre makes two important observations. The best known of the sites is Pléchâtel in Brittany where the outline of the timber structure and the surrounding enclosure strongly resembles that of the angled passage graves in the same region. At the same time, these timber 'houses' seem to be later in date than the tombs with which they are compared. It raises the intriguing possibility that their unusual architecture referred back to the stone monuments used in the past (Scarre 2011: 262–5). In this case the conventional sequence from houses to tombs may have to be reversed.

INSIGHTS FROM ETHNOGRAPHY

Chapters 2 and 3 emphasized some attributes of domestic dwellings which are rarely studied by archaeologists. A number of these features seem to be shared with monumental tombs. Perhaps it emphasizes the connections between these different kinds of architecture.

One theme that arose from the earlier discussion was the way in which houses could be thought of as living beings (Carsten and Hugh-Jones 1995; Herva 2009). Paradoxically, that may also apply to certain of the chambered tombs. Passage graves in Iberia and the west of France were sometimes decorated with anthropomorphic imagery, although some of the carved stones may have originally stood in the open air (Cassen 2009). Irish tombs could have similar associations, although they are rare. Breuil (1934) was the first to claim that there are faces and eyes among the carved designs. French allées couvertes illustrate a different practice, for they can be embellished with a pair of breasts linked by a kind of necklace, suggesting that they were considered as a female domain (Shee Twohig 1981; Villes 1997; Figure 29). The same applies to related structures in Northern France that were entirely subterranean. It seems unlikely that there were direct connections between all those areas. The common feature is that these different structures were 'animated'.

Occasionally, this belief was expressed in another way. In parts of Britain and Ireland, the treatment of the dead reflected the treatment of the dwelling. Thus, in southern England it is likely that both houses and corpses were allowed to decay. In Ireland, however, domestic dwellings were commonly set on fire and human bodies were cremated (Bradley 2007: 60–2; Figure 30). In both countries, their remains were placed inside a stone or earthen monument, but, unlike their English counterparts, the Irish sites contained deposits of cultural material which may have been introduced from a settlement.

Aveny

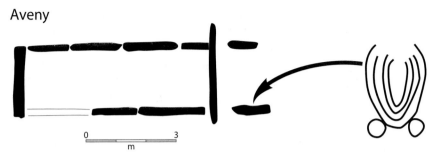

Figure 29 Plan of the megalithic tomb at Aveny, France, showing the decoration in its entrance.

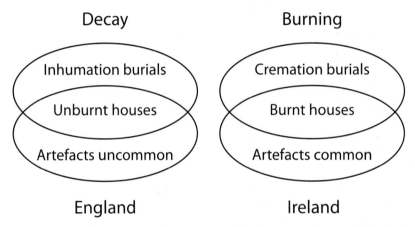

Figure 30 Regional contrasts in the treatment of the houses, artefacts, and the dead in Neolithic England and Ireland.

Another feature shared between houses and tombs was the significance of particular orientations. They could take many forms. At its simplest, long mounds were usually directed towards the rising sun, whilst passage tombs could have more precise alignments on the summer and winter solstices, and even the equinoxes (Ruggles 1999; Hoskin 2001). The orientations of Neolithic houses are rarely studied because they appear to be an entirely practical consideration. This may be unwise. It seems possible that the doorways of Linear Pottery longhouses were directed towards the regions from which the first settlers had travelled (Bradley 2002a: 26–8; Hauzeur 2006: 280–1). In that way, they recall the dwellings of the Pirá-paraná described in Chapter 2. During the Late Neolithic period, stone houses at Barnhouse in Orkney shared the same solar alignment as the nearby tomb of Maeshowe (Richards 2005).

CHRONOLOGICAL RELATIONSHIPS BETWEEN CIRCULAR AND RECTILINEAR TOMBS

It is clear that the two traditions of monumental architecture discussed in this chapter remained separate in some regions but overlapped in others. What was the chronological relationship between these buildings?

The area of overlap extends between Brittany, south Scandinavia, and the British Isles. The French evidence will be considered separately, but in other countries there seems to be some evidence of sequence. In Ireland, for example, court tombs, which are associated with long mounds and long cairns, were gradually replaced by circular passage graves. Their absolute chronology remains to be resolved, but it already seems likely that this development ran in parallel with the change from rectangular dwellings to round ones (Bradley 2007: 94–116). The same sequence has been identified in greater detail in Orkney—one of the few areas where the interiors of both kinds of monument resembled the inside of a house. Here, the transition is clearly documented and the link between the later dwellings and the last passage graves is strengthened because both were decorated in the same style: a style that extends to the pottery found with each kind of structure (Bradley 2007: 116–18; Darvill 2010: 139). In other parts of Britain long mounds lost their significance at about the time when rectangular dwellings were supplemented, or even replaced, by circular buildings. In this case the passage graves like those in Ireland are restricted to the north and west.

This contrasts with the sequence in Northern Europe, from Germany to Sweden, where the oldest monuments were probably long barrows and long cairns. They were supplemented by circular monuments during a secondary phase, although the rectangular plan sometimes remained the dominant form. Both kinds of cairn were associated with passage tombs. The interval between these successive structures was about two hundred years in Denmark (Schultz Paulsson 2010). There is a striking contrast with the situation in Ireland and Britain, for in south Scandinavia the change was accomplished without any obvious modification to the forms of domestic buildings, which still adhered to the rectilinear model.

The Northern European sequence provides only limited support for the idea that the forms of domestic buildings were monumentalized in the architecture of the tomb. There is no difficulty in accepting this model in the case of the earliest structures—the long barrows—but in subsequent phases there is too much variety to support a simple explanation of this kind. There remains a significant relationship between chambered tombs and the locations of living sites, but there is less to suggest a direct association between particular kinds of monument and particular types of dwelling. This is well illustrated by large scale excavations close to the Danish causewayed enclosure of Sarup where the

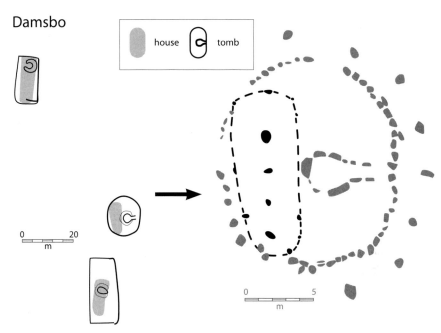

Figure 31 Chambered tombs overlying Neolithic timber houses at Damsbo, Denmark.

remains of small rectangular buildings were buried beneath both long cairns and circular monuments (Andersen 2009; Figure 31). Perhaps the connection between domestic architecture and the houses of the dead broke down sooner in Scandinavia than it did in other parts of Europe.

That is quite different from the situation in north-west France, where the two traditions of tomb building seem to have provided a source of contention at the beginning of the Neolithic period. Their relationship with one another has often been discussed, but the most important observation is probably that of Scarre (2004a) who has pointed out some striking contrasts in the archaeological sequence from one small region to another. It is because this was the area where the two main currents in the introduction of farming into Europe most obviously overlapped. They were associated with different kinds of domestic architecture—rectangular buildings in the Linear Pottery Culture and its successors, and, perhaps, a preference for roundhouses along the Atlantic coastline. That important contrast seems to be echoed in the forms of local tombs. The idea of the longhouse could have been perpetuated by the construction of long barrows (although the extent of any chronological overlap between them remains in doubt). The circular cairns associated with passage graves are likely to reflect a preference for circular dwellings, as they do in the Iberian Peninsula.

In any event, the people who constructed monumental tombs in north-west France reached at least two kinds of accommodation with these competing traditions. Both kinds of monument might be built on the same sites, as part of a larger cemetery, or round mounds and cairns might be incorporated within a larger rectilinear structure. Just as monuments of quite different external forms might be found side by side, there seems to have been no problem in conceiving composite buildings in which both rectilinear and curvilinear elements played a part. That applied to the internal organization of these monuments, as well as their outward appearance. To some extent, the same accommodation was achieved in parts of Britain.

THE CEMETERY AT BOUGON

The megalithic cemetery at Bougon in western France provides a good illustration of these processes (Mohen and Scarre 2002; Figure 32). It has been extensively excavated; human bones from the monuments still survive and the individual monuments have provided a series of radiocarbon dates.

By its final stage, the cemetery contained four stone-built monuments, separated from one another by the quarries that provided the material for their construction. The oldest structures date from the beginning of the Neolithic period around 4700–4500 BC, but they were reused many centuries afterwards. The original buildings were a small circular cairn with a single

Bougon

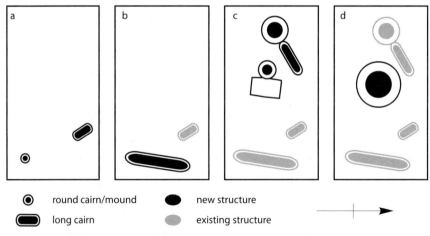

Figure 32 Outline sequence of the mortuary monuments in the cemetery at Bougon, France.

chamber and a passage, and a roughly rectilinear cairn that contained two more passage tombs. The first significant change was the addition of a roughly trapezoidal long cairn to the freestanding passage grave erected in the earliest period of activity. Although its corbelled chamber was retained, all trace of its circular perimeter was concealed within the new building. The result was that the site now contained two small rectilinear monuments.

In the following phase the architecture of Bougon changed again and two much larger circular cairns were constructed on the site. One covered a rectangular chamber which was offset from the centre and had an entrance passage which extended through four concentric walls, defining the edge of the monument. It was abutted by an oval cairn which provided evidence of at least two more passage graves. Another large round cairn was built alongside the monument, but it had only one chamber—again, it was not located in the middle of the cairn. During a secondary phase, a large rectangular extension was built onto the side of this structure. It overlay the position of one of the quarries, but still allowed access to the chamber.

Finally, in the mid-fourth millennium BC, approximately a thousand years after the first tombs had been built at Bougon, three of the structures saw a period of reuse, whilst the fourth—the large round cairn with its rectangular extension—was buried beneath a circular barrow. The interplay between round and rectangular forms had lasted almost a millennium, and it was only when the cemetery went out of use that the circular design prevailed. Until then, the people who used the site were able to draw on both the principal styles of architecture current in this region of France. Such a remarkable sequence poses problems of interpretation that will need to be addressed in the future.

SUMMARY AND CONCLUSIONS

This chapter began by discussing two unusual groups of monuments: the megalithic tombs at Aillevans in Franche-Comté and the underground structures described as *domus de janas* in Sardinia. Both involved the direct juxtaposition of mortuary monuments with what seemed to be domestic architecture. At Aillevans, a low cairn with a megalithic chamber was almost entirely encased within a wooden building which looked like a house. In Sardinia, where the remains of houses can be difficult to identify by excavation, they seem to have provided the prototypes for underground tombs whose features appear to represent the internal organization of a dwelling. Although these structures are exceptional at a detailed level, both raised questions that have a wider application. What was the relationship between domestic architecture and the forms adopted by monuments to the dead?

In a sense, the discussion covers familiar ground, for it has long been argued that barrows and cairns were conceived as representations of ancestral long-houses, although this hypothesis raises chronological problems (Midgley 2005: Chapter 6). There are also difficulties in working out the process by which domestic buildings that had been occupied over comparatively short periods were memorialized by such long-lasting constructions. The problem is made more severe by other factors. With the possible exception of the last long-houses in Northern Europe, their apparent prototypes had disappeared before most of the tombs were built. Moreover, the houses that were occupied at the time were smaller and less substantial than their predecessors, even when they were found on the same sites as these monuments. In fact, the situation is complicated even further because, in Scandinavia, the first long barrows were supplemented after about two hundred years by the building of passage graves, some of which were associated with circular cairns (Schultz Paulsson 2010). It follows that any direct link between the tombs and domestic architecture began to weaken *at an early stage in the Neolithic sequence*. That is particularly revealing as the forms of domestic dwellings in the same region remained the same (Jensen 2006a: 284–90). It follows that it is possible to talk of widespread traditions of rectilinear architecture that included both houses and tombs, but the link between them was by no means direct. Moreover, it diminished over time and, in some regions, circular monuments became the commonest form.

That is very different from the relationship between houses and mortuary monuments in Atlantic Europe and it seems ironic that this should not have been discussed in as much detail as the role of longhouses, for here there was a continuous—though poorly documented—tradition of circular dwellings extending throughout the currency of megalithic tombs. The links between them are best exemplified in the Iberian Peninsula and the West Mediterranean simply because those regions were well outside the area that was exposed to the alternative tradition of rectilinear buildings. It may be misleading that so much attention has been paid to the part of their distribution where both styles were used at the same time. The sequence in north-west France is certainly complex, but the relationship between houses and tombs is better studied in areas further to the south. Just as the first long barrows in Northern Europe were constructed in a world of rectangular buildings, the earliest passage graves in south-west Europe could have echoed the forms of the domestic structures of the same phase. It was further to the north—from Brittany to Ireland, and from Britain to Scandinavia—that both architectural traditions were juxtaposed. In France, Germany, Denmark, and Sweden elements of each style were eventually combined. By contrast, in Britain and Ireland circular tombs became the dominant form as roundhouses took the place of rectangular buildings.

If the links between houses and tombs became weaker during the archaeo-logical sequence in Northern Europe, along the Atlantic *they seem to have become even stronger over time*. There are several reasons for making this suggestion.

One point is especially important. Although the evidence is limited, it is likely that the architectural elements which most closely resemble domestic forms were a feature of the *later* monuments. Thus, Aillevans Dolmen 1 is among the last tombs in its region, the Sardinian *domus de janas* date from the Late Neolithic or the Copper Age (Lilliu 1988: 229–54), and low corbelled chambers like those at Los Millares belong to a developed phase in the evolution of megalithic architecture (Almagro Basch and Arribas 1963). On one hand, they are more like the structure of houses than their counterparts in the first tombs in north-west France; on the other hand, the late passage graves in Orkney also possessed high vaults (Davidson and Henshall 1989) and it would be unwise to make too much of this observation.

The plans of certain tombs recall those of domestic buildings. Whilst this applies to the outward appearance of many different monuments, their inter-nal features most closely resemble those of houses towards the end of the sequence. Again, Orkney provides a convincing example of this development, for the layout of the chambers in the local tombs is very similar to the organization of space inside the houses of the same period. These links extend to the orientations of both groups of buildings and their decoration.

The last point introduces another observation. It was only the chambered tombs along the Atlantic axis that were embellished with the carved and painted devices known as 'megalithic art' (Shee Twohig 1981; Bueno Ramirez and Balbín Behrmann 2002). Here, there is an important contrast to consider. The earliest designs were sometimes anthropomorphic and there is a growing body of evidence to suggest that they had originally been associated with standing stones in the open air. Sometimes these sculptures were broken and in many cases they were built into the tombs (L'Helgouach 1996; Cassen 2000). At this stage, there is little to suggest that they constituted a unitary scheme. By contrast, rather later tombs, from Portugal to Scotland, are embellished with designs that were obviously created *in situ*. They can extend from one orthostat to another and sometimes the basic pattern extend-ed across the whole of the interior. These painted or carved panels are associated with passage graves from Ireland to Iberia and, in many cases, are located inside circular mounds and cairns. Again, they belong to a developed stage in the Neolithic sequence (Bueno Ramirez and Balbín Behrmann 2002). Occasionally, they have features in common with the decorated pottery found at settlements (Bradley 2009: 99–102). There have been suggestions that 'megalithic art' might represent the internal decoration of a dwelling, but only in Orkney can this idea be substantiated (Bradley et al. 2001). If it has any merit, it provides another argument that circular passage graves became more like houses at a late stage in their history. It is difficult to take this argument further, but one important clue may have been overlooked. The insides of round cairns with passage graves were never decorated in Northern Europe. Perhaps this was because they were not thought of as representations of houses, for here *the domestic architecture of the same period was entirely rectilinear.*

There is a further indication that the relationships between houses and tombs became increasingly diverse. In north- and south-west Europe the use of passage graves is closely allied to the development of other traditions of circular architecture: traditions that extend to such massive constructions as Stonehenge (Cleal et al. 1995). They continued to develop during the Copper Age and even during the Bronze and Iron Ages. As they did so, they adopted novel forms. In Northern Europe, however, there is little to suggest that a similar process occurred. Significantly fewer large monuments were built (although there are many round barrows) and there is nothing to indicate that rectangular dwellings provided a significant source of inspiration for structures of other kinds. That remained the case until the Bronze Age. If the early Neolithic period witnessed a process by which houses were turned into tombs, from North Germany to Sweden that development went no further. From the West Mediterranean to Ireland, however, circular structures became more abundant and much more varied until they included some of the most impressive prehistoric structures anywhere in Europe. That distinctive sequence will be traced in Chapters 5 and 6.

5

Turning to Stone

STONE AND WOOD

The starting point for this chapter is a work by the German artist Joseph Beuys. '7000 oaks' is an installation which he inaugurated at Kassel, a city that had been damaged during the Second World War (Scholz 1986). Each tree was paired with a basalt stele which was quarried locally. In Beuys's conception, the installation would change its character over time. For the first few years the standing stones would be the dominant feature, but they would become less conspicuous as the oaks grew to maturity. After that, there might be two very different outcomes. Either new trees would be planted as the old ones died— that was the artist's plan—or a setting of monoliths would be all that remained with the stones themselves marking the positions of oaks that had disappeared.

Beuys was concerned with regeneration in a way that was entirely appropriate in a war-damaged city where the oak trees would gradually replace a setting of rocks. His work was informed by his interest in ecology and played on a contrast between wood and stone which is equally relevant to archaeology. They are very different materials from one another, but both were used in prehistoric structures and employed in distinctive ways. Wood is an organic substance and eventually decays. Stone, on the other hand, is inorganic and for that reason it lasts a long time.

The distinction is important in considering ancient architecture (Parker Pearson and Ramilsonina 1998). Of course, there were places in which only one of these materials was available, but there were others where the distinctive ways in which stone and wood were used are especially informative. Two examples illustrate the point. Neolithic houses in Northern Europe were timber constructions, but most of the tombs that accompanied them were made of local stone. In this case, the choice of building material suggests that these dwellings were thought to have a finite lifespan, whilst the tombs of their occupants would have a longer history. Similarly, the Neolithic longhouse at La Haute Mée in north-west France was built of wood but was accompanied by a granite menhir (Cassen et al. 1998). It seems as if the stone was intended to outlast the building and to indicate its site to later generations.

In such cases it seems likely that the choice of material was influenced by the life expectancy of the buildings. There are other examples in which the symbolic properties of wood and stone may have been equally important, as they clearly are in Beuys's work. During the Neolithic period, several long mounds in Britain, Ireland, and Denmark were associated with a distinctive kind of wooden structure (Madsen 1979; Noble 2006: 82–3; Figure 33). It was

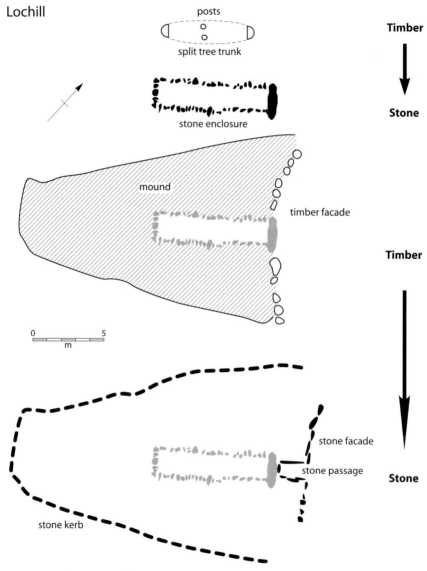

Figure 33 The structural sequence at Lochill, Scotland, illustrating the successive use of stone and timber.

formed out of a tree trunk which had been split in half and allowed to decay before it was replaced by a stone or wooden chamber containing human bodies. The corpses decayed, just as the tree had decayed, and only when both processes were complete were the remains covered by a mound. Occasionally, that earthwork was remodelled during a subsequent phase, and the timber and earthen monument was encased in stone. If the use of wood evoked the human lifespan, the rock was inert and unchangeable. In this case, it seems to have been connected with the dead. That relationship is evidenced in many parts of Europe where prehistoric stone settings are associated with human burials.

STATUES AND STANDING STONES

Beuys's '7000 oaks' is perhaps the contemporary counterpart of the settings of standing stones that occur in many parts of ancient Europe. Some of the earliest examples are associated with Neolithic tombs of the kinds considered in Chapter 4. How should they be interpreted?

The steles belong to two main groups. There are anthropomorphic examples which are sometimes called *statue menhirs*, and the undecorated monoliths which are described by the neutral term *standing stone*. Although their distributions overlap in time and space, important differences existed between them. Stones embellished with human features were most common in the West Mediterranean, in the Iberian Peninsula, and along the Atlantic coast of France (Mezzena 1998; De Saulieu 2004; Cassen 2009). The others were left undecorated and were usually found in the British Isles, although it is possible that the same conception extended to the megalithic tombs of Northern Europe (Scarre 2004b)

Their contexts differed, too. The earliest examples in the southern group were associated with passage graves, but statue menhirs might also be found with later single burials and/or with other funerary monuments. Both kinds could be erected close to chambered tombs and, less often, were situated inside them. Some stood in isolation, but others formed freestanding settings, such as stone alignments. In certain cases, it is clear that the monoliths were uprooted and were incorporated in the structures of the tombs themselves. Many were broken into fragments and it even seems possible that parts of the same stele were employed in more than one of the monuments. The common feature was that the stones had been shaped to resemble the human form. Although they underwent minimal modification, some represented entire bodies and others just parts of bodies, whilst a small number of examples featured drawings of artefacts, animals, and sea creatures of special significance at the start of the Neolithic period (Cassen 2000). It is possible that the dispersal of these fragments followed a similar procedure to the distribution of human remains within and between these monuments, but this cannot be proved. All too often the chambered tombs were cleared by excavators who did not keep adequate records, or were built on acid soils where bones do not survive. In the same way, it is by no means clear how rapidly the transition from the open air to the monument was accomplished. Some steles may have stood for a considerable period of time before they were reused (Scarre 2011: Chapter 4). In other cases, the interval may have been significantly shorter and, in any case, menhirs, alignments, and even enclosures formed out of monoliths had a lengthy history.

Anthropomorphic images were also created inside the tombs once those structures had been built. They took the form of both paintings and carvings. Examples were quoted in Chapter 4, and it is clear that the practice of making them remained important during the history of the monuments. There are many regional variations and, in some cases, similar designs are shared with decorated outcrops and rock shelters, and even with the motifs that feature on portable artefacts (Bradley 2009: 99–104). Perhaps the individual stones embodied the attributes of living creatures. If so, there is no way of telling whether they represented particular individuals, ancestors, or supernatural beings.

The northern tradition presents a very different picture. Decorated passage graves are recorded in Ireland, Orkney, and north-west Wales, but the designs associated with them are largely or entirely non-figurative. Whilst scholars have attempted to identify human faces and eyes among the carvings (for example, Breuil 1936), these motifs are rare and their interpretation is controversial. This observation is important, as half the megalithic art in Western Europe occurs in the Boyne Valley (Eogan 1986).

The distinction between the northern and southern traditions of megalithic art is especially puzzling as a certain number of the tombs share features in common. They were built in similar ways; examples belonging to both regional groups made use of reused stones and some of the same designs were employed in each of these areas. Thus, on one hand, there are plausible links between Irish monuments and those in Brittany and Portugal (Eogan 1990; O'Sullivan 1996), just as artefacts of Iberian origin or inspiration have been discovered in the Boyne Valley (Eogan 1990). On the other hand, what are lacking are unambiguous representations of the human form. The same applies to chambered tombs in Scandinavia, where the only carved motifs are cup marks on the capstones.

In fact, settings of undecorated standing stones play a greater part in British and Irish prehistory than they do in the archaeology of other parts of Europe. They can take several different forms. In the case of chambered tombs, individual monoliths may be located just outside the entrances, as they are at Knowth (Eogan 1986); the orthostats may be linked together to form a decorated kerb, defining the edge of the mound; or the stones can be laid out in a ring encircling the entire construction. The best known example of this arrangement is at Newgrange (O'Kelly 1982). More often, stone circles form freestanding structures, although they can also be bounded by a distinctive earthwork *henge* (Bradley 2007: 98–116 and 122–32; Darvill 2010: 152–8). By contrast, few stone circles of Neolithic date are recorded in continental Europe.

There is a little evidence that the standing stones of Britain and Ireland were significant in their own right. Cummings (2002) has shown how often stones with a rough outer surface were paired with those that were smooth; Lynch (1998) has demonstrated that some of the monoliths employed in stone circles were chosen for their distinctive colours; and Darvill (2002) has commented on the special role of rocks containing quartz. Similar concerns were important in other areas. Scarre (2004b) has observed that in north Germany and south Scandinavia the orthostats employed in passage graves were often separated by panels of walling, as if the individual stones were being put on display. Again, their shapes and colours appear to have been significant. On the west coast of Sweden a number of passage graves were organized around a series of striking relationships between the colours, textures and mineral inclusions visible in the raw material (Bradley and Phillips 2008). Again, it is possible that each orthostat was considered to have its own history.

It is paradoxical that the monoliths employed in the northern group of megaliths eschewed all reference to the body, when this was not true of those in the southern tradition. One explanation is that was inappropriate to depict human beings in this medium: a reluctance that clearly extended to portable objects of the same date in Britain and Ireland. Another possibility is that in both areas standing stones represented living creatures, but the monoliths in the northern group did not require any modification for that connection to be accepted. If so, the kerbs of Irish passage tombs and the stone circles in the British Isles might have been thought of as statues no different in kind from the anthropomorphic images in Western Europe.

In ideal circumstances, researchers can learn something from the ethnography of local communities, as especially powerful ideas may survive for long periods of time. That option is not available in the British Isles, but in this case a different approach is informative. Much is known about the folklore associated with prehistoric monuments. These sources cannot shed any light on the original significance of these structures, but they do suggest *which kinds of interpretation were considered to be plausible in the past*. In the case of standing stones and stone circles folk beliefs are revealing (Grinsell 1976).

These structures were most commonly interpreted as groups of people (sometimes they were soldiers, huntsmen, and dancers) who had been turned to stone. In other cases, the monoliths were originally supernatural beings. Certain stones possessed the ability to harm people or to cure them, and in several cases they could change their positions unobserved. As a result, they could never be counted. The common element in all these stories is that the stones were, or had been, alive and possessed the ability to perform good or evil acts. The fact they had never been modified to look like living creatures did not prevent such legends from developing at different places and times. Local communities had no difficulty in accepting that unshaped monoliths were people, but people who had lived long ago.

STONE CIRCLES AND STONE ALIGNMENTS

To a large extent, the contrast between uncarved steles and monumental sculptures corresponds to another distinction of direct relevance to this book. Although there are local exceptions, anthropomorphic steles are distributed from Brittany to the Mediterranean and can be organized in straight alignments. Unshaped monoliths are much more common in Britain and Ireland *where they are usually laid out in rings.*

The distinction between these two forms is of fundamental importance. There are many reasons for the contrast, but the most important point is that these monuments might have been perceived and used in different ways.

Apart from the presence of anthropomorphic sculptures, stone alignments have several characteristics. People might have moved along these rows, or they could have passed across them. In the first case, it seems as if the alignments led to a specific point or established a particular orientation. In the second, they presented a barrier and divided the area on one side of the monument from the space on the other side. All these elements are clearly documented in the archaeology of north-west France (Lecerf 1999; Cassen 2009).

Here, it seems as if some of the alignments extended the orientations of already existing long mounds. In other cases, the files of monoliths led towards, or between, large megalithic enclosures, themselves defined by a continuous circuit of standing stones (Figure 34). It seems possible that more lines of monoliths were added over time, so that what began as a prescribed path in between two files of uprights was elaborated by the construction of further rows until they amounted to a considerable monument in themselves. The significance of the terminals was emphasized by the increasing heights of the stones (Bradley 2002a: 102–9). The same also applies to simpler alignments that were composed of a single row of monoliths. The excavated alignment at Locmariaquer led to Le Grand Menhir Brisé, the tallest stele anywhere in Neolithic Europe (L'Helgouach and Cassen 2010).

When people moved along such alignments, they may have done so in procession. That would have involved a distinction between those who led and

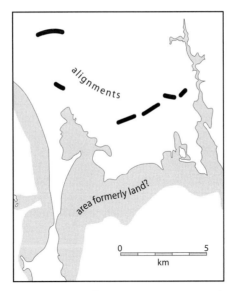

Figure 34 The siting of the Carnac alignments, Brittany, in relation to the Neolithic coastline.

those who followed after. The grading of the stones might have encouraged the grading of people; this would be especially significant if the monoliths were interpreted as creatures who had been turned to stone. It is unfortunate that so little is known about the enclosures at the ends of some of these avenues.

At the same time, the alignments, especially the most elaborate ones, formed a discontinuous barrier extending across large swathes of country. In one sense it could have confronted strangers approaching unfamiliar land, but a more radical interpretation has been proposed by Cassen (2009) in his account of the Carnac alignments. The largest examples run from east to west and follow a course running approximately parallel to the coast. They were built at a time when sea levels were rising rapidly and large areas of land were lost. In recent years, stone alignments have even been discovered by divers (Cassen et al. 2010). Cassen suggests that there was a direct relationship between coastal change and the erection of the stones. Perhaps they were conceived as a barrier against the sea, and the statues were intended to confront the rising water. That may be one reason why a few of the stones carry carvings of whales.

How were these constructions related to the circular monuments in the vicinity? There are two answers to this question. The first is that passage graves, which could be associated with round mounds or cairns, were offset from these linear constructions and were built some distance away; by contrast, long barrows were directly connected with the stone rows (Roughley 2004). At the same time, megalithic enclosures (which were once called

Kerlescan

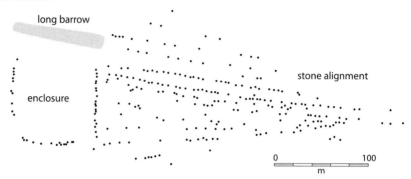

Figure 35 The megalithic enclosure, a long barrow, and the stone alignment at Kerlescan, Brittany.

cromlechs) were placed at the ends of these alignments (Figure 35). Although they have been described as 'stone circles' (Burl 2000), the term is rather misleading. Some of them were oblong or roughly rectilinear, whilst others were enormous horseshoe-shaped settings of uprights which were open on one side. They have very little in common with the rings of monoliths in Britain and Ireland, and, if they do have more distant parallels, they may be with smaller settings of standing stones in the Portuguese Alentejo, whose carved designs share features in common with Breton monuments (Calado 2002).

By contrast, the stone circles of Britain and Ireland are closely associated with round mounds containing passage graves and have no obvious connection with long barrows or long cairns. If the massive Carnac alignments overshadow the megalithic enclosures to which they lead, in this case the relationship is reversed. A small number of stone circles are approached by avenues, but they never consist of more than two rows of monoliths and few of them extend for any distance. The great avenues at Avebury and Shap seem to have been entirely exceptional (Burl 1993: 45–9). The enclosures themselves are different from the Breton sites with which they have been compared. They are bounded by spaced monoliths rather than a continuous wall of standing stones and are more or less circular. Their sizes vary considerably, from enormous freestanding circles like Long Meg and her Daughters in north-west England (Burl 2000: 119–22), to miniature settings bounded by an earthwork or rubble enclosure. The monoliths are never shaped to resemble the human body, but a very small number of stones are decorated with motifs that are found on natural outcrops or at chambered tombs.

Some of the larger stone circles have a formal entrance, marked by an unusually wide gap in the perimeter, and there are a few sites where its position is emphasized by a standing stone some distance away (Burl 2000). Otherwise, these monuments have no obvious orientation. However, the significance of certain directions may have been marked by the placing of unusually coloured stones or by the selection of monoliths with striking natural inclusions. Some were embellished with cup marks. Individual stones might also be paired across the circuit using pieces with distinctive shapes. The main feature which is shared between different regions is the grading of the stones by height, so that the lowest are towards the north east and the tallest to the south west. This configuration is well known in Scotland (Bradley 2000b, 2005a), but the most obvious example of this arrangement is found at Stonehenge, where it creates an alignment on the midwinter sunset (Cleal et al. 1995).

Such features are not found at every site, yet they provide the only indication of the grading of space inside these monuments. Apart from the centre, where there may have been a grave, there is no focal point, and these structures may not have been suitable for expressing distinctions between the people who used them. They may have entered the enclosure in procession, perhaps by following an avenue, but the form of the circle suggests that such differences were less important inside the enclosure itself. It may be that the circular plan was intended to play down the distinctions between different people, employing a similar principle to the seating plan at King Arthur's round table.

The same idea may be expressed by constructing the circles out of raw materials introduced from several sources. It suggests that different communities could have contributed their labour on equal terms with other groups. The two large stone circles in Orkney were built out of stones from a variety of places (Richards 2004), and the same is clearly documented at Stanton Drew in south-west England (Lloyd Morgan 1887). Of course, that does not make sufficient allowance for differences that were not expressed in the architecture of the monument. The quarrying and transport of enormous rocks was a process in which different communities could have competed to make their mark, whilst the finished structure—if it ever was 'finished'—was often too small to contain many people. Others must have been excluded.

Even with these qualifications, the contrasts between circles and stone alignments do appear to be real. Stone rows permit the grading of space as they lead from one monolith to another. That process is most apparent where the stones were shaped to resemble human beings. On one hand, the placing of these images with respect to one another could have expressed the relationships between different people in the past (Bradley 2009: 93–5). Stone circles, on the other hand, do not provide such an effective medium for emphasizing social distinctions and in this case none of the monoliths is explicitly anthropomorphic. They may have been regarded as human figures, but, if so, they were left unshaped and the separate components were treated on equal terms. If, as seems likely, they were the equivalent of Continental statue menhirs, they could have stood for *the community* rather than particular individuals.

STONE CIRCLES AND PASSAGE GRAVES

If Breton passage graves are set apart from the alignments, the circular stone settings in Britain and Ireland are closely integrated with chambered tombs (Figure 36). The relationship between them has been difficult to understand. The first stone circles are associated with cremation burials which date from the late fourth and earlier third millennia BC (Parker Pearson et al. 2009). That is the period of the last Neolithic passage graves. There were several monuments in which these structural elements were combined.

The evidence takes various forms, but the essential relationship is the same in every case (Figure 37). A circular mound or cairn containing a passage and a chamber is enclosed by a ring of monoliths. At most sites the circle is made up of standing stones set some distance out from the mound or cairn, but in the Hebrides, off the west coast of Scotland, they compose a *peristalith*, which marks the outer limit of the tomb itself (Henshall 1972: 140–2). Here, each orthostat is distinct from its neighbours so that the effect is similar to that of a stone circle. It is not clear whether these features were constructed simultaneously.

Other examples are more informative. Thus, a small passage grave at Callanish, in the same part of Scotland, was built inside an already-existing

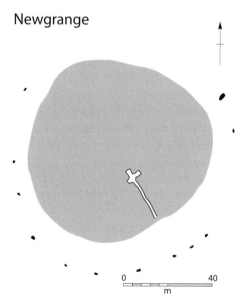

Figure 36 Outline plan of the passage grave and stone circle at Newgrange, Ireland.

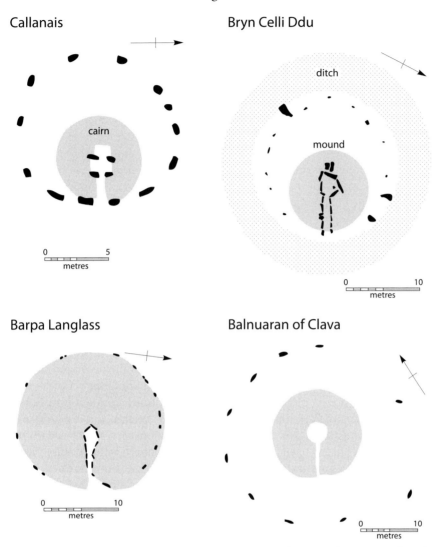

Callanais

Bryn Celli Ddu

cairn

ditch

mound

0   5
metres

0   10
metres

Barpa Langlass

Balnuaran of Clava

0   10
metres

0   10
metres

Figure 37 Plans of four chambered tombs in Scotland and Wales associated with stone circles. Monoliths are indicated in black and the mounds or cairns in light tone.

ring of monoliths, approached by two short alignments of standing stones and an avenue of paired uprights. It dates from about 2900 BC (Ashmore 1999). There is also a case in which a stone setting and a passage grave were built as a unitary design. Thus, in Burrow's recent interpretation of Bryn Celli Ddu in north-west Wales, a small passage grave was located towards one side of a circular ditched enclosure, in a position not unlike that of the tomb at Callanish (Burrow 2010). A setting of monoliths, several of them associated with cremations, was concentric with the earthwork and extended around most of the perimeter of the earliest mound. These burials date from 3300 to 2900 BC. In a subsequent phase, the chambered tomb was extended and its passage was modified to create a precise alignment on the midsummer sunrise. When it happened, the earthwork and the stone setting were buried beneath the mound.

A similar process may have been followed at Maeshowe in Orkney, another monument of about the same date which was enclosed by a ditch. In this case, no monolith survives *in situ*, but a substantial stone socket has been excavated beyond the perimeter of the mound. More importantly, the entrance passage is built out of four enormous slabs of rock and four more stones of similar proportions mark the corners of the chamber. They add nothing to the stability of the building and their presence is difficult to explain, but they are very like the uprights in a nearby stone setting at Stenness, which was built at about the same time. Richards has suggested that there had originally been a stone circle at Maeshowe (2005: Chapter 9). It was demolished when the passage grave was constructed and its remains were used to build the new monument. The completed tomb was aligned on the midwinter sunset. The sequence can be compared with that at Bryn Celli Ddu.

How often were monoliths reused in this way? It is hard to tell. The clearest evidence that the building material was taken from older structures is where they carry panels of decoration. The carved motifs continue down to the base of the stone where it was buried in the ground; parts of the decorated surface are obscured by the position of other stones; and there are a number of cases in which already-carved pieces seem to have been turned upside down. Robin (2009) has identified a number of examples in Ireland, but they do not resemble monoliths. Their characteristic decoration very rarely occurs on standing stones in the open air, and their proportions are by no means similar to those of the components of stone circles. Although it is obvious that rocks were being recycled in a structured manner, they seem to have been obtained from older tombs. As there is evidence for the enlargement of certain of these buildings (Eogan 1998), the decorated fragments may not have travelled far. Again, insular practice seems to have been different from that in continental Europe.

There is a distinctive tradition of Early Bronze Age architecture in northern Scotland, which also combines stone circles and megalithic tombs. The Clava Cairns include a number of passage graves surrounded by a ring of monoliths (Bradley 2000b). Like the kerbs of the cairns, the components of the circle are graded by height, with the tallest examples towards the south-west. They can be paired with the nearest kerbstones by colour, texture, or mineral inclusions. At the type site of Balnuaran of Clava both the passage graves are aligned on the midwinter sunset. Special significance seems to have attached to the number of stones employed in the main components of these buildings. Thus, the passage and the foundation course of the chamber both include twelve orthostats, whilst the edge of the cairn is supported by four times as many kerbstones: a total of forty eight. The same scheme extends to the number of monoliths in the stone circles on the same site and also to another cairn at Balnuaran of Clava where a ring of monoliths encloses a circular walled enclosure. Not only does this emphasize the unitary character of the design, the same convention extends to the well-preserved passage grave at Corrymony in the same part of Scotland (Piggott 1956: 174–84).

The structural sequence at Balnuaran of Clava is especially revealing (Figure 38). The passage graves were built first. Each had a circular cairn, a narrow entrance passage, and a domed central chamber. The edge of the monument was retained by a kerb which rose in height towards the entrance. The kerbstones were not embedded deeply in the subsoil and the lowest did not always have sockets. As a result, they would have been pushed outwards as the material of the cairn began to settle. To prevent the kerb from collapsing (as in fact happened at Corrymony) they were buttressed on the exterior by a substantial bank of rubble which continued across the entrance, making access to the chamber difficult. This must have happened soon after the original tombs were built. A stone circle was raised along the edge of this platform using this material as its foundation. In effect, the tomb was closed as the ring of monoliths was erected. From then on, those stones could have stood for the community whose dead were associated with the tomb.

When the Clava Cairns were investigated it was thought that they were Neolithic monuments and that the chambered cairns and stone circles would have been built simultaneously, as appeared to be the case at Newgrange. That was not correct. The Clava passage graves were built after the Neolithic period was over and were approximately a millennium later in date than the Irish tomb with which they had been compared. They may have been constructed in an archaic style because similar buildings of great antiquity were still accessible in the surrounding area and were being reused as burial places at the time (Bradley 2000b: 221–4). A new assessment of the archaeological sequence at Newgrange suggests yet another possibility (Stout and Stout 2008: 84–92). Here, a great tomb was built around 3000 BC, but the construction of a circle of monoliths was probably associated with secondary activity during the Beaker period. It seems possible that the people who established the stone settings at these two sites shared some of the same concerns. Whilst the entrance passages at Balnuaran of Clava faced the midwinter sunset, their equivalent at Newgrange was aligned on the midwinter sunrise.

If the stone setting at Newgrange was a later addition, the same interpretation may apply to a ring of 'fire pits' that surrounds a Neolithic passage grave on the Hill of Tara in Ireland (O'Sullivan 2005: 40–7). They also date from the Early Bronze Age and photographs of them in the course of excavation suggest that they were the sockets for a circle of standing stones which has since been removed. Such revisions raise a problem, for it means that superficially similar

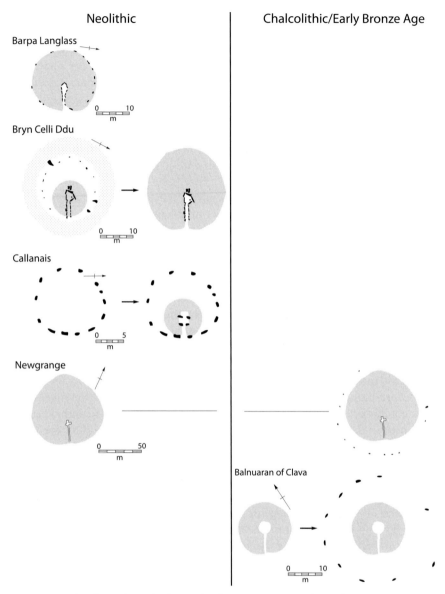

Figure 38 The chronological relationship between stone circles and passage graves in Britain and Ireland. The monuments considered in Figures 36 and 37 are organized according to the structural sequences identified at each site.

stone settings from Callanish and Bryn Celli Ddu to Clava and Newgrange date from quite different periods. Moreover, the detailed sequences identified at these sites contrast with one another. At Callanish, the stone setting was older than the chambered tomb, but at Bryn Celli Ddu both features were contemporary with one another, although the freestanding monoliths were buried when the passage grave was extended. At Clava, the stone circle was built very soon after the circular cairn, whilst its equivalent at Newgrange was not erected until a thousand years had elapsed since the construction of the original monument. Even so, several of the sites considered here—Newgrange, Maeshowe, Bryn Celli Ddu, and Balnuaran of Clava—were aligned on the solstices (Ruggles 1999). These structures cannot be attributed to a single 'type'. Did they come to resemble one another because they were linked by a common idea, that rings of unshaped stones were an appropriate way of commemorating the dead of the community? If so, their link with chambered tombs would be easier to understand.

STONE CIRCLES AND HENGE MONUMENTS

Robin (2009) has suggested that the internal structure of Irish passage graves can be thought of as a series of rings composed of different materials. Only the outermost skin was exposed when the mound was complete. He argues that the thresholds where the entrance passage breached these divisions were marked by carved designs. At a few sites, this process even extended to the raising of stone circles around the perimeter of the monument; elsewhere it is evidenced by the building of external platforms or other earthworks (Figure 39).

It seems as if a similar process involved those monuments that began as freestanding stone circles. It even drew on the character of the natural terrain around the structures themselves. Again, that interpretation depends on a new approach to the structural sequence at the sites.

For many years it seemed as if stone circles were simply the regional counterparts of the enclosures described as *henges*; such monuments are characterized by an external bank and an internal ditch. Burl argued that these earthworks were constructed in areas of softer subsoil where it would be possible to build an earthwork, but, where the rock was too hard to allow this, rings of monoliths were an acceptable alternative. He suggested that the two kinds of monument had complementary distributions (Burl 2000: 33–8). In his view, the concept of the henge developed first and stone circles were a later development.

There are two difficulties with this interpretation. The first is that the direct dating of cremated bone has allowed a number of ancient structures to be

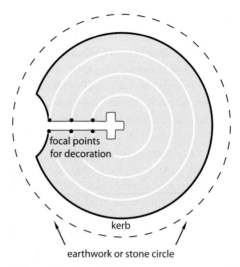

focal points
for decoration

kerb

earthwork or stone circle

Figure 39 The spatial organization of Irish passage graves, emphasizing the importance of concentric zones in the architectural design and their relationship to the
positions of the decorated surfaces.

studied in detail for the first time. This has established that circular settings of
monoliths, accompanied by human remains, were already being built between
3300 and 3000 BC (Parker Pearson et al. 2009). That is earlier than the first date
from the earthwork of a henge, for the ditch at Stenness was not dug until
about 2900 BC (Sheridan and Higham 2006). At the same time, it is clear that a
number of stone circles *were* enclosed by earthworks. Obviously, it would be
difficult to create settings of standing stones in regions where suitable raw
material was not available locally. However, it is obvious that considerable
banks could be constructed out of loose boulders, even where ditches were
difficult to excavate. The important question to ask is how the stone circles
inside these henges differed from those that remained unenclosed and the
order in which the separate components were established on individual sites.

The second issue seemed uncontentious. Henge monuments were defined
by an external bank and an internal ditch, encouraging the idea that they were
public arenas like the amphitheatres of the Roman period. People would have
been able to observe ceremonies taking place inside them, even if they were
separated from the participants by a barrier. There are several reasons why this
interpretation no longer seems satisfactory. Some are purely practical arguments. The earthworks of a number of henges seem to have been unstable and
there is evidence that that they soon collapsed. After that, they were no longer
maintained. The banks were especially high close to the entrance (or entrances) and would not have been able to bear the weight of a large number
of spectators. At the same time, there are indications of how the stones in the

interior had been raised. They could be located perilously close to the ditch and, in some cases, the orientations of their sockets show the direction from which they were pulled into position (Gibson 2010). It would have been impossible if the earthwork was already there. In other cases, there are stone circles whose plan is not concentric with the bank and ditch, suggesting that they had originally been conceived as freestanding structures. For instance, Arbor Low in the north of England was not precisely circular and may have had an entrance in between two of the tallest stones (Bradley 2011: 100–1). The earthwork that encloses this setting is closer to the monoliths on one side of the circuit than the other. Moreover, its construction changed the alignment of the monument by several degrees and established a new position for the northern entrance. In such cases, it seems likely that the bank and ditch were a subsequent development.

This is also suggested by radiocarbon dating. At Broomend of Crichie in north-east Scotland the stone setting inside an earthwork henge was not a ring but an arc of monoliths, approached by an avenue of paired stones which led between a stone circle (now destroyed) and a flat cemetery 500 metres away. The standing stones within the enclosure flanked the position of a shaft grave, but radiocarbon dating of vegetation cleared by fire when the bank was built showed the henge monument that surrounds these features was not constructed for another two hundred years, or possibly longer (Bradley 2011: Chapters 1–3).

A similar sequence has been established at the henge monument at Dyffryn Lane, close to the border between Wales and England (Gibson 2010). Here, there is stratigraphic evidence that a small stone circle was erected at an earlier date than the henge monument that eventually enclosed it. One of the uprights had already fallen when the earthwork was built. Again, the distinction is evident from radiocarbon dating. In a subsequent phase a mound was constructed in the interior, concealing the tops of the monoliths that remained intact. Not all henges need have been later than the settings of stones within them, but findings of this kind pose a challenge. Why was an additional circuit constructed around these monuments and how was it employed?

If the banks of henges were not intended as viewing platforms, why did they assume such a distinctive form? And how did their creation change the character of stone circles that had originally been permeable constructions?

Two hypotheses have been suggested to explain the distinctive configuration of the earthworks (Figure 40). Why was the bank located outside the ditch when this did not happen with other kinds of monument? One possibility is that this device represents a form of defence in reverse. In most circumstances an earthwork with an external ditch confronts the outsider—that is one of the characteristics of hillforts. In the case of Irish royal centres such as Uisneach, there is literary evidence that the internal ditch was intended to *contain* the powerful forces associated with locations where people came into contact with

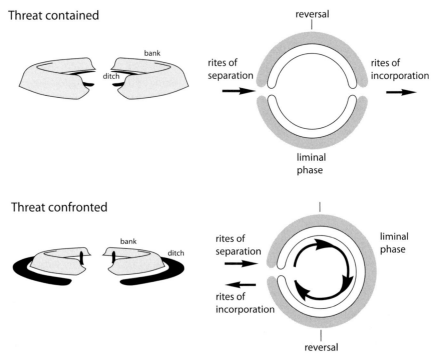

Figure 40 Alternative interpretations of the structure of henge monuments. The left-hand drawing illustrates the idea that these earthworks contained dangerous forces and prevented them from escaping. The other drawing shows how henges might have been used in the rites of passage.

the supernatural (Warner 2000). The same idea may well be relevant to henges, but in the case of those examples with stone circles it would not explain why this measure was taken so long after the monoliths had been put in place. Nor does it explain why it did not happen everywhere.

A second possibility is that the distinctive form of henges was intended to *reverse* the conventions observed on other sites where the earthworks had their ditches on the outside and lacked an external bank. Some of these structures were already old when the first henges were built, but they still seem to have provided focal points in the Neolithic landscape. At the same time, the new monuments had very few entrances—normally one or two—and they could be so narrow that people must have entered the enclosure in single file. There are sites where the banks were highest around the points where the earthwork was breached. The effect was very striking. Participants inside these enclosures were almost completely cut off from the outside world and the only glimpses of the surrounding area were through the entrance(s). At the same time, people outside the monument would have been unable to see what was happening inside it. The earthwork was not only a barrier, it was an enormous screen (Bradley 2011).

The reversal of everyday experience plays an important part in the rites of passage. Van Gennep (1909) contends that public rituals pass through three successive stages: a view endorsed by Turner (1969). First, there are the *rites of separation*, in which the participants are removed from their familiar settings. There follows a *liminal phase* in which the conventions of daily life are suspended or even reversed, before a final phase—the *rites of incorporation*—when the participants return to the wider world with new identities. There are several key elements in this scheme: seclusion, the crossing of boundaries, and the inversion of daily experience. Henge monuments supplied all three. They were secluded circular enclosures, almost entirely cut off from the areas around them; they were accessed through narrow gaps in a high earthwork screen; and the configuration of the enclosure was an explicit reversal of the forms taken by other monuments. Henges provide evidence of rituals that focused on the solstices and the commemoration of the dead. Both may have involved important changes of status, as one generation gave way to another or the sun changed its course across the sky. These are among the activities that van Gennep (1909) associated with the rites of passage. The liminal phase was the crucial element and the choice of this particular term is appropriate as the Latin word *limen* refers to a threshold or a boundary. It could certainly apply to the entrances leading in and out of these earthworks.

Another question relates to the difference between stone circles which were enclosed by henges and those that retained their original form. If certain settings of monoliths were hidden behind an earthwork screen, it did not apply to other sites where the perimeter of the monument was completely permeable. Watson (2004) has studied this phenomenon and has shown that larger, and apparently earlier, stone circles were often built at the centre of a natural basin with a continuous perimeter of high ground. Among the most obvious examples are Avebury and the Stone of Stenness, where this pattern is evident over an extensive geographical area. It can be identified on a smaller scale as well; here, the best known example is Stonehenge. On one level it seems as if the far horizon mirrored the configuration of the ring of stones. On another, it raises the possibility that the circle itself was conceived as a microcosm of a wider world. The addition of an earthwork barrier would have modified this relationship and sometimes it concealed the visual effect that had been contrived with so much care. Either the earthwork bank merged with a distant skyline, as it did at Avebury (Watson 2001), or it concealed it altogether, as happened at an enclosure like Mayburgh in north-west England (Topping 1992). The site might still be considered as a central point, but in one case this could be demonstrated visually, whilst, in another, it must have been understood as an abstract idea. What had once been public knowledge became increasingly restricted, and that restriction was expressed directly in the form and layout of the earthwork.

It seems possible that these developments were closely related to the society that built the henges. Not only did the construction of the earthworks place physical restrictions on who had access to these places, it also restricted knowledge of their significance and the ways in which they were used. That may not have been the case before. At the same time, the building of what were sometimes considerable earthworks must have placed great demands on human labour, and the execution of these undertakings would have required planning and coordination, even if it did not depend on coercion. The celebration of the dead inside these secluded locations would have highlighted the significance of certain people at the expense of others. A similar concern with important figures from the past was expressed by the construction of burial mounds. Some of them were contemporary with these monuments, but others were built after activity in these places had ceased.

SUMMARY

This chapter has involved some detailed arguments and, for that reason, it may be helpful to summarize its main conclusions. It began with the suggestion that stone settings were associated with the dead. It drew attention to the striking contrast between continental statue menhirs whose characteristic features referred to the human body and the aniconic tradition of standing stones which existed in the British Isles. That contrast extended into other media so that depictions of humans and animals could be found in many contexts in Atlantic Europe, but were virtually absent from Britain and Ireland. There was a further contrast between the insular stone settings and those on the continent. In Brittany, the West Mediterranean, and the Southern Alps, menhirs were often organized in rows, whilst many of the structures in Britain and Ireland were circular.

The contrast between statue menhirs and other standing stones had important implications. The settings of monoliths in Continental Europe may have referred to the qualities or achievements of *particular people* in the past, whilst their British equivalents made no such distinction. Here, all the stones were alike, leading to the suggestion that circular settings might have stood for entire communities rather than specific individuals. That association was maintained over a lengthy period, from 3000 BC to the mid-second millennium. Throughout that time, stone circles contained little archaeological material apart from human remains.

In some cases the contrast between insular structures and their continental counterparts went much further. The stone alignments of north-west France were closely associated with long mounds and at times they seemed to avoid the distribution of passage tombs. Their main connection with those particular monuments was when decorated menhirs were reused; these pieces could be isolated examples and need not have been taken from larger complexes. The Breton alignments were of special importance, and, although there were a few circular stone settings in north-west France, their frequency has been exaggerated. In any case, their architecture and chronology shared little in common with those in the British Isles.

By contrast, a few of the insular stone circles were directly associated with passage graves and also with earthwork enclosures. In both cases they contained human bones. It was clear that their connection with the dead was present from the outset. On the other hand, because such settings of monoliths remained a prominent feature of the landscape, structures of this kind were important for a long time and individual examples were reused. This was especially obvious in the case of megalithic tombs. Although a few stone circles were directly associated with passage graves, there were other cases in which they had been erected around already existing monuments. In some instances the interval between these periods of construction was a brief one—that was true at Balnuaran of Clava—but there were other sites where the chambered tomb was not enclosed until much later. Newgrange provides an example of this kind of sequence. Although insular passage tombs were decorated with 'megalithic art', it did not extend to the monoliths around them where cup marks were the only motifs. It is important to note that, in contrast to the situation in north-west France, this process of secondary embellishment did not extend to long barrows or long cairns.

A second development concerned the circular enclosures described as henges, which were peculiar to the British Isles. They took a quite distinctive form and should not be confused with the earthworks associated with the earliest stone settings where the bank was inside the ditch and the interior could be entered at several points. Strictly speaking, henge monuments had their banks on the outside and screened the interior from view. Most of these earthworks had only one or two entrances which, in some cases, could be extremely narrow. The people inside these monuments would have been cut off from the surrounding area. Many of these points had been appreciated for a long time. What was new is the recognition that these massive earthworks could enclose stone circles that had originally been freestanding monuments. Again, the interval between these developments could have been long or short—in extreme cases it was several hundred years. The construction of the earthwork constrained the ways in which these places could be used. In view of the link between rings of monoliths and the dead, it seemed possible that the new enclosures played a part in the rites of passage. They were where the conventions of daily life were reversed. What had once been permeable monuments became increasingly secluded. In its later stages this development ran in parallel with the construction of a new generation of burial mounds.

This account began by comparing the properties of wood and stone, and the different ideas they might have evoked in ancient society. It has considered the interpretation of stone circles and has traced their history over nearly 1,500 years. But they were not the only circular monuments in the British landscape over this extended period. There were also timber settings, which had very different associations. In contrast to the structures that have been considered here, they could be connected with the living and are found with the remains of feasts. It is not surprising that their architecture shares more features in common with the buildings found in settlements than it does with chambered tombs.

This theme is considered in detail in the next chapter, which investigates the relationship between domestic dwellings, 'Great Houses', and other circular monuments. It returns to the archaeological sequence in Sardinia, introduced in Chapter 4, and discusses the public architecture of other West Mediterranean islands before it comes back to the prehistory of the British Isles and the timber and earthwork monuments that were built there.

6

The Enormous Room

SEA AND SARDINIA

It is ironic that anyone studying the domestic architecture of Copper Age Sardinia must turn to underground tombs as a source of information, whilst the monumental 'houses' of the Bronze Age are among the most conspicuous structures anywhere in Europe. The contrast between these two periods introduces a new theme.

The first part of this chapter will study stone towers and related structures in the West Mediterranean. In every case they were associated with settlement sites and some may have been domestic buildings in their own right. Over time, they came to favour a circular plan. This section considers monuments in Sardinia, Corsica, and the Balearics and compares them with sites in Spain. It also asks whether they represent a single phenomenon.

The second part considers three groups of timber buildings in Britain and Ireland and the enclosures with which they are associated. In this case they date from different periods. Although they resemble one another on the ground, there were few direct connections between them and, in at least two instances, they are thought to have been ceremonial centres. These sites in the Mediterranean and the North Atlantic are considered together in the light of a recent analysis of monumental architecture in the eastern USA.

Both sections are designed to complement one another. The first considers the development of Great Houses in a series of well-populated landscapes. The second works at a larger geographical scale and studies the ways in which such buildings, and the earthworks associated with them, were related to a still more extensive area, until the most elaborate of all could be considered as microcosms of the wider world.

The growth of towers

Chapter Four discussed the *domus de janas* of Sardinia, the surprisingly realistic copies of domestic interiors provided for the dead during the Ozieri

Culture. They were lavishly decorated and have produced radiocarbon dates which suggest that they were contemporary with the later phases of megalithic art in Western Europe. At the same time, most of the Sardinian structures were roughly square or rectangular and only a minority were designed as depictions of roundhouses. That reflects the results of excavation at the comparatively few surviving settlements of the same date. By contrast, most of the *nuraghi* that became the main kind of domestic structure during the Bronze Age were circular, as were the small stone houses with which they are associated. How did those changes come about?

Two points are important in studying these distinctive sites. The first is that the subterranean tombs were not the only structures dedicated to the dead (Kolb 2005). Although their chronology is poorly understood, it is clear that megalithic 'dolmens' were built at ground level during the same phase. Where one kind of structure was excavated into the living rock, the other was built by raising large pieces of stone. Apart from their entrance passages, *domus de janas* were invisible, but the dolmens were a prominent feature of the landscape. The two traditions ran in parallel for some time. A second observation is that both the dolmens and *domus de janas* were reused for a long period after they were first constructed (Kolb 2005). That is one of the reasons why they have been difficult to date. It means that megalithic architecture would have been familiar to the occupants of Sardinia, even when these structures were old.

It is difficult to trace the evolution of the buildings in much detail, if only because their overall chronology is imprecise. Even so, there were several stages in the evolution of this style of architecture before the sequence was cut short as Sardinia was drawn into the Phoenician world.

The first stage has been mentioned already. It extended into the early second millennium BC. Here, the available evidence is biased towards the information provided by subterranean tombs. They offer an insight into the forms of domestic architecture that is more detailed than anything learned from settlement excavation. In common with other parts of the West Mediterranean, the houses adopted a variety of ground plans and seem to have been rectangular, oval, or round. They were contemporary with megalithic tombs, some of which were associated with circular cairns.

The archaeological sequence in Sardinia is controversial, but according to Webster (1996) and Blake (2001) the next phase saw the reuse of dolmens and *domus de janas*. On one hand, settlement sites remain difficult to discover and their characteristic forms were no longer imitated by underground chambers. On the other hand, this period saw the first development of monumental above-ground structures. Another particularly striking monument is Monte d'Accodi, where a massive rectangular platform was constructed and is approached by a ramp of 75 metres in length (Lilliu 1988: 255–9, Figures 62 and 63). It is not known how it was used, but elsewhere on the island there is evidence that circular and rectangular structures were built on a foundation of rubble. Their architecture anticipates that of later stone towers and, for that reason, these enigmatic monuments are known as *proto-nuraghi*. The presence of low platforms suggests that they might have been public buildings, but the forms of the circular and rectangular examples anticipate those of free-standing towers which are regarded as domestic sites.

That development is clearly evidenced during a third stage when circular and rectangular towers were widely distributed for the first time. Webster (1996) suggests that it happened between about 1800 and 1500 BC The first nuraghi seem to have been self-contained settlements and are found so widely that it is difficult to argue that they enjoyed any special status. Rather, they are distributed more or less evenly across the most productive land. It was only gradually that villages developed around them. The towers were built out of massive blocks and assume a variety of forms, although it is clear that at least some of them had corbelled roofs and rose to two or three storeys (Figure 41). They were accessed by corridors constructed in the thickness of the wall. Certain, but not all, of these structures were accompanied by newly built tombs, whose characteristic stonework was similar to the techniques used in building the towers. These tombs—*tombi de giganti*—contained a large number of inhumation burials and, like the Neolithic monuments discussed in Chapter 5, they reused older menhirs. A detailed study has shown that their positions are visible from many of the nuraghi, although they are usually

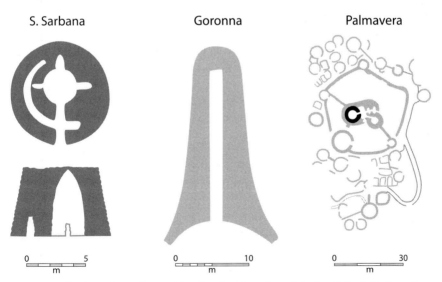

Figure 41 Outline plans of nuraghi and a chambered tomb in Sardinia. S. Sarbana is a stone tower and Goronna is a 'Giant's Tomb'. The plan of Palmavera shows the location of another tower in relation to the roundhouses outside it.

separated from one another by a distance of several hundred metres (Blake 2001). Even though they are often paired, there is a striking contrast between them. An increasing proportion of the nuraghi took the form of a circular tower. Although the forecourt of these megalithic tombs was concave, the core of the monument was rectilinear.

In Webster's scheme, the next stage in the Sardinian sequence is dated between 1300 and 900 BC and is much better known. This is when the nuraghi achieved their greatest architectural elaboration. They were more massive than their predecessors and individual examples could be enclosed by a defensive wall. The central building was often surrounded by roundhouses, all of approximately the same size. The nuraghi themselves were the central focus of the settlement and are associated with evidence of craft production and the consumption of food. They can also be found with quantities of metalwork which may have been deposited as offerings.

The buildings attributed to this phase have several new features (Webster 1996). There were greater architectural variations between different settlements than in earlier periods and now it is possible to infer the existence of a hierarchy among these sites, based on their structural elaboration and spacing across the landscape. Another feature was the presence of large numbers of houses around the central nucleus. These buildings were very similar to one another and their form contrasts markedly with the character of the central tower. At the same time, that focal structure was circular. It was massively built, but in plan it resembled an enlarged version of a domestic prototype. The resemblance would be all the more striking if the roundhouses had domed roofs, like those represented inside the *domus de janas* many generations before.

Not every site included a tower. Another reason for drawing attention to examples dominated by nuraghi is that there were other settlements where large groups of roundhouses occur in isolation. This evidence suggests two possibilities. The first is that the nucleated settlements associated with massive towers were of higher status than those in which such buildings were absent (Webster 1996: Chapter 6). They were also quite different from sites where a tower was the only structure. A second suggestion is that the roles of nuraghi may have changed over time. The earlier examples could be compared with independent farmhouses, albeit domestic dwellings built on an extravagant scale. The later examples may have been public buildings constructed in the midst of extensive settlement sites. The special status of the most elaborate nuraghi is shown by the fact that they are portrayed by models made of stone or bronze (Pirovano 1985).

Just as the latest nuraghi can be paired with *tombi di giganti*, they can also be associated with sacred wells where metalwork was deposited and animals were sacrificed (Lilliu 1988: 602–28; Figure 42). Again, they are complex roofed structures but in this case the dominant feature is a stone-lined shaft,

Sa Testa

Domu de Origia

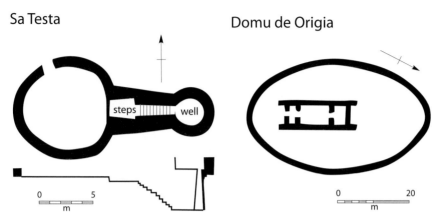

Figure 42 Plan and profile of the 'sacred well' at Sa Testa, and the plan of a stone shrine at Domu de Orgia, Sardinia.

access to which is provided by a flight of steps. Votive objects seem to have been suspended above the water, and others, perhaps made for the purpose, were displayed on the roofs of structures interpreted as temples or shrines (Lo Schiavo 2007). Whereas those shrines were rectangular, the buildings associated with the wells had a curvilinear ground plan which recalls the architecture of nuraghi and roundhouses. Megalithic tombs played a decreasing role in this final phase, but, again, the contrast between these different buildings can hardly have been fortuitous. The towers and the enclosures associated with sacred wells were generally circular or oval, as were the buildings in the settlements. The tomb had a concave forecourt, but the body of the cairn had a linear configuration which it shared with the temples.

This complicated pattern developed as Sardinia became increasingly integrated into a pattern of long distance trade which extended across the Central and West Mediterranean. It involved the export of large quantities of local copper. It was once supposed that Mycenaean *tholos* tombs provided the source of inspiration for the corbelled buildings. The chronological evidence rules out that idea, as close contacts with the Greek mainland did not develop until the first towers had been built. However, the intensification of long distance alliances may have accelerated social changes that had already begun (Giardino 1992).

Just as contacts with other parts of the Mediterranean precipitated social changes in Sardinia, the establishment of Phoenician colonies may have brought that process to an end between 900 and 500 BC. Nuraghi were no longer constructed. That is not to say that they lost their importance entirely as some examples are associated with deposits of valuables of similar significance to the offerings at the sacred wells. Although the evidence is limited, Blake (1999) has suggested that a few of the latest towers were reused as cult centres at the time. By that stage the pattern of settlement was changing, but it is a moot point whether the roles of nuraghi might have altered even earlier. Is it possible that by the end of their history the most complex examples were not only public buildings located at the heart of large settlements? Might they have become sacred monuments in their own right? It is an intriguing idea, but one which will be difficult to evaluate.

The language of size

Nuraghi are not the only circular towers in the Bronze Age of the West Mediterranean. There are others in Corsica, the Balearics, and Southern Spain, and further examples may occur in the south of Italy and on the island of Pantellaria (Lewthwaite 1985; Patton 1996). Each kind has a local name. The Corsican monuments are *torri* and those in the Balearic Islands are *talayots*. The towers of La Mancha are known as *motillas* and the stone monuments of Apulia are *specchie*. Possible counterparts include the *sesi* of Pantellaria. The main groups occur on islands whose inhabitants could communicate with one another by sea—the closest connections between the architecture of these monuments were between Sardinia and its neighbour, Corsica.

Together with the Sardinian nuraghi, these monuments are sometimes considered as a single phenomenon, although differences of chronology between these areas make it a difficult argument to sustain. Lewthwaite (1985) considers almost all these forms of architecture together; the only exceptions are motillas. He compares these structures from Italy to the Balearics and even suggests parallels among the fortified settlements of south-east Spain. For Lewthwaite, the stone-built monuments can be treated as a single phenomenon, albeit one which developed over a long period and was subject to local variations. Other writers have taken a different view. Kolb (2005) restricts himself to the structures found on West Mediterranean islands and, like Lewthwaite, he does not discuss the motillas of the Spanish mainland. However, he refers to Mycenaean tholos tombs as examples of Bronze Age monumental architecture. A similar approach is found taken by Patton (1996) in his account of stone monuments in the Mediterranean.

Perhaps the best way of discussing the nature of these buildings is to focus on Sardinia, where the structures are best preserved and have been investigated for the longest time. The other traditions can be characterized by comparing their diagnostic features with the development of nuraghi set out earlier in this chapter.

At the outset, two of the local traditions mentioned by Lewthwaite (1985) are best omitted from the account. At present, little is known about their architecture and chronology, and for many years there was doubt whether the buildings in question were freestanding towers associated with domestic sites or whether they were associated with the dead. They are the specchie of Apulia and the sesi of Pantellaria. The Mycenaean tholoi are much better known, but in this case they can be left out of the discussion because they are so obviously tombs. The account that follows is limited to settlements.

The remaining examples are found in areas with a tradition of circular domestic buildings, although other forms can be represented and were sometimes more common than roundhouses. Even then it is not easy to consider them as a coherent group. The motillas of La Mancha epitomize the problem. They occur on fertile soils and were massive stone monuments associated with food production and the storage of agricultural produce (Fernández-Posse et al. 2000; Bénitez de Lugo Enrich 2010). Their main feature is a stone tower which was frequently surrounded by a circular walled enclosure; in some cases, the limits of the motilla are marked by more than one circuit of defences. Despite the circular outline of many—but not all—of these enclosures, the central towers may be approximately round or square, and the houses that have been excavated inside the enclosure walls can also be oval or rectangular with apsidal ends. The emphasis on a circular ground plan that characterizes the later nuraghi is not so evident here. Nor is it clear how far motillas were isolated buildings, as there is evidence of external settlements and clusters of storage pits which remain too little known (Bénitez de Lugo Enrich 2010). Even though this combination of an open settlement and a central tower recalls the evidence from Sardinia, any close comparison would be misleading as the motillas date from an earlier period than the superficially similar structures on the island. There is another problem, too. Like many settlements of the same date in the south of Spain, motillas can be associated with human burials and one of the excavated examples was constructed over a cave (Bénitez de Lugo Enrich 2010). It is not clear whether these sites should be interpreted entirely in terms of food production and control over resources.

Corsican torri are of similar age to the nuraghi and share the same basic plan as those structures (De Lanfranchini and Weiss 1997; Costa 2004: 114–18). As their name suggests, they are also circular towers and, like their better known counterparts, they seem to have been spanned by corbelled roofs. Again, the upper levels were accessed through corridors constructed in the thickness of the wall. They are found in the part of the island closest to Sardinia.

Like nuraghi, torri are associated with settlement sites which include roundhouses, as well as other kinds of buildings, but the towers never attained the complexity of the later examples in Sardinia. They may also have played a more specialized role, for access to their interior was restricted. At the same time, there is a striking link with the *tombi de giganti* found on the neighbouring island, for, at the Corsican site of Filitosa, statue menhirs were reused in building the monument (Costa 2004: Chapter 6). The links between these architectural traditions can be misunderstood. The Giants' Tombs in Sardinia were monuments to the dead and the reused fragments may have represented ancestral figures. Those at Filitosa included sculptures of armed men. Again, this may have involved a reference to the past, but it seems just as likely that the sculptures were incorporated in the torri as an expression of political power.

The stone monuments of the Balearics contrast with those of Corsica and Sardinia, although most authorities consider that they represent a similar phenomenon. In this case, two main kinds of structures can be found together. There are the stone structures known as *talayots,* or watch-towers, as well as tombs in the shape of an upturned boat which are peculiar to Menorca (Gili et al. 2006). These *navetas* date from 1100 to 850 BC whilst talayots were used between about 900 and 600 BC, meaning that their histories ran in parallel with those of the last nuraghi and torri.

The talayots can be associated with settlements. They take several forms: all are essentially towers but they can be circular or square in outline and their profiles may be vertical or stepped. Although their outward forms can resemble the monuments discussed in Corsica and Sardinia, they were built in a different way. They did not make use of corbels. Instead, the roofs of all three types were supported by a pillar in the middle of the floor (Figure 43). It is by no means clear how they were used, but at Son Fornés (Gasull et al. 1984) it was suggested that they were places where the inhabitants of the settlement came together at feasts.

The navetas raise some of the issues discussed in Chapter 4. They are stone-built tombs in the shape of a boat and are associated with large numbers of unburnt human bones. On Menorca, their distinctive architecture seems to have been inspired by a local tradition of domestic dwellings which were occupied between about 1650 and 1050 BC. The two kinds of structure do not appear to have been contemporary with one another, so this may be a

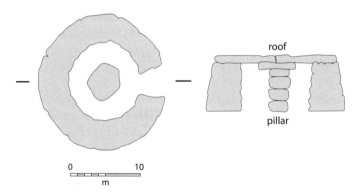

Figure 43 The structure of a Majorcan talayot with its central pillar.

further instance in which the architecture of stone tombs copied the appearance of houses inhabited in the past.

There are several ways in which the connections between the monuments in these different regions have been interpreted, but none of them does much to account for the ways in which space was organized in and around these buildings. That is because these discussions have been based on general theory and are excessively abstract.

Two related themes can be identified in these accounts. One focuses on the distinctive character of islands and suggests that their independence and isolation are reflected by a special concern with massive construction projects. In places whose natural resources would not allow a process of political expansion, more effort was devoted to monument building (Patton 1996). This approach is indebted to Polynesian anthropology. A second approach emphasizes the legacy of megalithic tombs that would have been apparent to the inhabitants of Sardinia, Corsica, and the Balearics. People were already accustomed to living in a world of stone constructions and were familiar with the techniques of acquiring and using the raw material. In that case, it would have been natural to continue the process (Kolb 2005).

There are problems with both approaches. The emphasis on the distinctive identity of islands is fundamentally flawed, for it is evident that the places discussed here were by no means isolated. Sardinia was a major source of obsidian in the Neolithic period and it and the Balearics produced large quantities of Beaker pottery; Sardinia was also a major source of copper which was traded over a considerable area. Similarly, there are finds of North African ivory from Majorca and Menorca. At the same time, none of these islands was especially remote from the European mainland and people who were accustomed to travelling by sea would have had little problem in moving between them. This discussion overlooks a more important point. Bronze Age monumental architecture is not a special feature of the Mediterranean islands, as Patton's book contends. Whether or not the inhabitants of Sardinia or Corsica were aware of the Spanish motillas, those structures were as elaborate as any he considers and yet they are located in an extensive and fertile plain. Indeed, current fieldwork is identifying even more complex stone and earthwork monuments of the Chalcolithic and Early Bronze Age periods in Portugal (Jorge 1998; Valera in press).

Kolb (2005) studies almost the same selection of architectural traditions as Patton, but is more concerned with the way in which they were inspired by earlier megalithic tombs than he is with the details of their construction. His analysis emphasizes the size and spacing of the buildings. Like Webster (1996), he studies the amount of work needed to build them. Their objective is to interpret Bronze Age social organization. The debt to Polynesian anthropology is obvious in Kolb's research, for he employs much the same model in his account of the West Mediterranean as he did in an earlier investigation of monuments in Hawai'i (Kolb 1997). His study areas may have included megalithic tombs, but the specific character of the nuraghi, torri and talayots would seem to be a secondary concern. Some of the most useful observations have been neglected in the search for general principles.

Two of the more puzzling features of these buildings suggest another approach to the evidence. It is difficult to distinguish between the ritual and domestic associations of these buildings and yet there is little evidence that any of the towers were set apart from the settlements of the same period. Even those nuraghi that were not surrounded by houses appear to have been inhabited. At the same time, one of the distinctive features of these monuments—especially the stone towers of Sardinia and Corsica—is that they share the circular plans of the houses occupied during the same period. In Sardinia, there are indications that roundhouses became increasingly important over time so that they are virtually the only kind of domestic building in the villages associated with nuraghi.

Polynesia has provided the principal source of analogy in discussions of these buildings. Perhaps the archaeology of the eastern USA has more to offer as a basis for comparison. In 1997, DeBoer published an analysis of the ceremonial centres of the Hopewell Culture. His argument was simple. The massive earthworks that have commanded so much attention from archaeologists were massively enlarged versions of a domestic prototype. They were conceived in the image of the house and adopted exactly the same ground plan, but they were enclosures and mounds rather than roofed buildings. They could be described as the 'Great Houses' of communities who assembled there on special occasions.

The same principle can be identified among the rectilinear buildings in the Late Neolithic of western France and again in Early Medieval Europe (Bradley 2005b: Chapter 2). In the Bronze Age of the West Mediterranean it may have extended to circular constructions. They could have played many different roles, from dwellings to ritual centres and from defended food stores to small fortresses. What they share is their relationship with the dwellings that were inhabited at the same time. There may have been few direct connections between the people who built the towers in different regions, but the design of those buildings illustrates a common process. Many of the circular monuments constructed during the Bronze Age in south-west Europe adopted domestic buildings as their prototype. This may be a case, like those considered in Chapter 2, where the 'house' provided a symbol for a larger community. That would be true whether or not these buildings were inhabited. They could have provided the settings for public events. It may be that individual examples also played a role as ceremonial centres, but the available evidence is not sufficiently detailed to support this argument.

These structures have been treated as anomalies, but they deserve much closer study from archaeologists concerned with prehistoric monuments, for two of the local sequences are particularly striking. In the Balearics, the layout of boat-shaped houses was copied in the building of tombs, whilst the archaeological sequence in Sardinia shows how the forms of circular dwellings were elaborated in the architecture of towers. In this case, the sequence is even more unusual. Some of the earliest monuments were underground and the latest rose into the sky.

THE ROUND EARTH

Circles, ringworks, and royal centres

A similar process can be illustrated by the prehistoric archaeology of Britain and Ireland, but here there are two important differences. The stone towers of the West Mediterranean were located at the heart of the settlement pattern, whilst most of the 'Great Houses' in the British Isles were set apart from the domestic landscape and have more in common with the ceremonial centres considered by DeBoer (1997). At the same time, structures which resemble one another in plan were built at quite different times and any direct connection between them may be illusory.

The recognition of this distinctive phenomenon arises out of a history of confusion. For many years 'timber circles' have been accepted as one of the principal types of monument built during the Neolithic period. Some were surrounded by the earthworks known as henges and others by massive palisades. For a long time prehistorians believed that these features represented a unitary phenomenon, but recent work does not support this conclusion. Like the stone settings discussed in Chapter 5, the timber circles may have been enclosed *during a secondary phase* (Gibson 2010). Even so, the link between them appeared so strong that archaeologists believed that these sites could be identified by air photography. In most cases the ditch and bank were visible, but any post sockets had to be detected by other methods.

That approach turned out to be misleading; during the 1970s and 1980s a number of earthwork monuments investigated as Neolithic henges turned out to date from the Late Bronze Age. Today they are described as 'ringworks'. Like henges, they could be associated with circular timber buildings, some of them of unusual size, but the ringworks were between 1000 and 1500 years later than the monuments with which they had been compared. Instead of dates around 2400 BC, these examples were constructed from about 1100 to 800 BC (Bradley 2007: 206–10).

Other excavations undertaken in the 1970s were discovering the same combination of timber settings and circular earthworks in Ireland, where sites like Navan Fort (Waterman 1997) and Knockaulin (Johnston and Wailes

2007) had been identified from literary evidence as the royal centres of the Early Medieval period. These projects showed that such places had a longer history, extending back into the pre-Roman Iron Age or even the Late Bronze Age. They featured large enclosures with an external bank and an internal ditch which recalled the layout of a henge. As the Irish earthworks were associated with enormous timber settings, it was tempting to postulate a continuous tradition of monumental architecture which went back to the Neolithic period (Gibson 1995, 2000). The case found little support.

The resemblance between all three groups of monuments raises an important question. If they were largely or entirely independent phenomena, how did such similarities arise?

The obvious starting point is to consider the timber structures of the Neolithic period. They raise two important issues for any discussion of architectural 'continuity'. Some—but not all—were surrounded by considerable earthworks and those banks and ditches would have survived as landmarks during later phases. For that reason their characteristic forms could be copied and their remains could be reused, but this would not explain the presence of *circles of posts* in all three periods, as no trace of them could have survived for such a long time. It is true that a few Neolithic examples were replaced by settings of monoliths of the kind studied in Chapter 5, but this evidence has nothing to contribute to the discussion. Neither the Late Bronze Age ringworks nor the royal centres of the Iron Age are associated with stone circles—all the structures inside them were built of wood.

Neolithic monuments

The best starting point is to reconsider the origin of circular architecture in Britain and Ireland during the Neolithic period. It is not quite clear when this happened and there is no reason to suppose that rectilinear structures were supplanted by curvilinear buildings and monuments at the same time in every area. Most of the rectangular houses of the Early Neolithic period date from the first half of the fourth millennium BC. By contrast, what little evidence there is of early roundhouses first appears in the Middle Neolithic phase (Bradley 2007: 94–8). For example, the structures buried below the principal monument at Knowth must have been in use around 3000 BC. From that time onwards there are examples of circular domestic buildings, although others were roughly oblong or square and continued to take that form until the Early Bronze Age. After that, roundhouses became the norm, although the first examples are seldom well preserved.

Some confusion is created by the fact that Late Neolithic dwellings can have a rectangular floor plan and a curving exterior wall, but this was not the only kind of house occupied during that period. Another type is well documented.

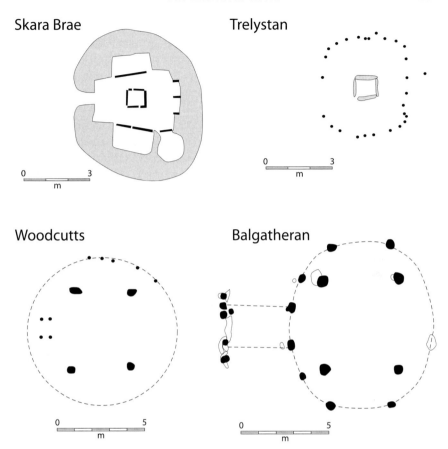

Figure 44 Plans of Late Neolithic houses and timber circles in Britain and Ireland. The house at Skara Brae is constructed of stone, but the other structures are defined by postholes and stakeholes. Like the example at Skara Brae, the building at Trelystan has a stone-lined hearth.

It has a roughly circular plan, with a clearly marked entrance, and at its centre is a square hearth or setting of posts. Buildings that conform to this arrangement are found from Wessex to Orkney and are equally widely distributed in Ireland (Bradley 2007: 119–21). They could be built in wood or stone (Figure 44).

Features of this kind are also associated with ceremonial centres, although they were often built on a much larger scale. Recent work in Orkney sheds some light on this practice. The Late Neolithic settlement at Barnhouse contained a number of examples of this type, but one of them was larger and architecturally more complex than the rest (Richards 2005). The excavator suggests that a further example was located at the centre of the Stones of Stenness: a nearby site whose distinctive character was discussed in Chapter 5.

This idea is supported by a more recent discovery at the Ness of Brodgar. Here, a series of structures of similar proportions was grouped together inside a massive walled enclosure. It was in between two stone circles, each of them inside a henge. They are interpreted as public buildings (Card 2010).

The same contrast can be identified at Late Neolithic sites in southern England, where the available evidence is so widespread that it is best to focus on the results of just one project. Recent work at Durrington Walls has identified the remains of small square or circular structures which are similar in size and construction to those in settlements (Parker Pearson 2007). The excavators suggest that they were occupied over short periods and by people who did not normally live on the site. They had come there to participate in special events. A similar argument was put forward by DeBoer (1997) to account for the deposits of artefacts found at Hopewell ceremonial centres.

At the same time, enormously enlarged versions of this simple prototype are recorded at several monuments in Wessex and at other sites in Britain and Ireland (Figure 45). The biggest were both inside, and outside, the earthwork enclosure at Durrington Walls. The largest example had been constructed before the henge was built. Like the houses described earlier, the Southern Circle had a clearly marked entrance and at its centre there was a setting of four large posts. It was approached by a ditched roadway. The remains of this structure were associated with a large number of artefacts and a considerable quantity of bones (particularly those of pigs), which the excavators interpret as the remains of feasts. There is evidence that a certain number of the animals had been killed around midwinter. That is of particular interest as the timber structure was aligned on the rising sun on the shortest day of the year (Parker Pearson 2007). Other monuments of this kind seem to be directed towards the solstices.

Although this particular structure was eventually enclosed by the henge, it is revealing that similar circles of posts, some of considerable dimensions, have been excavated outside that enclosure. Only Woodhenge—the most elaborate of all—was surrounded by an earthwork and here, again, the bank and ditch may have acted as a monumental screen. The two components were not necessarily built simultaneously (Pollard and Robinson 2007).

Two other monuments in this area shed light on the relationship between domestic dwellings and public architecture. The first was located within a circular enclosure inside one of the entrances to Durrington Walls (Thomas 2007). It was a lightly constructed building which resembled the Late Neolithic houses on the same site. It was larger than those structures, but it did not assume the monumental proportions of the timber circles there. Perhaps it played a specialized role, such as the house whose existence is postulated inside the Stones of Stenness. The example at Durrington Walls is especially interesting as it was originally enclosed by a bank with an external ditch. In a

Durrington Walls

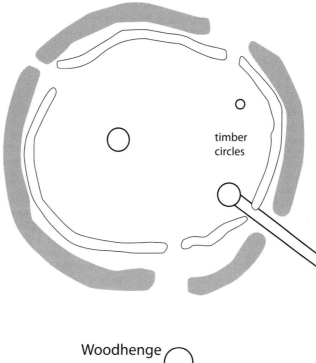

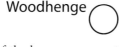
Woodhenge

Figure 45 Outline plan of the henge monument at Durrington Walls showing the likely positions of the entrances, the avenue leading into the enclosure from the south-east, and the sites of four timber settings. Like Woodhenge, which was enclosed by a bank and ditch, the two structures inside the eastern sector of the monument were massive constructions. The structure inside the north-west entrance was surrounded by a ditch. It was built on a much smaller scale and bore a greater resemblance to a domestic building. It was only in a secondary phase that the surrounding earthwork was provided with an external bank. The ditch of Durrington Walls is shown in outline and the bank in light tone.

later phase, the earthwork was rebuilt with its ditch on the inside, turning this small enclosure into a henge.

Although there may have been monoliths within the earthwork at Wood-henge (Pollard and Robinson 2007), none of the other buildings was replaced in stone, but not far away was an even more famous monument. Chapter 5 suggested that Stonehenge was associated with the dead. At the same time its architecture is unique because the monoliths have been carefully shaped and are connected by lintels which are fixed to the uprights using carpentry joints. This does not happen at any other stone circle and it seems clear that

Stonehenge was designed as a copy of a wooden building. It was entirely different from the stone settings discussed earlier in this book, for the uprights were linked together to create a single design (Cleal et al. 1995)—the individual monoliths may not have been regarded as statues in their own right. The distinctive form of the final monument would have resembled that of the timber circles nearby. If so, they cannot have been roofed.

How were such monuments related to the landscape around them? It is difficult to tell; this relationship may have been subject to considerable regional variation. The small houses at Durrington Walls were occupied discontinuously and over short periods, and it may be that in Wessex the main density of Neolithic settlement was in the coastal basin to the south of the chalk where the ground was less exposed and the soils were more productive. It is also where the widest range of artefacts is found (Field 2008: Chapter 9). It is likely that these large monuments were at the margins of the ancient landscape and were visited on special occasions. Another reason for taking this view is that in many parts of Britain timber circles and related sites are found in places that were particularly accessible from the surrounding area. They were commonly located along the major rivers and close to confluences. There is little to suggest that such monuments were central to the pattern of settlement.

In summary, the timber circles of southern England appear to have been modelled on a domestic prototype. They followed the same proportions as domestic buildings, although there is some doubt whether the largest examples were roofed. They may have been used discontinuously and it is clear that they provided the setting for feasts. These structures could be directed towards the position of the sun at the turning points of the year. They may not have been located in the midst of the settled landscape, and it is possible that some of them were built towards its limits in regions where land use was less intensive. They were visited by large numbers of people on specific occasions and similar gatherings would have been required to supply the labour and raw materials needed to build them. A few timber structures were replaced in stone, but outside southern England this was not particularly common. Similarly, certain of the largest buildings were enclosed by henges, but it may have happened at a later stage. The connection between these earthworks and timber settings was by no means uniform and it is clear that many of the wooden monuments remained entirely open.

Late Bronze Age and Iron Age monuments

Again, so much information is available and the best way of exploring the main themes is by focusing on a few sites.

The first large scale excavations of Late Bronze Age ringworks took place at Thwing in north-east England (Manby 2007) and at Mucking in the

Mucking   Thwing

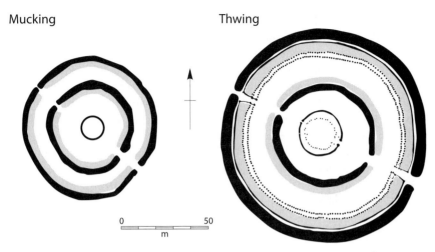

0 ————————— 50
            m

Figure 46 Plans of the Late Bronze Age enclosures at Mucking and Thwing, England. The positions of the banks are indicated in light tone.

Thames Estuary (Evans and Lucy in press; Figure 46). Thwing had been identified as a henge monument on the basis of air photography, whilst the enclosure at Mucking was discovered in the course of gravel extraction. It was originally described as an Iron Age hillfort before it was backdated to the Bronze Age.

Both enclosures shared some of the same features. Each was circular and had two concentric ditches, breached by a pair of entrances, one opposite the other. At Mucking, the central area of the inner enclosure contained a dense concentration of postholes, as well as a circular gully which was interpreted as the foundation for a timber building; no entrance was identified. The corresponding position at Thwing was occupied by a more massive circular structure. It was so large that it is not certain that it could have been roofed. At its centre was an exposed boss of chalk, surrounded by an irregular ditch. It was associated with a cremation burial (Manby 2007). It is difficult to reconstruct the configuration of the enclosure banks at Mucking because the site had been badly damaged, but the outer enclosure at Thwing had an internal rampart, retained by vertical posts in the same manner as the defended sites of the Late Bronze Age. The ditch of the smaller enclosure, however, was inside the bank. There was evidence of metalworking at both these monuments and the enclosure at Mucking may also have been associated with salt production. It seems likely that large-scale food consumption took place at Mucking and Thwing. At Thwing, this is shown by a considerable deposit of animal bones in the ditch terminals of the inner enclosure. At Mucking, the argument depends on the changing character and quantity of pottery associated with the earthwork perimeter. The site may have been used more intensively when the earthworks had decayed. The excavation report (Evans and Lucy in press) suggests that the enclosure may have begun as a high status residence, located within an area of open settlement. In a later phase it assumed a more specialized role and was used as a public monument. At Thwing, the inner enclosure was the first to be built. It has been compared with a henge, whilst the outer ditch and bank have more in common with hillforts.

Mucking and Thwing were extensively excavated, but, with the exception of their double ditches, their characteristic features have been identified at other places in England. In several cases there is evidence that they formed only parts of larger settlements. Although none of their sites includes the remains of a henge, in two cases they were built next to the positions of Neolithic causewayed enclosures, and it may be that their locations were selected because the remains of those earthworks could still be identified (Bradley 2007: 207–8).

At about the same time as the English ringworks were built, a series of circular ditched enclosures was established in Ireland. They remain little known, partly because so many are recent discoveries, but one important research excavation is of special relevance to this discussion. It was at Rathgall, where a Late Bronze Age hillfort was defined by two widely-spaced banks and ditches. At its centre was a circular building, defined by a narrow gully which resembles that at Mucking. Like the central structure at Thwing, it contained cremated human bones, but in this case they were associated with a gold ring. The artefact assemblage from Rathgall is exceptionally rich and, again, there is evidence of metalworking (Raftery 1984: 58–9). On one level the finds are unusual, but the basic form of the monument has parallels at other sites. The spaced defences seem to be a characteristic of Irish hillforts, whilst the basic configuration of a circular enclosure with a round-house at its centre is found elsewhere (Bradley 2007: 216–19). Sometimes these earthworks were accompanied by open settlements, like the sites already considered in England.

One of these enclosures is of special importance as it was the first of a series of circular earthworks, each of them enclosing a roundhouse, established at Navan Fort in Northern Ireland (Waterman 1997). Here, there is a continuous structural sequence extending from the end of the Bronze Age to the first century BC. During that time, the site changed its character. Although these earthworks continued to be built, circular enclosures or buildings of different sizes were joined together to form a figure-of-eight (Figure 47). This distinc-tive layout is a characteristic of the ceremonial sites of the late pre-Roman Iron Age; on the Hill of Tara it even extends to the combination of a large enclosure and a prominent mound (Newman 1998). Such groups of earthwork monu-ments are commonly described as 'royal centres' but that term reflects the role of these places in early medieval literature and it is not clear which of their structures (if any) were newly built at that time (Schot et al. 2011).

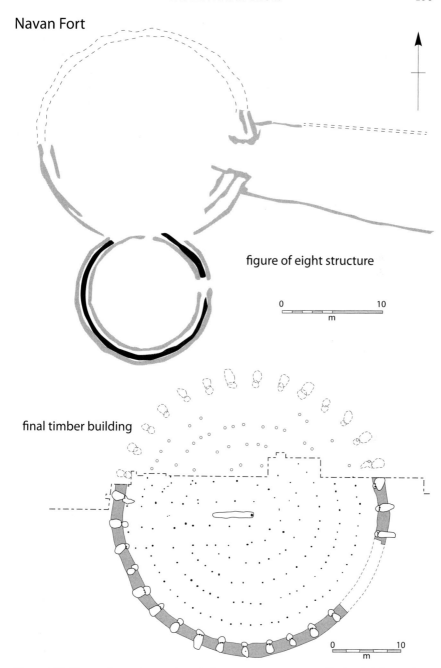

Navan Fort

figure of eight structure

0   10
m

final timber building

0   10
m

Figure 47 Plans of two successive timber structures eventually buried beneath a mound and cairn at Navan Fort, Site B, Ireland.

Navan Fort has two other features which have sometimes been compared with those of English henges. The entire complex is bounded by a circular enclosure with an external bank and an internal ditch. Indeed, its form is so reminiscent of a Neolithic monument that it has taken excavation to establish its true date (Mallory 2000). There are similar enclosures at the royal centres of Rathcroghan and Knockaulin. Inside them were immense circular buildings, some of which were approached by an avenue or roadway not unlike that leading into the Southern Circle at Durrington Walls (Johnston et al. 2009; Waddell et al. 2009).

These enclosures occupy similar positions in the landscape. They can be situated on hills, but perhaps more important are the views that can be seen from them (Fenwick 1997). They extend a great distance in all directions. Like the large stone circles discussed in Chapter 5, these are circular monuments at the centre of what appears to be a circular world. There is one important difference from their Neolithic counterparts. The settings of monoliths were usually located in valleys or basins so that the impression of a circular landscape was created by a horizon of hills. In this case, that relationship is reversed, and, although distant landmarks can be recognized, the views from the Irish site extend across large areas of lower ground. Whether or not these places were 'royal' in the pre-Roman Iron Age, it is right to think of them as 'centres'.

How were they used? It is surprisingly difficult to tell as they have not produced many finds of artefacts or food remains. Even so, certain features recall the roles played by other circular monuments. The quantity of animal bones from Knockaulin suggests that feasts took place there; as at Durrington Walls, pigs were well represented (Johnston and Wailes 2007, Chapter 13). Similarly, there is evidence for metalworking from that site, although it is mainly associated with a late phase when the timber buildings were no longer used. It seems possible that some of the enclosures had celestial alignments, but the best evidence of this comes from a small enclosure at Lismullin rather than the nearby site at Tara (O'Connell 2009). Otherwise, the main activity was the erection of a series of circular buildings. The largest of these was at Navan Fort (Waterman 1997). It was well preserved but lacks any evidence of a central hearth. Instead, its place was taken by an enormous post. The clearest indication that this was a specialized structure comes from the way in which it was treated. Not long after the building was put in place it was filled with rubble. It was then destroyed by fire and its remains were buried beneath a considerable circular mound.

It is difficult to tell how closely the forms of these buildings reflected the organization of the domestic dwellings of the same period. That is because ordinary occupation sites have been difficult to recognize. It has happened for two reasons. Pottery was no longer made in Ireland, so that Iron Age settlements are most often identified as a result of radiocarbon dating (Becker 2009).

At the same time, it is likely that use of the landscape changed at the end of the Bronze Age so that particular places were occupied less intensively and for shorter periods. Despite these limitations, enough is known to show that the main kinds of settlement did not alter completely. Circular enclosures were still being built and the main kind of domestic dwelling remained the round-house (Becker 2009). For those reasons there is no doubt that the distinctive buildings associated with the royal centres really were Great Houses whose form was modelled on a familiar prototype. Indeed, the contrast between the massive structures associated with sites like Navan Fort, Tara and Knockaulin and those found in ordinary settlements provides the strongest argument for the special character of these buildings.

If the enclosed roundhouses of the Late Bronze Age had been accompanied by more extensive settlements, the royal enclosures of the Irish Iron Age seem to have been set apart. Like Neolithic timber circles in lowland England, they may have been located in special places to which people had to travel. Indeed, Raftery has suggested that a timber road preserved in the bog at Corlea was 'part of a pilgrims' highway linking two great ceremonial centres' (Raftery 1984: 204). On a smaller scale, embanked roads or avenues lead towards a number of these enclosures.

The oldest literary sources in Ireland can be misleading. They suggest a number of important roles for these places, in particular the inauguration of kings, but they refer to a period when many of the earthworks were already ancient and may not necessarily shed light on their original functions. It is obvious that they were important monuments in the Irish landscape, but by the time they enter history their roles may have been reinterpreted. There is no substitute for conducting fieldwork on these sites.

Uisneach again

One of the excavated examples has not featured so far in this chapter, although it provided the starting point for the book. It is Uisneach, the centre of Ireland in the ancient sources (Schot 2011). Although it was excavated eighty years ago, it has all the characteristics of these places. It includes a large circular enclosure, ring barrows or mounds, and the two conjoined earthworks ap-proached by an embanked road. The hilltop commands an enormous view, so that it would be easy to believe that it was the centre of the world. Like all the monuments treated in the second part of this chapter, it could have been considered as a microcosm of the land around it.

Uisneach was the capital of Midh, which was in the centre of Ireland, bounded in every direction by provinces that reached to the coast. Is it possible that this conception of space went even further? If Uisneach was the centre of

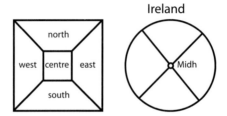

Figure 48 Two schemes summarizing the subdivision of ancient Ireland with Midh at its centre. Both show the same geographical relationship, but the right-hand drawing is based on a circular archetype.

Ireland and Midh was the middle kingdom (Rees and Rees 1961), was the island itself imagined as another circle: a round world, set apart and entirely surrounded by the sea (Figure 48)? Of course there is no way of telling, but this idea might suggest something of the pervasiveness of the circular archetype among the inhabitants of ancient Europe.

Part III

Circular Structures in a Rectilinear World

7

Significant Forms

Most of the problems investigated by prehistorians involve material that has been known for a long time. Thus, artefacts, settlements, and monuments have been placed in chronological order and their distributions have been mapped. Taken together, the results of this work constitute an 'archaeological record' which can be analyzed and interpreted with the aid of different theories. Only occasionally is the nature of that record entirely transformed. It has happened in some regions where large-scale excavations are necessitated by commercial development, but it is in Central and south-eastern Europe that the transformation has been especially dramatic. This has happened for two reasons. The first is a consequence of political changes which have allowed archaeologists to employ aerial photography for the first time. The second has been the use of large-scale geophysical survey which has often been inspired by the discoveries made from the air. Taken together, these new methods have identified largely new classes of prehistoric monument and have shed fresh light on those that were already known.

An unexpected result of these developments has been the discovery of enclosures dating from the Neolithic period. Until twenty years ago their distribution was largely confined to West Germany and Austria. Now that restrictions on flying have been lifted, it has been possible to undertake aerial reconnaissance in other areas and similar monuments have been found in considerable numbers in East Germany, Slovakia and Hungary (Andersen 1997: Chapter 5). At the same time, the rapid development of geophysical survey has had dramatic consequences. It has shown that some of the prominent tells that were already recorded were bounded by considerable earthworks. The reason that these discoveries were so surprising is that the enclosures were circular, while the houses of the same date were rectangular. The same situation arises in other regions and periods. What was the significance of curvilinear structures in a right-angled world? Part Three of this book investigates this relationship.

The oldest circular enclosures probably originated during the earlier fifth millennium BC. There are some striking contrasts between them. This section illustrates the point by considering two recently investigated sites: the Rumanian tell at Uivar (Schier 2008) and the Hungarian tell at Polgár-Csöszhalom (Raczky and Anders 2008). Both are compared with the evidence of earthwork enclosures described by the German word *Kreisgrabenanlagen* and the English term *roundel*.

Chapter 2 commented on the formation of the settlement mounds known as *tells*. They were created by the practice of building new houses over the remains of their predecessors. It seemed possible that dwellings were replaced at regular intervals, perhaps when one of the inhabitants died. The abandoned houses were often destroyed by fire (Stepanovic 1997) and the structures that replaced them occasionally included human remains (Bailey 2000: 151–2, 194–6). It was not by chance that these settlements developed into conspicuous mounds and, in a way, this process monumentalized the history of the communities who lived there. Such structures are a special feature of southeastern and Central Europe.

Recent fieldwork has shown that traditional ideas about these sites have been rather misleading. Not only was the growth of settlement mounds a deliberate strategy, there were occupation sites where it did not occur. The houses in these 'flat settlements' were no different from those discovered at tells, but these places did have a distinctive character. They can be very extensive and complement better-known sites that have dominated archaeological research for many years (Chapman and Gaydarska 2006). There is a further complication, for excavation, geophysical survey, and the collection of surface artefacts have shown that groups of domestic buildings can also be found beyond the limits of the tells, so that the mounds themselves form only the most prominent parts of larger villages. At the same time, this work has also shown that certain mounds were ringed by ditched enclosures. Again, they have been identified by geophysical survey and dated by excavation.

Although circular enclosures are a feature of the fifth millennium BC, it is important to emphasize that it was their geometric form that was new, rather than the existence of a boundary around a settlement—that can be found in earlier phases (Chapman and Gaydarska 2006). In fact, the chronology and distribution of circular structures are quite distinctive. They have been identified at the outer edge of the distribution of tells and were constructed towards the end of the period in which this kind of site was occupied.

The enclosures are a recent discovery and it remains to be seen how often they occur. One place where earthworks of this kind have been investigated is Uivar in Romania (Schier 2008; Figure 49). The extent of the settlement is known from a combination of geophysical survey, coring, and sample excavation. It seems to have had two components. The mound itself is formed from the remains of about seventy houses, but around its edge was a massive,

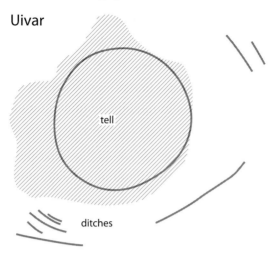

Uivar

tell

ditches

Figure 49 Simplified plan of the tell and surrounding earthworks at Uivar, Romania. The shaded area was occupied by houses.

ditched enclosure. There were further ditches which were roughly concentric with that earthwork and extended 100 metres from the mound. They may have been of slighter proportions, but were supplemented by palisades. The outer earthworks also enclose an area which was partly free of houses. The overall sequence remains to be elucidated, as it is clear that the earthworks were renewed on several occasions and that the innermost circuit cut across the positions of older dwellings.

The excavator interprets the inner enclosure as a defensive barrier, which is entirely plausible in view of its considerable size; it was no less than seven metres wide and four metres deep. The houses were densely distributed across the area of the tell and were associated with a great number of artefacts. There can be no doubt that the site was intensively occupied. There are a number of indications that rituals were performed there and a concentration of wild animal bones was found in the entrance to the innermost enclosure. Similarly, some, but by no means all, of the houses had been burnt. Uivar may have enjoyed a special status in the late Neolithic period, but there is no suggestion that it was anything other than a settlement.

Polgár-Csöszhalom, in Hungary, shares some of the same features, but in other respects it is quite different (Raczky and Anders 2008; Figure 50). In this case, the site consists of an extensive flat settlement with a comparatively low tell towards one end. It was bounded by no fewer than six concentric ditches which created a circular enclosure with four entrances spaced at equal intervals around the perimeter. According to the excavators, not all the ditches were in use together as the tell had increased in size during the course of occupation. Inside the enclosure were the remains of sixteen burnt houses.

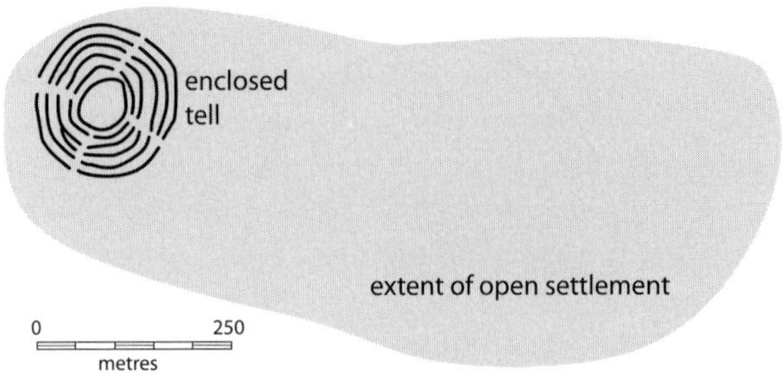

Polgár-Csőszhalom

Figure 50 Outline plan of the tell and open settlement at Polgár-Csöszhalom, Hungary.

The open settlement was approximately six times the surface area of the tell and lacked an earthwork boundary. A substantial sample has been investigated, making it possible to compare the ways in which the two parts of the site were used. Although houses of similar form were found in both areas, those associated with the enclosure had been decorated. The two groups of buildings were organized in different ways and seem to have had different histories from one another. The structures on the mound were arranged in a radial pattern with their long axes orientated on the centre, but those outside it were laid out in rows. All the buildings associated with the tell had been set on fire, but this did not apply to any of the sixty houses investigated in the other part of the settlement. The excavators suggest that the enclosure was employed on special occasions and that only the dwellings in the surrounding area were routinely inhabited.

There were other contrasts between the contents of the two main areas at Polgár-Csöszhalom. The enclosed area contained all the finds of copper ornaments, as well as a spondylus shell bracelet. There was evidence for the grinding of haematite, apparently for pigment, and the assemblage included unusual artefacts of kinds which are sometimes associated with the dead. There was evidence for the destruction of numerous ceramic vessels, but their equivalents in the flat settlement were less often damaged. On one hand, the bones from the enclosure are dominated by those of wild animals, in contrast to the domesticates associated with the houses outside it. On the other hand, structured deposits of artefacts could be found in both parts of the site; the same applies to finds of figurines. Taken together, these observations led the excavators to conclude that the enclosed mound 'was not the scene of everyday activities. The prominent mound and the system of ditches and walls that surrounded it carried a symbolic meaning' (Raczky and Anders 2008: 49).

They compare this earthwork with the Central European roundels, whose distribution complements that of the latest tells. They were built and used over a restricted period between 4900 and 4700 BC, although superficially similar

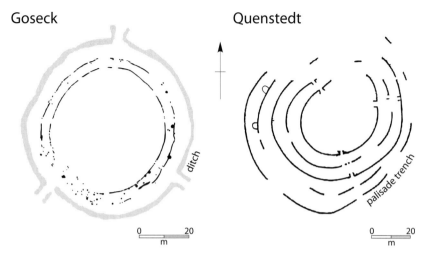

Figure 51 Plans of the circular monuments at Goseck and Quenstedt, Germany.

structures date from later phases (Petrasch 1990; Trnka 1991; Doneus 2001; Biehl 2007). Like the earthwork at Polgár-Csöszhalom, roundels were usually circular. In some cases, the perimeter conformed to that template exactly. They were defined by banks, ditches, or palisades; sometimes all three were used in combination (Figure 51). In certain instances the bank could be on the outside. A number of enclosures had pairs of entrances, placed directly opposite one another. Roundels had a completely different layout from the domestic sites of the same period, although houses can be found in the vicinity. These monuments have been compared with the henges of the British Isles (Behrens 1981; Bertemes and Spatzier 2008), but the two groups are separated by at least a thousand kilometres and up to two thousand years. They may have shared a similar significance in the past, but there can have been no connection between them.

How were the roundels used? In most cases they were cut off from their surroundings by a screen which concealed the interior from any people outside. At Goseck in southern Germany it seems to have been two and a half metres high, so that no one could have seen over it (Biehl 2007). The only points of access were through narrow entrances which might have admitted only one person at a time. These features might be emphasized on a monumental scale. The roundel was the one circular element in a world characterized by rectangular buildings. There are a few sites at which both these elements are juxtaposed, but it is much less common for longhouses, or any other kind of structure, to be found inside the enclosures themselves. When it does occur, the alignment of the houses conforms to the axis of the monument. Some of the roundels have entrances directed towards the cardinal points (Pászter et al. 2008; Biehl 2010). This distinctive arrangement contrasts with the situation in settlements of the same date where all the dwellings share a common alignment.

In the past, scholars have proposed functional interpretations of these monuments and roundels have been interpreted as stock compounds. This idea does nothing to explain the labour devoted to their construction. In any case, the entrances could be too narrow to allow the passage of large domestic animals—excavation at Goseck found no evidence of enhanced levels of phosphate (Biehl 2007, 2010). In the same way, roundels cannot have been used for defence. Like the henge monuments of the British Isles, some had external banks and internal ditches.

In fact, the circular monuments combine two distinctive features. They have a continuous outer boundary which, like the sky, extends in all directions from the viewer. In principle, it would be possible to watch the movement of the sun from the interior of the monument. It would achieve a powerful effect, for the light would be concentrated as it passed through the entrance. That has been demonstrated by modern surveys and reconstructions, but it is important to emphasize that this effect does not occur at every site. In the past, other examples may have been directed towards natural landmarks like hills.

The enclosures have been studied by archaeoastronomers (Pászter et al. 2008). Some of the monuments seem to have been aligned on the heavenly bodies, although the arguments for solar alignments are easier to substantiate than claims that their positions were related to the moon or stars. It is true that they were built by early farmers, but it is unlikely that they played any practical role. It is improbable that the earthworks and palisades were built in order to establish a calendar or that they were used to define fixed points in the agricultural cycle. There is an obvious weakness in such an argument, for roundels could not have been designed and built *unless that information was known in the first place*. Because such arguments fail, in recent years there has been a greater willingness to view their circular configuration in other ways. Were they places where ceremonies took place? Perhaps the alignment of these structures was determined by the timing of festivals.

That might be suggested by the material associated with them. There are the remains of feasts, in particular, cattle bones. There are also human remains. Whilst some consist of complete burials, other deposits contain parts of bodies which show signs of violence. Biehl (2010) has suggested that they represent sacrificial deposits. There are also quantities of artefacts, including worked stone, broken ceramic vessels, and figurines. Large-scale excavation has begun to identify the places in which it was appropriate to deposit cultural material. The openings leading into these enclosures provided one such focus. Entrances (and perhaps exits) could have held a special importance. At Goseck they were associated with deposits of pottery, worked flint, animal bones, and human remains (Biehl 2007). There was also evidence of pits containing a layer of ash where cooking probably took place. In this case the enclosure had three entrances, two of which were aligned on the midwinter sunrise and sunset respectively.

There are several levels on which it is appropriate to compare such structures with enclosed tells. One is their distinctive ground plan. Although there may have been many reasons for constructing circular enclosures, these examples are extremely stereotyped. The circuits of banks and ditches can be precisely geometrical in layout; their perimeters are reinforced by palisades and the entrances were often paired across the interior of the enclosure. They may be extremely narrow, and in the case of Goseck and Uivar they were associated with special deposits of animal bones. The orientation of some of these enclosures also suggests that they played a specialized role. Even the layout of buildings on the enclosed tell at Polgár-Csöszhalom differs from their arrangement in the surrounding settlement and in this case the structures on the mound had been set on fire.

The contents of these monuments are distinctive. The tell at Polgár-Csöszhalom contained a series of artefacts that were not represented in the open settlement around it. In the same way, it contained a large number of wild animal bones, a feature that also characterized the entrance to the inner enclosure at Uivar. Similar arguments apply to the excavated roundels, which contain placed deposits of faunal remains, complete and partial human burials, and a distinctive range of artefacts.

How should these similarities be interpreted? For Raczky and Anders:

> The new excavations suggest that Polgár-Csöszhalom represents a synthesis of two, previously separate structures: an organic conflation of the . . . circular ditch system which is characteristic in Transdanubia; and the tell mounds which are typical for the southern Great Hungarian Plain (2008: 39).

It may be possible to take this argument further. It was not a new development to enclose the buildings on a tell; only the circular design was novel. Both the examples considered here are found towards the edge of the geographical distribution of settlement mounds and were established at a late stage in their history. In one case, a densely occupied mound was enclosed by a series of ditches which seems to have extended beyond the occupied area. In the other, a tell developed towards one end of a large open settlement and was enclosed by a still more regular system of earthworks. In this case, the mound itself may have played a specialized role.

Is it possible that the same idea was taken up in neighbouring areas where tells were never established? Could the roundels have represented this kind of settlement in a world that was very different? It is worth comparing this evidence with the enclosures of the Linear Pottery Culture. Few adopted a circular outline, but some of the first examples were associated with groups of longhouses. When the pattern of settlement changed and that type of building went out of favour, earthworks of similar form were still constructed, but now they may have acted as ceremonial centres. In a sense they *ritualized* the features of settlements of a kind that had been occupied in the past and, in doing so, they invested these forms with a new significance (Bradley 1998: Chapter 5). A similar process may have influenced monuments that were used concurrently, but in different areas. The roundels might have represented a transformation of the idea of the tell in the same way as chambered tombs recreated the appearance of domestic dwellings.

BARROWS, SANCTUARIES, AND SHRINES

So far, this chapter has considered the juxtaposition of rectangular and curvilinear structures and the reasons why the circular archetype may have been significant. This section discusses a series of monuments in which those forms were combined. In this case, they date from the Iron Age and Roman periods.

The growing importance of square and rectangular structures began in the La Tène phase of the Iron Age and was expressed in a series of different media. There were four of these. The best known are *Viereckschanzen*. As the German name suggests, these were square or rectangular ditched en-closures. There is no agreement over their roles in prehistoric society, nor is there any consensus over the geographical extent of this phenomenon. Some scholars prefer to restrict the discussion to a series of monuments in Central Europe, while others include possible examples further to the north and west (Buchenschutz et al. 1989; Bittel et al. 1990; Bittel 1998; Wieland 1999). It may be that these distinctive earthworks were used in a variety of ways. Some contain timber buildings that have been identified as temples and others include wells with votive offerings. Such sites can occupy isolated locations, or they may be associated with Iron Age cemeteries. At the same time, there are earthworks of similar form which were only part of a larger settlement. They could have fulfilled entirely mundane roles, but an example inside the oppidum at Manching was associated with a deposit containing a sword (Sievers 1991).

These enclosures have been compared with a second series of Iron Age sites in Gaul which are normally interpreted as sanctuaries (Buchenschutz et al. 1989; Brunaux 1991; Wells 2007). In this case, the archaeological evidence is less ambiguous. Like Viereckschanzen, they can be associated with small timber buildings, but the main characteristic of these sites is that they contain large numbers of discarded weapons, animal bones, and a quantity of human remains. The treatment of the artefacts and bones is particularly unusual (Brunaux 2009). For example, at Gournay-sur-Aronde (Brunaux et al. 1985) it seems as if the weapons had been nailed to the perimeter fence before they were deposited in the ditch. The bones from such sites can include a large number of skulls. Many bodies show signs of injuries and may be the remains of defeated war bands. At Gournay the distribution of faunal remains was organized according to species and was probably the result of sacrifices. In a subsequent phase, most of these monuments were replaced by Roman temples.

Both kinds of earthwork contained specialized buildings. At the same time, there were square barrows and rectilinear enclosures associated with burials. Again, both are a special feature of the La Tène phase of the Iron Age where they are widely distributed in Western and Northern Europe (Stead 1979: 29–35; Wilhelmi 1990). The burial mounds were frequently added to existing groups of circular barrows, some of considerable antiquity. Square barrows were usually associated with inhumations. For the most part they were used in regions with a well-established pattern of rectilinear architecture, but in north-east England, and perhaps more widely, such monuments are associated with roundhouses. At Garton Slack it seems as if mounds of this kind were built on the sites of older dwellings (Bradley 2007: Figure 5.17). The chronologies of square barrows and burial enclosures overlapped, but were not the same. Although this kind of burial mound went out of favour before the Roman period, those enclosures had a longer history. In most areas it ran in parallel with a change from inhumation to cremation. It suggests a preference for rectilinear structures, even in regions where the circular archetype had been well established.

There is also evidence for a *combination* of circular and rectangular elements in the monuments of the Late Iron Age and Roman periods. It may be significant that one of the principal bodies of evidence is provided by a series of cult buildings with a wide distribution in north-west Europe. Their hybrid character is obvious because they are among the features called 'Romano-Celtic' temples (Horne and King 1980; Faudet 1993). They are equally distinctive in structural terms. They adopt a variety of ground plans, one of which took the form of a circle inside a square. These distinctive structures have a lengthy history and Blair (1995) argues that monuments of this form were created in Britain from the Iron Age to the Anglo-Saxon period.

Again, the evidence is so extensive that the main issues are best highlighted by discussing individual examples. Each of them typifies a wider pattern. There are rectangular enclosures associated with circular buildings, and circular mounds which were delimited by rectilinear earthworks during a subsequent phase. In certain cases rectangular structures were erected within them. Two pairs of monuments are discussed in each of these categories. They have been chosen because they illustrate developments on both sides of the English Channel.

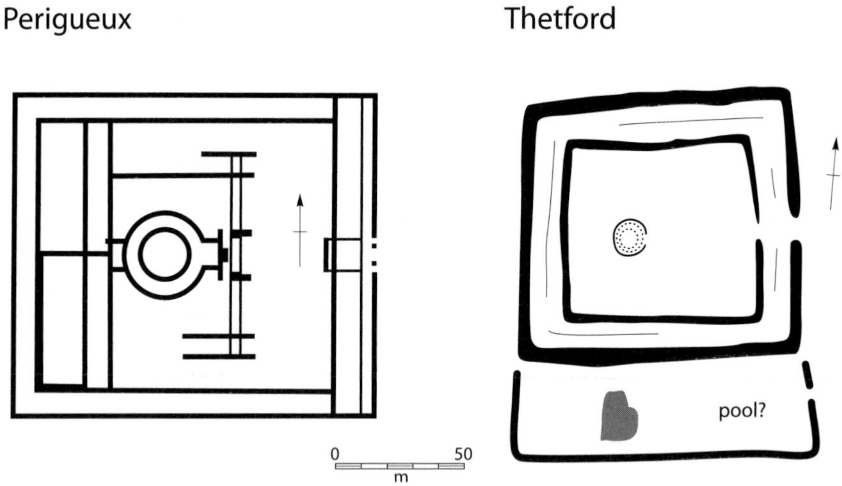

Perigueux   Thetford

Figure 52 Outline plans of the temple complexes at Perigueux (France) and Thetford (England). The structure at Perigueux was built of stone. At Thetford, a large timber building was inside a ditched enclosure.

Circular temples have a restricted distribution in the Roman provinces and are found mainly in England and in Northern and Central France (Lewis 1966; Faudet 1993; Verger 2000). They are entirely absent from the Iberian Peninsula and also from the Mediterranean coastline of Gaul. The best known example of a circular temple within a rectangular temenos is Le Tour de Vésone at Perigueux, where the building was erected in the late-first to early-second century AD and abandoned about a hundred years later (Coupry 1977, 453–6; Horne and King 1980: 446–7; Figure 52). This was a massive structure with a circular central tower, seventeen metres in diameter. It was approached through a monumental entrance. Little survives of the enclosure around it, but it was rectangular in outline and measured 140 by 120 metres. An altar reveals that the temple was dedicated to the spirit of Augustus and to the Great Mother. Unlike most comparable monuments, it was inside a major town. Buildings with a similar plan are by no means common, but a number of circular or polygonal examples have been identified by air photography in France. They were situated within square or rectangular enclosures, and both types had the same distribution.

Another well documented monument was at Thetford in Eastern England (Gregory 1991). It went through several successive phases and was probably constructed not long after the Roman invasion of Britain. It seems to have replaced a series of domestic enclosures and houses and was accompanied by a series of small circular barrows. The principal monument had two major elements: a rectangular enclosure whose perimeter may have been reinforced by planting trees and a circular structure in the centre of the site. In a

subsequent phase that building was supplemented by four further constructions of similar type. The main example was massively built and had two
entrances located opposite one another. These buildings bear little resemblance to Late Iron Age or early Roman dwellings in the surrounding region,
although their form recalls that of domestic architecture. They are surely Great
Houses of the kind considered in Chapter 6 and can be compared with those
established at about the same time in Ireland. There are few finds from the
enclosure at Thetford, but the site is associated with Late Iron Age coins,
Roman coins, and brooches. Despite the considerable scale on which the
timber structures were built, there is no evidence that any of them were
replaced in stone. However, it is possible that a Late Roman shrine, now
destroyed, may have existed nearby. This was the findspot of an exceptionally
rich hoard of treasure (Johns and Potter 1983: Chapter 1).

The monument at Thetford recalls the distinctive outline of Romano-Celtic
temples in Gaul. They combined a rectangular enclosure with a central
building which was circular in plan; however, there are major differences
between them. The example at Perigueux was an enormous structure which
closely resembles a tower. The buildings inside the rectangular enclosure at
Thetford recall the configuration of a domestic dwelling. It was only the scale
of the structure that was exceptional. One reason for any contrast between
such temples in England and Gaul may be their relationship to established
traditions of architecture. Although circular burial mounds had a wide distribution in Iron Age France, in Britain similar monuments were uncommon
after 1100 BC (Bradley 2007: 197–200). Although they do occur around the
enclosure at Thetford, it seems that a more likely prototype is provided by the
roundhouses of the later prehistoric period.

The treatment of round mounds raises similar issues. A useful starting point
is the Belgian site of Ursel-Rozenstraat (J. Bourgeois 1998; Figure 53). Here,
the main feature was an Early Bronze Age round barrow which was rebuilt in
the Late Bronze Age or Early Iron Age. During the Late Iron Age the perimeter
of the mound was incorporated in a square ditched enclosure with a larger
rectilinear enclosure alongside it. The smaller one was almost empty, but its
neighbour was the site of a cemetery of about seventy cremation burials which
date between the first century BC and the abandonment of the site a hundred
years later. Another burial was placed in the ditch around the older barrow.
This deposit was inside a small mortuary house, defined by a ring of posts.
Several relationships seem to be significant here. The Bronze Age monument
was enclosed and respected but was not reused as a cemetery, for almost all the
burials were in a rectilinear earthwork outside it. The one exception was
located on the outer limit of the mound and was associated with a *circular*
construction. Again, the interplay between squares and circles seems to have
been significant.

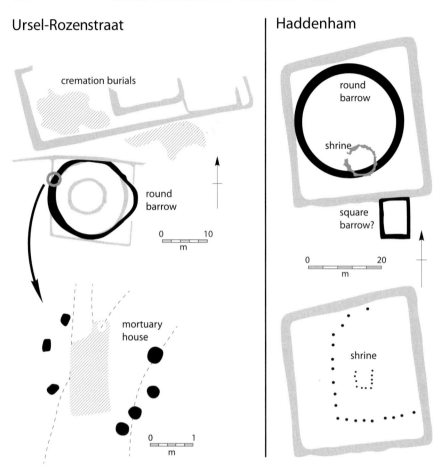

Figure 53 The reused Bronze Age round barrows at Ursel-Rozenstraat (Belgium) and Haddenham (England). The principal barrow ditches are indicated in black and later rectangular enclosures in light tone.

A final example of this relationship is provided by an excavated monument at Haddenham in Eastern England (Evans and Hodder 2006: Chapter 7). As at Ursel-Rozenstraat, the earliest structure here was an Early Bronze Age round barrow. During the late Iron Age or early Roman period a small square enclosure or mound was constructed against its flank and then the entire mound was redefined by a square ditched enclosure of Roman date. An octagonal shrine was erected on top of the mound. It was associated with deposits of pottery, coins, brooches, and animal bone typical of Romano-Celtic temples. Most of this material dates between AD 150 and 300. The circular barrow had been remade as a rectangular monument, but the sequence did not end there. In the later third century or the earlier fourth century the stone structure on the Bronze Age mound was replaced by a small rectangular building made of wood and then by a circular shrine. They were associated with the same range of deposits.

This site at Haddenham illustrates the full complexity of the relationship between rectilinear and circular structures in Roman Britain. Not only was an ancient round barrow selected for reuse, it was surmounted by an octagonal shrine. At the same time, the limits of the mound were redefined by excavating a square ditched enclosure. Eventually, its distinctive outline was reflected by the construction of a square timber building, yet even that was replaced by another wooden shrine whose circular outline reflected an older tradition of domestic architecture. The accommodation between squares and circles took many different forms, but some of the places where it was achieved most effectively possessed a specialized character.

ISMANTORP AND EKETORP

That was equally true of Late Iron Age structures in the Baltic.

Öland lies near to the east coast of Sweden. The island contains an abundance of impressive monuments, most of which are dated between the late first millennium BC and the Viking Age. Among them are numerous cemeteries with cairns and stone settings, and a series of circular stone forts. Throughout this lengthy period the inhabitants of Öland took advantage of its strategic setting and accumulated extraordinary material wealth. It is represented in the archaeological record by the finds from the burial grounds (Näsman and Wegraeus 1976) and by votive deposits like that at Skedemosse (Hagberg et al. 1977).

Towards the centre of the island is a monument which has attracted discussion for almost four hundred years. It is of special relevance because of its distinctive ground plan (Andrén 2006). The stone ringfort of Ismantorp is a circular enclosure, with a massive defensive wall broken by numerous entrances. It contains the remains of ninety-five well-preserved rectangular buildings (Figure 54). They fall into two main groups. Roughly half define a circuit attached to the defences. They are separated from the central area by a road which runs parallel to the perimeter wall and surrounds a second group of buildings with a less regular layout. At their centre was an open area containing a small semicircular structure. Here, excavation has located two pits and the socket for a massive wooden upright. Ismantorp preserves traces of outworks beyond the walled perimeter, but the monument seems to have been conceived as four concentric circles, with a large post at their central point. With the exception of the miniature structure towards the middle of the site, all the internal buildings were rectangular.

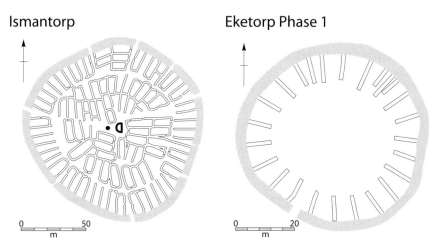

Figure 54 Plans of the stone ringforts at Ismantorp and Eketorp (Öland, Sweden), illustrating the distribution of rectangular buildings inside them.

That combination of circular and rectilinear elements has a wider significance on Öland. Ismantorp was used between about 200 AD and the seventh century and was probably the earliest of the twenty or more stone forts which are a distinctive feature of the island. Their architecture is difficult to interpret. The best known example is the fully excavated site of Eketorp (Borg et al. 1976). Like Ismantorp, it consisted of a circular walled enclosure associated with a large number of rectangular houses. In this case there were only three entrances. At its heart was a circular space largely devoid of artefacts. Eketorp had a longer and more complex history than Ismantorp, and its period of use extended through the Viking period into the early Middle Ages. The defensive circuit was rebuilt on three occasions when new structures were erected in the interior. Here, there was plentiful evidence of craft production. The original outer wall was replaced by a larger enclosure which followed the outline of its predecessor. By the eastern entrance was a pool.

Both the structural elements recognized at Ismantorp and Eketorp occur at other sites. Nearly 2,000 houses of similar form have been identified from their surface remains. They are located some distance away from the ringforts and are commonly associated with field systems. All the domestic buildings are rectangular, but the stone forts adopt a circular plan. This contrast has seldom been addressed, and the definitive report on Eketorp suggests that the forts were built in this way because the level topography would present no obstacle to an attacker (Borg et al. 1976: 32). It is true that one of these sites was built against a cliff so that the defensive circuit was incomplete, but there seems no obvious reason why the other sites should not have been rectangular or square

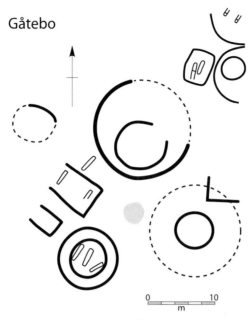

Figure 55 Plan of the cemetery at Gåtebo, Öland, Sweden, illustrating the interplay between circular and rectilinear monuments. The small oval features are graves and the area defined by light tone is a small mound.

in plan. That is especially puzzling as their defences seem to have been modelled on Roman prototypes.

The juxtaposition of circular and rectangular forms is also a characteristic of the cemeteries of Öland, for here the stone monuments assume a variety of forms (Figure 55). Whilst circular structures are always in the majority, there are also less common rectangular stone settings. There are other arrangements of monoliths in the form of a boat. The occasional pairing of round and rectilinear elements is of particular interest as it is represented in a different way at the ringforts. It even seems possible that the rectilinear cairns and platforms were constructed in the image of the house. How were these features related to one another? Fortunately, the contents of the graves have been studied in detail and provide important chronological evidence. It suggests that most of the square or rectangular stone settings date from the pre-Roman and Roman Iron Ages. While there are later examples, the circle became the dominant type during the period in which the forts were occupied. At the same time, another distinctive kind of stone setting was built at the edge of some of the cemeteries. This was the 'tricorn': a form which is also represented on metal artefacts. Andrén (2004) has suggested that this design represents the roots of Yggdrasil, the tree that in Norse mythology connects nine different worlds. Thus, the cemeteries include rectangular monuments whose form recalls domestic architecture, a large number of circular cairns, and a version of the *axis mundi*.

All three types of structure were associated with the dead. Were similar elements represented at the ringforts?

Andrén, who has undertaken fieldwork at Ismantorp, has drawn attention to its unusual layout. Far from being an obvious example of military architecture, the wall is breached by nine gateways, only three of which provide direct access to the centre. That number may be significant, as he suggests that the earliest enclosure at Eketorp may have been polygonal rather than strictly circular and that there were nine corners in its exterior wall; the field evidence is ambiguous because of subsequent rebuilding. It is clear that Öland is associated with a number of unusually richly furnished graves whose chronology extends from around 400 BC to AD 1050. Among the monuments found in the cemeteries are stone circles associated with cremation burials. They are distributed from northern Germany to Middle Sweden. As Andrén says:

> They normally consist of an uneven number of stones, above all, five, seven or nine stones, but the number varies regionally. On Öland, where investigated graves have been dated to the period 200–550 AD, nine stones in the circles predominate (2006: 54).

The number may be significant in other ways. Literary evidence suggests that important sacrifices had to be made at nine year intervals and that they involved the slaughtering of nine animals. In Old Norse cosmology a sacred tree connected nine different worlds. Its roots were depicted by stone settings in the major cemeteries of Öland (Andrén 2004). In the same way, the god Odin is credited with performing nine different kinds of magic (Hedeager 2011: 7).

These ideas are especially relevant to Ismantorp. Despite a long history of fieldwork on the site, very few objects have been found there (Andrén 2006). The interior has been investigated by excavation, geophysics, and metal detector survey, yet the only diagnostic finds were a spearhead deposited in a pit at the centre of the monument and an arrowhead from the semicircular building beside it. In the same area there was a hearth and a pit associated with animal bones. By contrast, the excavation at Eketorp produced enormous quantities of artefacts and food remains. At first sight the two monuments seem to be entirely different from one another, yet their architecture has many features in common.

These comparisons also extend to points of detail. At Eketorp there was a large assemblage of animal bones from the pool outside the eastern entrance. They are interpreted as a votive deposit. In the same way, there was a curious stone setting in front of one of the principal buildings. It has been identified as the support for a wooden figure or perhaps a standing stone. Here, there was a hoard of gold artefacts of the kind associated with pagan shrines in

Scandinavia (Fabech 2006: 28–9). There was another upright post in the middle of Ismantorp. The two weapons were deposited nearby and so was a collection of faunal remains. Andrén emphasizes the significance of this observation. He suggests that:

> Ismantorp can be interpreted as a representation of the world. The post in the centre of the fort corresponded to the world-tree, whereas the nine gates symbolised the nine worlds surrounding the world-tree (2006: 36)

How was this strange monument related to the better known site at Eketorp?

It is often suggested that Ismantorp was a ceremonial centre, but Andrén prefers the idea that the structure of the ringforts was influenced by Roman military architecture. He makes two further points. In Iron Age Scandinavia the conduct of war was ritualized. It was governed by strict conventions concerning the identity of the participants, the conduct of the conflict, and even the timing and location of encounters. The distribution of plunder and the exchange of hostages were governed by similar protocols. For Andrén, 'Ismantorp…: functioned as an occasionally used army camp, inscribed with cosmological meanings' (2006: 37). Eketorp may have had a similar significance, but in this case it was occupied more intensively and for a much longer period.

His second argument represents an equally radical departure from the orthodoxy. Andrén makes the important point that even the stereotyped plan of a Roman fort was originally the expression of a cosmology—it was no accident that so many of these sites were organized according to the cardinal points (Rykwert 1976). It might have been the expression of a Roman world-view, but it was conceived in a society in which rectilinear architecture was the norm. That template was transformed in South Scandinavia where the circle had a greater significance. The walls and gates of the ringforts might be copies of structures inside the Roman Empire, but the spatial organization of the interior was entirely different. The distinction between them is the contrast between rectangles and circles which was first discussed in Chapter 3.

The evidence of the burial grounds may be relevant here. There was a similar pairing of circular and rectilinear elements, but in this case it was associated entirely with the dead. If, as Andrén suggests, Ismantorp was the earliest ringfort on Öland, that contrast may have extended into a new medium. Perhaps the first defended enclosure played a more specialized role than its successors. Fabech (1998) has suggested that in Iron Age Scandinavia ritual activity changed its context over time. The earlier votive deposits were connected with traditional locations such as bogs, whilst the latest were associated with high status settlements and even with specialized buildings. She applies that argument to the gold hoard from Eketorp. It may be no accident that the earliest enclosure there was constructed beside a natural pool and that it marked the position of one of the entrances. During the first millennium AD ritual and ceremony became more closely integrated with the political process. It may be that the early ringfort at Ismantorp and the later monument at Eketorp mark different stages in that sequence.

AN OVERVIEW

This previous section compared two ringforts on Öland. The relationship between them is not unlike that between enclosed tells and roundels. Eketorp was densely settled, but Ismantorp was not. At the same time, both these sites observed the same conventions in the organization of space. No doubt each of them played a specialized role, but the symbolic character of Ismantorp is obvious because of its unusual configuration. However, it is only comprehensible because it was the ritualized expression of the same ideas as Eketorp. The differences between them are simply ones of degree. Perhaps the same applies to the comparison between Uivar, Polgár-Csöszhalom, and a roundel like that at Goseck. It may also apply to the connection between roundhouses and the circular temples of the Iron Age and Roman periods. If so, it may be right to consider them as examples of a wider phenomenon.

Certain features are obvious in the case of all these structures. The dwellings of the Navajo discussed in Chapter 2 provide a point of comparison. Like the post at the middle of Ismantorp, their roof supports are identified as an axis mundi. Similarly, the outline of the house refers to the dome of the sky and its orientation reflects the position of the sun. Perhaps the roundels assumed a circular outline because it was suggested by natural phenomena. There are many possibilities, but they include the movements of the sun and moon, the contrast between day and night, and even the passage of the seasons on which life depends. Such structures provided an image of the daily cycle, but they were also integrated with the solstices. For many people these are the most significant times of year. The circular dwellings discussed in the New World may be directed towards the sunrise as a source of illumination, but the east is also associated with the renewal of life.

Similar arguments apply to the circular monuments known as *Great Kivas* in the south-west USA. They are especially relevant, as the largest examples are often paired with the massive rectilinear buildings described as Great Houses. Perhaps the best known examples are in Chaco Canyon (Van Dyke 2007; Figure 56). Great Kivas are subterranean or semi-subterranean structures which were used in communal rituals. They are between ten metres and twenty-five metres in diameter and were organized around a north-south alignment, although others are orientated from north-east to south-west. The kiva was completely roofed and often had an altar at its centre and a

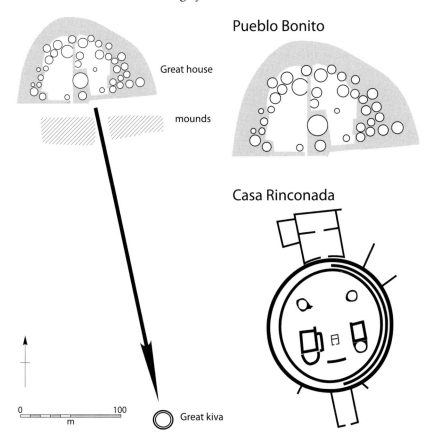

Figure 56 The spatial relationship between the Great House of Pueblo Bonito and the Great Kiva of Casa Rinconada (south-west USA).

bench extending around the perimeter wall. Certain examples were directed towards the solstices.

Two points are particularly relevant here. The circular shape of the Great Kiva was probably a reference to the sky, whilst its subterranean structure placed it at the meeting point of the earth and the underworld. At the same time, many of these monuments were paired with rectilinear public buildings so that the contrasts between them assumed a special significance. Their relationship is described by Van Dyke (2007). Both types of structure are paired and their shapes complement one another; one kind of building is accessible, while the other is not. Great Houses are above ground and seem to reference the sky, but the Great Kivas are subterranean and are also related to an underworld.

Similar ideas may be relevant to structures in Europe, where Andrén (2006) takes a comparable approach to the ringfort at Ismantorp. The roundel in

Central and south-east Europe might also have been considered as the centre of the world. Again, its layout might have been intended as a microcosm of the universe. The same may have been true of circular buildings and mounds in the late prehistoric and Roman periods. It is why they were so different from the rectangular buildings occupied at that time.

This chapter has been concerned with the character of circular monuments in regions and periods characterized by rectilinear architecture. Thus, the ringforts of Öland were associated with longhouses, as were the Neolithic roundels of Central Europe. The enclosed tells were also populated by rectangular dwellings and so, to a large extent, were the settlements of the Late Iron Age and Roman periods in north-west Europe. Circular enclosures and buildings were comparatively rare outside Britain, Ireland, and parts of Iberia. That is not to say that such structures necessarily played a specialized role. No interpretation can be based on their shapes alone.

There are two reasons why this is true. The first is really self evident. Rectilinear structures, from Classical temples to Christian cathedrals, can be laid out according to cosmological principles in the same way as ringforts or roundels. In the prehistoric period that would certainly apply to Viereckschanzen, square barrows, and Iron Age sanctuaries, but this argument is equally relevant to the stereotyped layout of Roman towns and forts, with their orthogonal plans and cardinal alignments (Rykwert 1976: Chapters 3 and 4). Indeed, more is known about the rituals employed in founding a city than can possibly be inferred from the evidence of prehistoric archaeology (Rykwert 1976: 65–71).

At the same time, it is easy to forget that circular plans can result from practical considerations, as well as more arcane ones. Roman public buildings were sometimes accompanied by the distinctive circular structures known as *comita*, but it happened because they were used for assemblies (Stamper 2005: 38–9). A circular plan is well suited to this purpose, even when the proceedings of such meetings are completely secular. Again, rectangular enclosures can be built because their outline fits into the grid pattern of the surrounding fields, or they may be designed so that new plots can be butted on to older ones. In the same way, the construction of a circular enclosure makes the most efficient use of the available labour. The perimeter of a circle will always be shorter than that of a rectangle enclosing the same amount of space. That applies to domestic compounds and to the defences of hillforts. A circular plan also allows people to survey the surrounding area more efficiently than a square one. That is why the Chalcolithic forts of the Iberian Peninsula were equipped with semicircular 'bastions' (Kunst 2006).

In some cases other sources of information are available; it is these that suggest that certain of the circular structures played a specialized role in a rectilinear world. Several features characterize the sites that have been discussed in this chapter and, without those features, the argument would fail.

The first is the orientation of specific structures. That was a characteristic of the roundels of Central Europe, whose entrances might be directed towards the rising and setting sun at the turning points of the year. It is a characteristic that they share with other prehistoric enclosures in Europe, although there seems to have been no direct connection between them. In some cases the nature of the banks and ditches provides a further clue. The six concentric earthworks at Polgár-Csöszhalom can hardly be explained in purely practical terms when they delimit such a small part of the settled area. A similar argument applies to the circuits at Uivar. Not all these earthworks were in use together because the size of the interior increased over time, but the complexity of their perimeter surely calls for comment. The same is true of the earthworks and palisades that define the edges of the roundels, just as it applies to the distant copies of Roman military architecture that characterize the ringforts of Öland. Ismantorp is particularly significant here, as a comparatively small enclosure had nine separate gateways. In this case the interior contained nearly a hundred houses, yet the only artefacts found by fieldwork were two offerings of weapons.

In fact, the distinctive deposits associated with some of the circular enclosures provide another reason for treating them as special, especially where, as at Polgár-Csöszhalom, they can be compared with the contents of an adjacent settlement. In this case it is not only the composition of these assemblages that stands out, but the distinctive contexts in which they were deposited. Thus, the enclosed tell in Hungary was associated with large numbers of wild animal bones, whilst its Romanian counterpart had similar material in its entrance. Roman temples include large numbers of coins and brooches and are associated with the remains of sacrificed animals. In the same way, there were finds of weapons beside the central post as at Ismantorp and a group of gold artefacts close to a similar feature at Eketorp. That need not mean that these ringforts were entirely specialized constructions, but, as Andrén argued in the case of Ismantorp, some of the activities that took place there may have taken on the formality of rituals. It happened to different extents in different places, and the distinction between special ceremonies and more mundane practices must have been a matter of degree.

CODA

Finally, this discussion has introduced two issues that require a more extended treatment. It will be provided by the chapters that follow. The first topic is the distinctive character of mounds or cairns, as opposed to buildings or enclosures which include open spaces. That contrast was especially apparent in the Iron Age archaeology of Öland and calls for more discussion. There are other examples of this relationship in Northern Europe and Chapter 8 will discuss the relationship between Bronze Age round barrows and longhouses in the Netherlands, Denmark, and Sweden.

The second issue was chronological change: a topic that was especially important in the discussion of Romano-Celtic temples where there was evidence of an interplay between roundhouses and rectilinear structures. To what extent were the roles of circular buildings affected as rectangular constructions became more important? Chapter 9 considers this question in relation to Iron Age Sicily, Roman Britain, the Castro Culture of Iberia, and Early Medieval Ireland.

When all these issues have been explored it will be possible to review the results of this enquiry as a whole.

8

The Attraction of Opposites

THORNY DOWN AND DE BOGEN

One of the best known accounts of the psychology of perception is Richard Gregory's book *Eye and Brain* (Gregory 1998). It is relevant to this chapter because it uses an example from archaeology to illustrate the way in which the mind creates visual patterns. The author considers the methods by which excavators distinguish between the remains of rectangular and circular buildings.

He considers the Middle Bronze Age settlement of Thorny Down in southern England, where different scholars have inferred the existence of different types of buildings on the basis of the same field evidence. The original excavator was uncertain of the precise form of the settlement (Stone 1941), but, in later years, Piggott identified the site of a large rectangular house there (1965: Figure 87) and Musson recognized circular structures (1970: 267; Figure 57). Gregory's summary of their method is as follows:

> Science and perception work by knowledge and rules, and by analogy . . . [In the case of Thorny Down] some of the holes in the ground might be ancient post holes; others might be rabbit holes, to be ignored. One group of archaeologists accepted close-together large holes as evidence of a grand entrance. They were altogether rejected by other archaeologists. One group constructed a large rectangular hut; the other, a small rectangular hut, and a circular building. 'Bottom-up' rules—holes being close together and forming straight lines or smooth curves, and 'top-down' knowledge or assumptions of which kinds of buildings were likely—affected the 'perceptions'. Both could have been wrong (1998: 11–12).

The identification of a rectangular building at Thorny Down took place at a time when it was believed that the Netherlands had been settled from England during the Bronze Age. The argument was based on pottery styles and the distribution of metalwork (Theunissen 2009). Most likely there were contacts in both directions. As the Low Countries were characterized by a tradition of rectilinear architecture, what could be more natural than the construction of a longhouse at a site on the Wessex chalk? Dutch prehistorians attempted to find similar links between domestic architecture on both sides of the North Sea

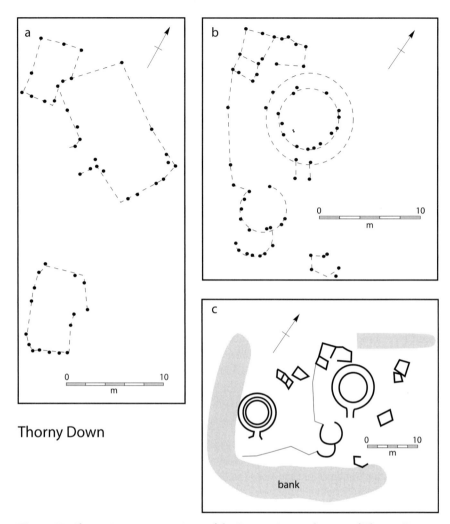

Figure 57 Alternative reconstructions of the Bronze Age settlement of Thorny Down, England, based on the post holes found in excavation: (a) the structures identified by Piggott (1965), and (b and c) those recognized by Ellison (1987).

and soon they identified roundhouses of British type in their excavations. More recent research (Theunissen 2009) suggests that this interpretation was over-optimistic. In order to create such patterns, they had selected a series of unrelated features from a wider distribution of postholes. Attitudes have also changed in British archaeology, so that the most recent interpretation of Thorny Down (Ellison 1987) dispenses with any rectangular dwellings. Instead, it suggests that the settlement contained two large circular houses.

De Bogen

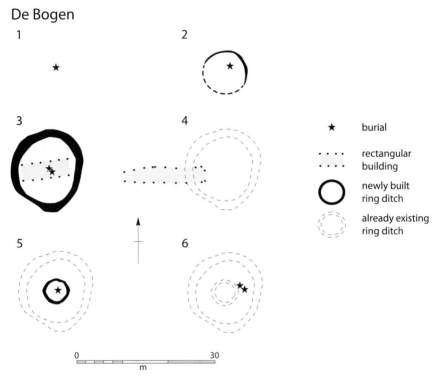

Figure 58 The structural sequence at De Bogen, the Netherlands, showing the changing relationship between circular mounds or enclosures, burials and rectangular timber buildings.

Similar discussions have centred on the Dutch site of De Bogen (Bourgeois and Fontijn 2008; Meijlink 2008). Here, the ambiguity extends from the forms of domestic buildings to those of more specialized structures. When the results of fieldwork were first published, the excavator identified a number of timber circles, as well as longhouses, round barrows, and inhumation burials whose chronology extended from the Late Neolithic period to the Iron Age. A more recent review of the evidence, which is endorsed by Meijlink (2008), suggests a simpler interpretation (Figure 58).

It now appears that the earliest feature was a pit associated with Bell Beaker pottery, faunal remains, and a small amount of human bone. It dates from about 2000 BC. In a second phase, in the mid- to late-second millennium BC, its position was reused by a circular enclosure or mound. A further burial, or burials, may have been deposited at the time. The next development took place not long afterwards and involved the construction of a larger monument, surrounded by a ditch. A rectangular timber building, which is described by its excavator as a 'house', was built within its area. At its centre were the burials of an adult man and a child.

The pairing of a circular mortuary monument and a rectilinear building was repeated during the next phase at De Bogen when a wooden longhouse was aligned on the position of the older barrow and extended to the edge of the mound. It was similar to the other structures in a Middle Bronze Age settlement excavated on the same site and was associated with a quantity of domestic pottery. After an interval, the remains of this barrow were supplemented by a smaller ring ditch containing the burial of a man accompanied by a rapier, a pot, and two bronze arrowheads. It happened around 1000 BC, but the sequence did not end there, for five or six hundred years later, during the Iron Age, two more graves were dug. In this case the existing earthwork was left unaltered and the burials were not associated with any buildings.

On a superficial level the changing interpretation of De Bogen depends on the acceptance of the most striking patterns among the excavated postholes and the rejection of other, less regular configurations; it is also supported by radiocarbon dating (Bourgeois and Fontijn 2008). There is little doubt that rectilinear houses had been paired with circular enclosures or mounds, but there was no longer any evidence for the rings of posts originally identified by the excavator.

Despite this revision, the juxtaposition of rectangular and circular elements remains the most striking characteristic of the site. It raises important questions of interpretation. To what extent must these distinctive structures be considered separately? Were the rectangular houses necessarily associated with the activities of the living and circular monuments with the dead, or was their relationship actually more complicated? How is the difference to be interpreted? A similar pairing of round and rectilinear monuments occurs in other parts of prehistoric Europe where it is commonly observed in cemeteries. The account that follows considers these questions in more detail and places a special emphasis on the evidence from the Bronze Age of the Netherlands and south Scandinavia.

STORA KALVÖ

An illustration of the same principle is provided by the monuments on an island located a short distance off the coast of south-east Sweden. Stora Kalvö has seen little archaeological investigation, but contains a remarkable series of stone structures attributed to the Bronze Age (Bradley and Widholm 2007: 33–5; Figure 59).

They can be divided into four different groups. On the high ground towards the southern end of the island there is a pair of circular cairns. One is

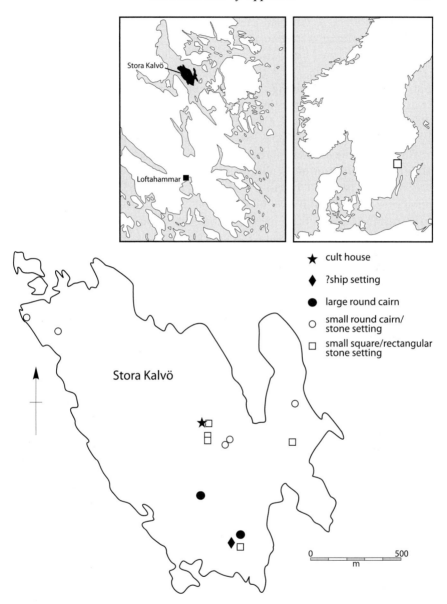

Figure 59 The siting of Bronze Age (and possibly Iron Age) monuments on the offshore island of Stora Kalvö, Sweden.

associated with a rectangular cairn and a possible ship setting. A larger monument complex is close to a former inlet of the Baltic. Some of the same elements are repeated here. There are two circular stone settings, two square settings of similar size, and a massive rectangular enclosure which was built out of rubble. The remaining monuments on Stora Kalvö occur in pairs, but in each case they are separated from one another by a distance of about 300 metres. One consists of a rectangular stone setting and an equally small stone circle. The other includes two circular stone settings.

Although these monuments have not been excavated, again they illustrate a striking juxtaposition of rectilinear and circular elements. One of the large round cairns is found together with a rectangular stone setting and with another structure which may be in the form of a ship. A further rectilinear stone setting is not far from the small ring of standing stones, whilst the main group of structures on the island has no fewer than five separate components: two circular settings, two square settings, and an elongated rectangular enclosure or 'house'. In this case, the shapes of these structures are unambiguous, for, unlike the wooden buildings at Thorny Down and De Bogen, all of them were made of stone.

At first sight it would be easy to identify the largest construction on the island as the remains of a longhouse and to suggest that the other monuments were associated with the dead, but the character of the building is not consistent with this interpretation. It does have the dimensions of a domestic dwelling, but it lacks an entrance. Unlike its counterparts in excavated settlements, it was built of stone rather than wood, and there is no indication that it had a roof. Similar constructions in Sweden and Denmark are usually associated with cairns and some provide evidence of fires, the production of metal artefacts, food preparation, and cremation burials. Whilst these enclosures are about the same size as the buildings inside Bronze Age settlements, they have quite different orientations (Victor 2001, 2002). Because they are associated with cemeteries they are commonly described as 'cult houses'. Although their characteristic form was inspired by a domestic prototype, they appear to have played a more specialized role (Svanberg 2005; Goldhahn 2007: Chapter 9).

They are best known during a period between 1350 and 1000 BC in which barrows and cairns were substantial structures, but in this part of Sweden the connection with funerary monuments continued into the first millennium BC when rectilinear stone settings were built on a smaller scale. This may apply to some of the examples on Stora Kalvö. If the round cairns were associated directly with the dead, did the shapes of the rectilinear structures still refer to the forms of domestic architecture (Widholm and Regnell 2001)? If so, it is difficult to say how long this contrast was observed—the monuments themselves may still have been used in the Iron Age. In neither period is there any evidence of settlement on the island itself. For that reason it is likely that the dead were brought there from the mainland.

MORTUARY HOUSES AND CULT HOUSES

Small rectangular stone settings are paired with circular cairns at many other sites in south Scandinavia, but excavation has shown that buildings of similar dimensions were also constructed of timber. Again, they are interpreted as 'cult houses' (Victor 2002). They are rarely found at settlements, but they are associated with round barrows and cairns, and with one of the specialized enclosures identified as Late Bronze Age hillforts: Odensala Prästgård, near Stockholm (Olausson 1995). They have been studied in most detail in Denmark where one of the best preserved of these buildings was at Grydehøj (Nielsen and Beck 2004; Figure 60).

Here, the principal monument was a round barrow which was enlarged by the construction of a kerb in the second millennium BC. At the beginning of the first millennium a rectangular structure, measuring only six metres by five, was constructed alongside the mound. It had a wall of upright posts and sods. A central upright supported the roof and behind it there was a fireplace and a small semicircular compartment within which pottery sherds and a limited quantity of burnt bones were deposited. Outside the building were a number of features that have been interpreted as 'cooking pits'. During the same phase at least three cremation burials were inserted into the barrow. One was in a small stone cist; another was in an urn; whilst the third was deposited inside a small pit. There were no grave goods with any of these deposits.

A recent account of the site considers the interpretation of this building:

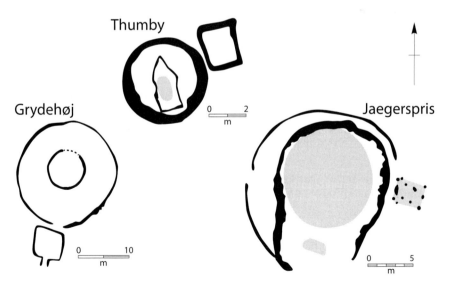

Figure 60 Bronze Age round barrows associated with rectilinear timber structures at three sites in Denmark. The mound at Thumby also covered a boat-shaped grave.

> One could imagine that ceremonies took place inside and outside the house, which may have been connected with the burials, as well as the preparation of food. The semicircular room at the back of the house could have been a sacred space. In front of it there was a fire...Such *mortuary houses* and the cult associated with them may have been widely distributed (my emphasis; Jensen 2006b: 86-8, translation by C. Nimura).

That is certainly suggested by other sites where small rectangular buildings are paired with Bronze Age round barrows in Denmark. They could be built either of wood or of stone; in a few cases, structures of this kind were buried beneath the edge of the mound when the earthwork was extended. More than one example can be associated with a single monument.

Although these buildings echo the rectangular ground plan of domestic dwellings, they were built on an altogether smaller scale than the longhouses of the same period. In southern Sweden there may be indications of a complex archaeological sequence in which the large rubble 'cult houses' were sometimes paired with considerable round cairns during the Early Bronze Age. Famous examples include those at Kivik (Larsson 1993) and Hågahägen (Victor 2002: Chapter 7). In the Late Bronze Age, however, human remains are often associated with smaller circular stone settings, and it seems as if the rectangular structures were also conceived on a more limited scale. Like the wooden building at Grydehøj, they may have played a role in the rites of passage. They may even have provided mortuary houses or platforms where the corpse was laid out before it was consumed on the pyre. Alternatively, they might have been places where offerings were displayed when the funeral took place.

A similar interpretation might shed light on the character of the first timber building at De Bogen, but may not apply to its successor on the same site. The earlier structure resembles a rectangular house in plan, but it fitted exactly into the space defined by a Middle Bronze Age ring ditch. It is not clear whether that earthwork was originally an enclosure or whether the wooden construction was buried beneath a barrow. In either case it is clear that it contained two inhumation burials. Again, its interpretation as 'mortuary house' seems entirely appropriate (Meijlink 2008).

More doubt attaches to a second timber building which was aligned on the older monument at De Bogen. There is nothing to distinguish it from the longhouses associated with a nearby settlement and in this case it was associated with finds of pottery and did not include human remains. Although it was orientated on an existing round barrow, the mound itself was not reused until a subsequent phase. The people who erected the building may have chosen this location in order to associate it with an older earthwork, but there is nothing to suggest that it played a direct role in funerary ritual.

MORTUARY HOUSES AND DOMESTIC DWELLINGS

The characteristic forms of cult houses or mortuary houses may have referred to those of domestic buildings, even when these structures were built on very different scales. What of the dwellings of the living and their relationship with prehistoric round barrows?

The round barrows of continental Europe were constructed in regions which were characterized by rectilinear domestic buildings. The contrast is striking, but the relationship between these separate elements was by no means consistent across time and space. Such differences are particularly apparent among the earlier examples, for the distribution of circular burial mounds in the Chalcolithic and Early Bronze Age periods complemented that of a series of flat cemeteries in Central Europe, whose positions may not have been marked by any monuments (Häusler 1977). In Bronze Age Scandinavia there was a striking contrast between a few very large barrows and cairns and an abundance of smaller structures that could be found in the same places (Widholm 1998).

JUXTAPOSITION, SUCCESSION, AND BELIEF

It is difficult to establish how closely round barrows and round cairns were related to the houses occupied by the living and it seems unlikely that any one model can accommodate all the available evidence. Rather, people living in different regions found their own ways of expressing relationships with the dead. Although there are many areas of uncertainty, the most striking contrasts are easy to identify. They are epitomized by obvious differences in the chronologies and distributions of these features. They are also expressed through the shapes of the various structures.

The spatial relationship between longhouses and round barrows is, perhaps, the simplest to recognize, although that does not make the interpretation of this evidence any easier. The dead may have been buried among the remains of their settlements; they may have been celebrated by monuments only a short distance from the domestic buildings of the same period; or they could have been set apart from the living. The contrast between Stora Kalvö and De Bogen illustrates the range of variation. In the first case, the dead could have been taken from settlements on the Swedish mainland for burial on an offshore island. In the second, people seem to have inhabited a longhouse which was aligned on an earlier round barrow and extended to the edge of that mound.

The same contrast can be recognized between the monuments in different regions of Northern and north-western Europe. Perhaps the evidence is most thoroughly recorded in Denmark where the forms and contents of Early Bronze Age barrows have been documented in a series of volumes by Aner and Kersten which began in 1973, but, although the field evidence is often of high quality, its interpretation poses problems.

Certain points are generally accepted. It is clear that many of the Danish mounds were constructed at the heart of the settled landscape, with the result that excavation has found evidence of houses, fences, or cultivated fields preserved beneath them. Indeed, Kristiansen (1990) has suggested that much of the landscape was being farmed by this period. In the same way, Rasmussen (1993) has argued that settlements and ploughed fields were so extensive that barrows might have been constructed over them entirely by chance. That is why some of the houses whose remains were buried below these mounds date from a significantly earlier period than those earthworks and why the positions of certain round barrows are so different from those of these buildings. Both writers accept that the dead were buried in a landscape that had been occupied by the living (and one which may still have been settled), but they do not consider that the juxtaposition of these particular elements was especially significant.

Such pragmatic arguments were a reaction against an older idea that the barrows of the dead were deliberately built over the dwellings of the living. Rasmussen and Kristiansen also questioned the significance of the plough furrows preserved below the mounds. Did they really provide evidence for the practice of 'ritual ploughing', as an earlier writer had suggested? This practice is recorded in classical literature and the Vedic hymns, but that is no reason to suppose that it happened in Northern Europe (Pätzold 1960). Even now there is no consensus. Kristiansen rejects this interpretation, whilst Rowley-Conwy (1987) draws on the evidence of experimental archaeology to suggest that the mounds must have been built immediately after the ground was tilled. For that reason he considers the relationship between round barrows and plough furrows to be of special significance.

It is not easy to assess these arguments, but it seems unlikely that all the excavated evidence can be dismissed as the result of chance. There are a small number of Bronze Age longhouses whose ground plans seem to have exerted a direct influence over the size and position of a later round barrow (Figure 61). There are even instances where the layout of the dwelling seems to have determined the siting of the graves beneath the mound that took its place (Bradley 2005b: 23–8). Thus, the bodies were buried in relation to the position of its doorway or even that of a cellar. Moreover, there are also cases in which the axis of the building seems have been determined by the alignment of the plough furrows preserved beneath the barrow. That makes sense if these buildings were placed in a cultivated landscape, but it is harder to explain why the same applies to the orientations of the graves. The plans published by Aner and Kersten (1973–1986) show that it applies to more than half the

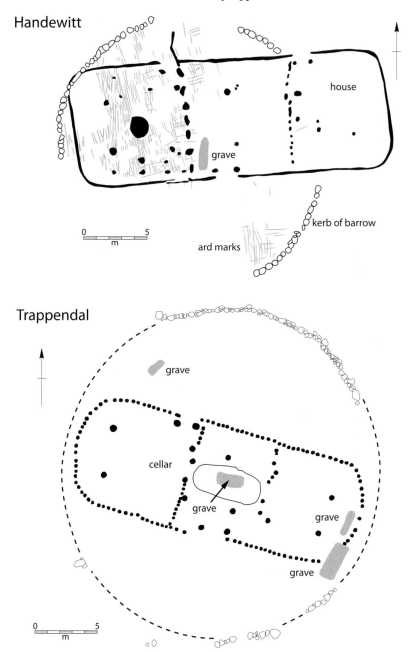

Figure 61 The relationship between Bronze Age longhouses and round barrows at Handewitt, north Germany, and Trappendal, Denmark.

burials under mounds where plough marks have been identified. It suggests that the act of cultivation and the burial of the dead were linked in a significant manner. As the direction of cultivation also influenced the orientation of longhouses, this must have serious implications for the relationship of barrows to domestic dwellings.

Another way of thinking about this evidence is to consider the link between death and fertility. As Bloch and Parry (1982) have emphasized, the ethnographic record often documents a connection of this kind. It seems as if particular communities believed that life could be considered as a finite resource, with the result that the death of one individual would release the fertility required for someone else to be born. Alternatively, the dead could have been integrated into the natural cycle of death and regeneration on which the continuity of society would depend. By burying them in a ploughed field their remains could be treated like the seed corn that was planted there and would grow to maturity. That may be an explanation for the use of arable land as a suitable place for building round barrows.

Later cremation burials in Northern and north-eastern Europe suggest a similar idea, for they were sometimes placed inside ceramic vessels which assumed the form of a domestic building. Like their Italian counterparts discussed in Chapter 3, they were originally identified as models of ancient dwellings and for that reason they were described as 'house urns'. Whilst the Southern European examples bear a strong resemblance to the dwellings identified by excavation, the same cannot be said of their northern counterparts. In this case the models are entered by a door part way up the outside wall; others represent buildings raised on stilts (Figure 62). They bear no resemblance to the longhouses documented by excavation in the areas where these pots are found; in the circumstances they are best interpreted as representations of grain stores (Bradley 2002b). If this is correct, their role in mortuary ritual surely refers to basic ideas about death, fertility, and regeneration. The burnt bones were placed in these containers, just as cereals were kept in the granaries. In short, they emphasize the same beliefs as the association between burial mounds, graves, and cultivated land.

Another observation has been made in the excavation of round barrows in the Netherlands, Denmark, and parts of southern Sweden. Many were constructed of turves. Again, Kristiansen has provided a mundane explanation for this practice (1984: 94). He thinks of it in relation to the conspicuous consumption of pasture, in the same way as the construction of these monuments represented a substantial investment of human labour. That may well be true, but there is another possibility to consider. If the sods used to build the barrows were taken from areas of grazing land, they would have been manured by domestic animals, so their selection might make a reference to the agricultural cycle in the same manner as the consumption of ploughed fields.

Figure 62 Bronze Age 'house urns' in the form of a granary.

The argument could be taken even further. During later periods turves were used as stable bedding and were spread on cultivated fields as a source of manure. In the Netherlands this led to the creation of what are known as *plaggen* soils (Groenman-Van-Waateringe and Robinson 1988). It is uncertain when this practice was first adopted although it is thought that it developed in the Early Medieval period, but it is possible that the sods employed to construct round barrows were also considered to be fertile. At the same time, the construction of turf-built mounds may have followed a specific sequence. They were constructed out of living matter. Once it had been built into the mound it decayed, and, on those sites where the barrow was capped by a layer of inert material excavated from a ditch, the pieces of turf would have been deprived of nutrients. In that way the barrow went through the same process of change as the bodies buried underneath it (Bradley and Fraser 2011).

DEGREES OF SEPARATION

If certain burial mounds or cairns were near the settlements of the same date, others were located according to quite different criteria. Again, the evidence from Early Bronze Age Denmark has a special significance.

The results of excavation make it clear that the construction of a round barrow must have drawn on the labour of a significant number of people. It is unlikely that the workforce came from a single settlement. For that reason it would be wrong to suppose that each barrow commemorated the members of only one community. Although these earthworks were built in a populated landscape, their importance may not have been restricted to the people living in the vicinity.

Recent research has added substance to what was really an old idea: one that was first proposed in the early years of research on the Bronze Age of Northern Europe (Johansen et al. 2004). Although circular mounds are often considered singly, as the positions of graves containing a particular set of artefacts, those monuments also conform to a wider system and were apparently laid out in lines that extend for long distances across the landscape. They probably followed the course of roads which first influenced the distribution of burial mounds during the Late Neolithic period. They form the component parts of an extended network which may well indicate the principal routes along which people travelled in the past. As a result, certain locations must have enjoyed more extensive connections than others, especially when the evidence of these lines of mounds is considered together with the courses of navigable rivers. At the same time, the regions where the roads converged contained the most varied assemblages of grave goods. They included artefacts of exotic or unusual types and sometimes made use of non-local raw materials. To that extent, the siting and associations of the barrows were determined not only by the presence of settled land but also by the wider pattern of communication. That is particularly obvious in Jutland.

A possible explanation is proposed by Oestigaard and Goldhahn (2006) who question the conventional assumption that the objects buried with the corpse were the personal property of the deceased. Instead, they suggest that the variety of funeral gifts reflects the alliances that the dead person had formed. It follows that the inhabitants of certain areas enjoyed more extensive contacts than others. It may be why the most varied grave assemblages come from monuments that occupied a pivotal location in the pattern of movement across the terrain. The barrows in which they were buried may have occupied areas of farmland, but that was not the only factor that influenced their siting. The monuments by which the dead were remembered were addressed to a wider audience.

A stronger case for distancing the dead from the living is provided by the monuments on Stora Kalvö, which have already featured in this account. That site is unusual because such remains are so frequent and so well preserved, but its archaeology conforms to a wider pattern, for many offshore islands along the west coast of the Baltic and the Atlantic coast of Scandinavia are associated with Bronze Age cairns. Some of the ground would have been unsuitable for sustained occupation and other parts of the archipelago were too small to support a resident population. In eastern Sweden this was still the case in the Viking period when they were used as seasonal pasture and provided the sites of fishing camps (Bradley and Widholm 2007: 21). In any case, the sea level was significantly higher during the Bronze Age so these islands would have been even less extensive than they are today. It is unlikely that the people buried on the islands had lived there. Perhaps the archipelago was associated with the dead.

Stora Kalvö is by no means the smallest island in the Baltic archipelago, but it does contain an exceptional number and variety of monuments. It shares this characteristic with the nearby site of Hellerö on the mainland, but with one important difference. Whist the monuments found there include a number of cairns and a ship setting, there are also the remains of an early field system (Sigvallius 2005). It raises the possibility that the south-east coast of Sweden was farmed during the Bronze Age, while small offshore islands were used mainly as cemeteries. Although there are many more cairns on the mainland, there is certainly a contrast between the stone monuments off the coast and the timber longhouses found in inland areas.

CHRONOLOGICAL PATTERNS

Just as individual mounds had their histories, so did the houses occupied by the living, and these histories may have been equally relevant to the relationship between settlements and round barrows. Certain points are particularly significant. It is not clear how long these dwellings were occupied and what happened to the material of which they were constructed. Some of the longhouses may have been repaired or rebuilt on the same sites, but others were replaced in a different location (Gerritsen 1999). Again, there is disagreement about the length of time over which these buildings would remain structurally sound and it is not certain that they were abandoned every generation in the way that has been suggested for the Neolithic dwellings whose remains were incorporated in tells (Arnoldussen 2008: 92–4). Even with these qualifications, there seems to be a general sequence among the domestic buildings of the Bronze Age. No matter how long individual dwellings were inhabited, most of them changed their locations over time. That was particularly true in the late second and early first millennia BC.

How was this related to the history of the mounds? If the siting of these earthworks was determined by beliefs about regeneration, it might be natural for older plots to be abandoned and for barrows to take their place. It is not necessary to suppose that it occurred every generation, but it would be reasonable to infer that both processes formed part of the same ritual cycle and that their relationship to one another was coloured by more basic beliefs about the connections between the living and the dead. Of course, such ideas will have differed from one part of Europe to another. This chapter has already presented some evidence of a fairly rapid alternation between houses and barrows in Early Bronze Age Denmark, where certain mounds overlay the positions of fields. The fact that plough furrows are still identifiable in the surface of the buried soil shows that little time can have passed between the act of cultivation and the building of these monuments. That is also the case where the layout of the barrow reflected the organization of the domestic dwelling whose remains were preserved beneath it.

A very different sequence has been recognized in the southern Netherlands (Bourgeois and Fontijn 2008; Figure 63). For many years it seemed likely that Dutch round barrows dating from the Middle Bronze Age were directly

Eigenblock-West

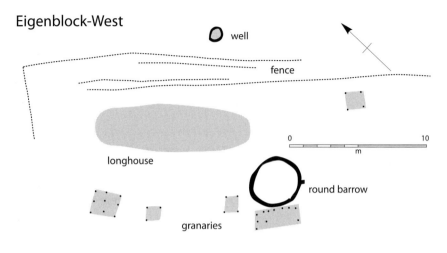

Itford Hill

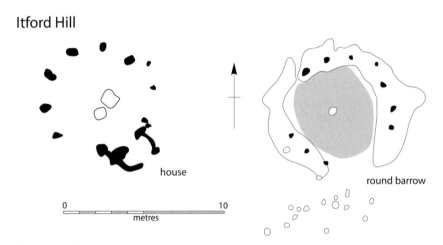

Figure 63 The spatial relationship between timber houses and round barrows at Eigenblock-West, the Netherlands, and Itford Hill, England. The barrow at Eigenblock-West is older than the settlement, whilst the roundhouse at Itford Hill is contemporary with the nearby burial mound. Postholes associated with this barrow are indicated in black and pits containing cremation deposits are indicated by open symbols.

associated with the settlements of the same period. They have certainly been found together, but recent research suggests that, whilst their spatial relationship to one another may have been significant, they were not constructed simultaneously. The mounds, some of which incorporate timber circles, were built between 1800 and 1400 BC, and the groups of well-preserved longhouses between 1400 and 1100 BC. It follows that the mounds were not intended to commemorate the occupants of the settlement, although their earthworks might be reused in later phases. In fact, groups of domestic buildings were associated with the monuments of the past. De Bogen provides an example of this relationship, for here a newly built house was aligned on a long established round barrow (Meijlink 2008). No burials can be attributed to this particular phase, although some examples date from an earlier period and others were added afterwards.

If the positions of newly built longhouses were influenced by the proximity of older round barrows, a similar process may already have happened in the development of cemeteries. Few of those mounds are found in isolation and new research has shown that many of them were built in close proximity to existing examples (Bourgeois and Fontijn 2008). The older monuments could also be of Middle Bronze Age date, but there are other cases in which they were constructed during the Neolithic period. Just as new earthworks were created alongside older ones, the original monuments could be reopened to receive secondary burials. The process extended so far back in time that it is unlikely that anyone knew the identities of the first people commemorated by the mounds. The same could well be true when the earliest longhouses were built close to the barrows. They may have stood for a past that no one could remember. The inhabitants of these settlements need not have been the descendants of the people who were buried nearby.

In this case the contrast between rectilinear longhouses and circular burial mounds is well documented. It was obviously significant, but the two kinds of structure were not contemporary with one another. In fact, the few monuments that were built at the same time as the houses take a quite different form and consist of roughly oval mounds or enclosures associated with human remains. They enclose settings of upright posts and may have been designed to mirror the forms of domestic dwellings (Bourgeois and Fontijn 2008). The resemblance between them can easily be exaggerated and, in any case, such structures are rare. Similar features occurred in greater numbers during the Late Bronze Age and Early Iron Age when smaller houses were built (Roymans and Kortlang 1999: 42–53).

ROUND BARROWS AND ROUNDHOUSES IN THE BRONZE AGE OF BRITAIN AND IRELAND

This chapter began with an account of an excavation in southern England. This was at the settlement of Thorny Down. The ways in which the site was interpreted were influenced by more general ideas about the cultural connections between Britain and the Netherlands. Thus, studies of Thorny Down identified a rectangular building similar to those in the Low Countries. In the same way, Dutch archaeologists recognized roundhouses of British-type in their own excavations. They also discovered timber circles.

Some of these ideas have fared better than others. Although there is general agreement that the principal buildings at Thorny Down were roundhouses, there are few Dutch archaeologists who still claim to recognize dwellings of British inspiration. However, a small number of timber longhouses have been identified in lowland England; in this case the field evidence is convincing (Bradley 2007: 193–5). With this exception, there is a striking contrast between the structures built in mainland Europe and those in Britain. Rectilinear architecture occurs on the continent and circular buildings in the British Isles.

That contrast concerns the forms of houses, but it does not extend to the cemeteries of the same period, for on both sides of the English Channel and the North Sea burial mounds were usually circular. The same applies to many of the specialized structures, usually post circles, with which they are associated. It would be easy to suppose that different forms were appropriate in different contexts, so that round barrows were associated with the dead and rectangular houses with the living, but that cannot be entirely true. In the Netherlands, a few elongated mounds and enclosures may reflect the ground plans of nearby houses (Roymans and Kortlang 1999; Bourgeois and Fontijn 2008), but in Ireland and Britain domestic dwellings and barrows share the same circular outline (Bradley 2007: 197–200). Thus, the contrast between these different forms was by no means universal.

The best way to appreciate the distinctive pattern in mainland Europe is to compare it with the evidence from the same period in Britain. That is possible because land use in both regions seems to have changed during the later second millennium BC (Brinkkemper and van Wijngaarden-Bakker 2005; Bradley 2007: Chapter 4; Darvill 2010: 211–23). It was when settlements became more apparent in the archaeological record, agricultural production intensified, and houses were increasingly durable. It was also during this phase that barrows and domestic sites occurred together.

The British evidence needs to be set in a wider context. Circular structures had been favoured since at least the Late Neolithic period and took a variety of different forms, from the great post settings associated with large henge monuments to some of the small domestic buildings of the same date. Earthwork enclosures also favoured a circular outline, together with settings of monoliths. Round barrows were important, too. The earliest date from the late fourth millennium BC, but most examples span the period between the adoption of Bell Beakers around 2400 BC and the end of the Early Bronze Age, nearly a thousand years later (Garwood 2005). After that time, some of the older barrows were reused for cremation burials and smaller mounds were constructed (Bradley 2007: 1197–200). Outside Ireland their creation seems to have lapsed by the beginning of the Late Bronze Age, around 1100 BC. Like those on the continent, earlier barrows were associated with inhumation burials and their successors mainly with cremations.

This broad outline conceals some important areas of uncertainty. The first is represented by the circular timber settings associated with a number of these mounds, from the Beaker period to the middle of the Bronze Age. They have been interpreted in different ways (Ashbee 1960: Chapter 5). They may have been mortuary enclosures in which corpses were displayed before they were buried; they could have been enclosed cemeteries whose remains were covered by mounds during a later phase (Garwood 2005); they may even have been the remains of fences which retained the material of the barrow. All these arguments are plausible and, in particular cases, they may be correct, but another possibility has been suggested. Could these enclosures have been conceived as the houses of the dead? The possibility is worth entertaining where the barrows overlie collections of artefacts similar to those found in settlements.

At this point it becomes apparent that the field evidence from British sites can be just as difficult to interpret as its counterpart in Northern Europe—and for very much the same reason. Unless they were built of stone (as sometimes happened in the uplands), Early Bronze Age roundhouses left little trace behind. Often, all that can be recognized are groups of postholes and stakeholes. Whilst many of the timber settings associated with burial mounds may have played a specialized role, others could be the remains of domestic buildings. That is more likely to be the case where they are associated with pits and hearths like those found at open sites (Gibson 1982: 27–48). However, these observations pose a special problem. Just as Dutch excavators were influenced by the expectation that round houses of British type would be found in the Netherlands, fieldworkers in southern England were keen to identify post circles similar to those associated with barrows in the Low Countries. The points made in Gregory's study of the psychology of perception are particularly relevant here, for the excavated evidence is subject to more than one interpretation.

There is another possibility to consider. Were the forms of the later round barrows in Britain and Ireland conceived as copies of domestic buildings? Could the mounds themselves have been thought of as the dwellings of people in the past? It raises some of the issues discussed in Chapter Four, but this time the context is very different.

A few observations do seem to be securely based. During the Middle Bronze Age settlements were often paired with burial mounds in southern England (Bradley 2007: 197). In contrast to the evidence from the Netherlands, both were employed together, although there are certain cases in which older barrows were reused during this phase. Nearly all the deposits were cremations and were frequently associated with pottery vessels of exactly the same types as those found in the nearby houses. The burials were generally in groups and were most often located on the south side of the mound. In certain cases this is where there was a causeway in the barrow ditch. The earthworks were of approximately the same size as the houses, and, where the ditch was broken by an 'entrance', it might share the orientation of the porch leading into those buildings (Bradley 1998: 148–60). In certain instances the outline of the barrow was emphasized by a setting of posts, but this is rare. Few of the cremation burials contained deposits that can be described as grave goods, but the comparatively unusual metal artefacts from the cemeteries are of the same types as those associated with occupation sites, where they could be deposited with some formality in abandoned dwellings or in a ditch enclosing the settlement.

Similar arguments may apply to Irish 'ring barrows' (Waddell 1998: 365–8). Although the name might suggest that they were mounds, they were, in fact, small circular enclosures with an entrance and an external bank. Like the monuments just discussed, they are associated with cremation burials and can be found in the same areas as Bronze Age settlements, although the chronology of these earthworks extends as late as the Iron Age (McGarry 2009). They are relevant because they are roughly the same size as the circular houses that have been discovered in recent years and, for the most part, share the orientation of their doorways. In this case there is a further factor to consider. A number of the Irish settlements were bounded by circular enclosures. Their extent varies from one site to another, and the smallest contain only one house. These compounds were usually defined by a shallow ditch with a bank on the inside (Bradley 2007: 216–17). The ring barrows reversed this convention. Perhaps this was done in order to signify the contrast between a space inhabited by the living and an area devoted to the dead. Both kinds of structure adopted a circular outline, but the distinction between them is obvious. Where English settlements were sometimes accompanied by mounds of similar proportions to domestic dwellings, the Irish counterparts of those buildings were embanked enclosures. In their different ways, both may have been considered as the dwellings of the dead.

BARROWS AND HOUSES IN NORTHERN EUROPE: A SPECULATIVE MODEL

If the situation in Britain and Ireland was truly exceptional, how did it compare with the norm? The final section of this chapter returns to the relationship between burial mounds and houses in the Netherlands and south Scandinavia.

Two observations require more discussion. The first is the relationship between rectilinear buildings and circular burial mounds. It took several forms and clearly changed during the course of the Bronze Age. Even so, it is evident that there was no simple contrast between round barrows and other structures. A significant number of monuments in Denmark and Sweden were accompanied by square or rectangular buildings of wood or stone. The earlier examples could be the same size as domestic dwellings, whilst those built during the Late Bronze Age usually were smaller. They differed in other ways, too, as the first cult houses were open enclosures formed of rubble, while some of the later structures consisted of platforms or cairns. It is particularly striking that monuments of these kinds are rarely, if ever, found in isolation. They accompany cairns or occur on sites where human remains are found.

Perhaps the use of these distinctive monuments played a special role in mortuary ritual. Their forms appear to refer to domestic architecture and yet they are associated with the dead. It seems possible that they were used at an intermediate stage in the rites of passage, in between the removal of the body from a settlement of rectilinear buildings and its burial in a circular barrow or cairn. The shapes of these buildings referred back to domestic architecture, but their siting shows that they must have played an integral part in the funeral ceremony. The same duality was noted in Chapter 7 which discussed the Iron Age burial grounds of Öland.

A second issue is the siting of Bronze Age round barrows and round cairns. This chapter has considered the extent to which they were distanced from the world of the living, but, apart from those monuments built on offshore islands, it has said little about their placing in the topography. That information is especially important in parts of Sweden where concentrations of funerary monuments follow the coast, sometimes to the exclusion of inland areas. The structures on the mainland can overlook the sea, but they also follow the courses of rivers and lakes. In many cases they were placed on the highest available ground, even when it made their construction difficult (Gerdin 1999). On one level it suggests that proximity to settled land was not an important criterion, but, on another, it may say something about a wider system of belief. The monuments that followed the shoreline may have been located there because it was where the land met the water. In the same way, the siting of other structures could have been directed to the sky. These observations are significant because the same elements were important in Scandinavian rock art (Bradley 2009: Chapter 8).

The comparison is intriguing for a number of reasons. According to Kaul (2004), Bronze Age cosmology placed a special emphasis on the movement of the sun. It rose out of the sea at dawn and during the day it travelled across the sky until it set. It returned to its point of departure during the night when it was carried by a ship which passed beneath the water. These beliefs appear to be documented by drawings on decorated metalwork and by others carved on

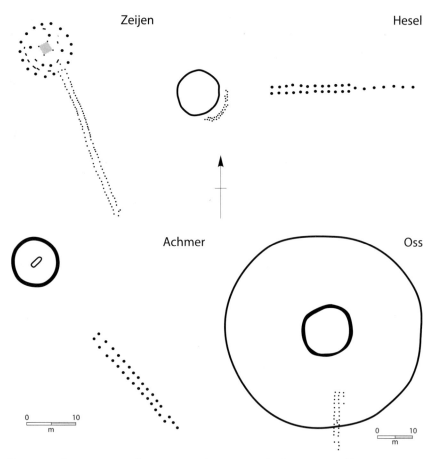

Figure 64 Bronze Age and Iron Age timber avenues leading to round barrows at four sites in Germany and the Netherlands.

rocks at the water's edge. Taken together, these sources suggest the existence of a three-tier cosmology which explained the relationship between the land, the sky, and the sea. Bronze artefacts illustrating this scheme are found in round barrows and round cairns from north Germany to southern Sweden. The same emphasis on the position of the sun is evident in the Early Bronze Age in southern Denmark where Randsborg and Nybo (1984) suggest that graves containing inhumations were aligned on the sunrise and sunset.

    One of the distinctive features shared between decorated artefacts and rock carvings is the importance of circular motifs. They have been interpreted as drawings of the sun and both media feature designs in which they are carried by a boat or some kind of cart. In some cases, the circle is subdivided to form a 'wheel cross'. It may be no accident that the same pattern can be recognized at a small number of stone settings. Geoglyphs of this kind are rare and poorly dated (Hyenstrand 1969; Wangen 1998), but their very existence raises the question whether the layout of circular cairns was intended as another reference to the sun. On one hand, it is difficult to take the argument further, as discoveries of decorated metalwork and rock art extend across only part of the overall distribution of circular monuments. On the other hand, new research suggests that similar beliefs extended into Central Europe and beyond (Meller 2004).

Lastly, there are a few more structures which combine circular and linear elements. At a series of sites extending from Germany to the Netherlands and Denmark round barrows are approached by avenues consisting of two parallel rows of posts (Thörn 2007: 149–86; Figure 64). They might have led from the settlements, but this has never been established. Their chronology is imprecise and individual examples have dates extending from the Late Neolithic period to the Late Bronze Age or even the Iron Age. What they do share is an emphasis on alignments towards the east and west. They also avoid northerly orientations, leading Thörn to suggest 'a link with the rising and setting sun' (Thörn 2007: 202). The number of sites is limited but, if he is correct, this may provide another reason for supposing that the curvilinear monuments of Northern Europe formed *only one element* in a system of belief that was also expressed in other media.

In that case the differences of shape that preoccupy students of visual perception could have become a matter of life and death.

9

The New Order

OBSERVATIONS IN AFRICA

How would someone who had been brought up in a roundhouse adapt to life in a rectangular world? The experience of a servant working for a family in Malawi shows how difficult it could be.

Her predicament is described in a book entitled *Women's Work in Heathen Lands*, published in 1886. Jan Deregowski quotes the following extract:

> In laying the table there is trouble for the girl. At home her house is round; a straight line and the right angle are unknown to her or her parents before her. Day after day therefore she will lay the cloth with the folds anything but parallel with one edge of the table. Plates, knives and forks are set down in a confusing manner, and it is only after lessons often repeated and much annoyance that she begins to see how things might be done (Laws 1886, quoted by Deregowski 1973: 180–1)

That simple story introduces a larger issue. Under what circumstances did people make the transition from a world of circular structures to one of squares and rectangles, and how were their lives affected by that process? It is surprising how much attention had been paid to structural changes among ancient buildings and how little to the political and social circumstances in which they happened. One way of approaching this topic is not only studying the advantages offered by new styles of architecture, but also asking which important features might be lost.

That is too rarely considered. Many of the approaches described in Chapter 2 emphasized the possibilities offered by the change from circular to rectangular buildings. Houses could be larger and could accommodate more people; they would be easier to maintain; they could be expanded as the number of inhabitants increased and space was subdivided; in many cases rectilinear dwellings could be inhabited over longer periods than roundhouses.

None of those arguments is unsatisfactory in itself, but all are incomplete because they do not take into account the motives of the people who chose to live there. Chapter 2 also showed how houses could be used to emphasize subtle distinctions among their inhabitants: differences that were based on age, gender, and social standing. Such dwellings might be considered as models of the cosmos—even their orientations and elevations had a significance that extended beyond any practical considerations. As Chapters 4 and 6 have argued, such buildings were a source of inspiration for a series of specialized monuments, from burial mounds to temples, and from underground tombs to arenas. Subsequent chapters illustrated the interplay between circular buildings and rectilinear constructions in a series of different societies. All these studies made a similar point. In changing from one style of architecture to another certain beliefs may have been allowed to lapse. If not, they might have continued, but in a different form. Although such interpretations were influenced by ethnographic analogies, all of them were based on archaeological evidence.

One of the best ethnographic sources is Lyons's study of domestic architecture in North Cameroon. It provides a well-documented account of the changing relationship between round and rectangular houses as she observed it in the late 1980s (Lyons 1996) One of the strengths of her analysis is that she was well aware of the archaeological implications of her research.

Lyons studied 200 domestic compounds which were inhabited by four ethnic groups. Each had a different history, but the Wandala, who were comparative newcomers, had assumed the dominant position in society. They adopted rectilinear buildings through contacts with Moslem communities rather than European colonists, but a major influence was the use of such structures in government and local administration. Although the Wandala were the first to take up these new forms, other inhabitants of North Cameroon emulated their distinctive houses as a way of raising their own status at a time of economic and social tensions. When Lyons undertook her survey, the Wandala had the highest proportion of rectangular dwellings, whilst the other groups occupied a greater number of roundhouses. In 1986, circular structures accounted for between thirty and fifty per cent of the domestic buildings. It may be that long-established communities preferred to maintain their links with the past, if only to distinguish themselves from other people.

In fact, certain existing practices continued despite the change. Although new Wandala compounds contained rectangular houses, the functions of the separate buildings were still divided along traditional lines (Figure 65). Thus, their internal organization was much the same as that of groups of roundhouses. At the same time, changes in domestic architecture might emphasize important divisions among the inhabitants. Thus, the men's rooms were generally rectilinear, but some of the women's dwellings in the same settlement might be circular; in that respect, they resemble the Nankani buildings discussed in Chapter 2. As new styles of architecture became more common among the Wandala, the status of roundhouses diminished so that they were

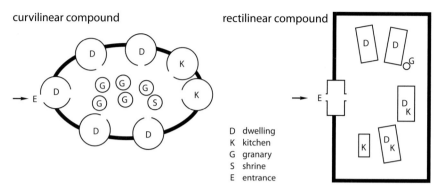

Figure 65 The relationship between contemporary rectilinear and curvilinear compounds in Cameroon.

constructed of cheaper materials. In the end they were relegated to use as kitchens or animal pens.

It would be easy to interpret these changes in purely functional terms, but there are serious problems in doing so. If the rectangular buildings studied in North Cameroon were thought of as a source of prestige, they were more expensive to build than roundhouses and were also less durable. It was claimed that some of these changes developed out of practical concerns—it would be easier to arrange large pieces of furniture in a rectilinear dwelling; it would be possible to roof these structures with corrugated iron—but Lyons's observations did not bear out either of these claims. Instead, she saw the adoption of rectangular buildings as part of a political strategy by which a dominant group like the Wandala associated themselves with the style of architecture employed by the political elite. That is why such structures were common beside roads and in other places where they could easily be seen. In time, some of the remaining communities followed the same practice. They emulated the changes instituted by the Wandala with the intention of improving their own positions in society. As a result, by the time of Lyons's survey rectangular architecture was taking the place of more traditional forms.

FROM HUTS TO HOUSES

Similar changes in domestic architecture were discussed by the contributors to a monograph with the title *From Huts to Houses* published in 2001 (Brandt and Karlsson 2001). It contained the proceedings of a conference held by the Norwegian and Swedish Institutes in Rome. The editors were at pains to point out that the aim of the conference was 'to examine the causes and effects of architectural transformation processes in general, and not only in Iron Age Italy' (Brandt and Karlsson 2001: 7), but in some ways the contents of this volume reflect the setting in which it was conceived. Although its remit was not limited to the Mediterranean, over sixty per cent of the papers deal with Etruscan and Roman archaeology and four of the others are about Greece. It is hard to escape the impression that the book is really about the evolution of buildings in the Classical world.

The title raises another problem:

> The organisers of the seminar and also the editors of this volume are aware that the title 'From Huts to Houses' is capable of causing confusion. It implies both a processual development in architecture from the simple to the complex, which is not always the case, and that we are dealing with two different categories of building for living, and this is not the case (Brandt and Karlsson 2001: 7–8).

They explain that the English title of the book refers to two terms which are in common use in Italian archaeology: *capanna* meaning 'hut' and *casa* meaning 'house'. That was understandable as the conference took place in Rome, but the adoption of this terminology emphasizes the assumption, which is made by some of the contributors, that architectural history is primarily concerned with building technology. The main emphasis—but by no means the only one—is on practical issues. Unlike Lyons's research, these chapters describe a physical process and rarely consider its implications.

In fact, the title of the book provides a reasonable description of the case studies from Italy and Greece. The papers concerned with Mediterranean archaeology trace the development of rectangular stone buildings from smaller curvilinear structures which were sometimes built of wood. The early houses often had oval footprints and are best evidenced in Etruria where they are also represented by ceramic models. From *Huts to Houses* is more concerned with the construction of ancient buildings than it is with their significance for the people who used them, yet a number of the papers describe what may have been a wider process in Southern Europe. One of the clearest examples comes from a new study of Iron Age Sicily (Hodos 2006).

It is an ideal place in which to observe the interplay between different architectural styles. Many of the inhabitants lived in settlements of circular houses—a tradition that was already well established in the Bronze Age. Others favoured rectangular dwellings. The island saw two phases of colonization during the Iron Age. Initially, Greek colonies were established at a number of locations along the coast and then others were founded by Phoenicians. These developments extended over a long period of time, from the late-eighth to the sixth century BC, and, as they happened, parts of the indigenous population withdrew to the mountainous interior of the island where they established new settlements and fortifications. Not only did they try to avoid the incomers, they seem to have defended themselves against them. Even so, it is clear that artefacts and other commodities passed between the separate communities and, over time, the antagonism broke down.

The contrasts between these different groups were expressed through their domestic architecture. At first, the native inhabitants continued to build roundhouses, whilst both groups of colonists favoured rectangular buildings. Eventually, those structures became more complex and echoed some of the characteristics of Greek architecture. At Monte Saraceno de Ravanusa, for instance, rectilinear dwellings replaced a series of circular buildings and were laid out on a grid. There was an obvious difference between the styles of building favoured by the colonists and the traditional forms maintained by indigenous communities. This contrast retained its power despite the fact that contacts between these two groups increased. It seems as if the distinctions between them were expressed through their use of space, and it was only gradually that they became less significant.

The contrast was never complete. As Hodos says,

> While elements of Greek forms of architecture and town planning were adopted over the course of the seventh and sixth centuries, they were utilised in ways that accorded with local needs and preferences, sometimes side by side with traditional architectural forms . . . : Individual settlements used only particular aspects of Greek architectural and urban ideas, and not necessarily the same ones as on a neighbouring site (2006: 112).

The contrast diminished until it virtually disappeared and rectilinear dwellings were favoured in most parts of Sicily, but the change was a subtle one and can easily be misunderstood. If roundhouses went out of favour as the original inhabitants assimilated a new architectural style, circular buildings continued to be built and were sometimes constructed on a larger scale than before. They were no longer dwellings but shrines and are associated with a distinctive material culture, including votive offerings and the remains of sacrificed animals (Figure 66). The change happened gradually. At first, circular buildings of the traditional form were approached through a rectangular portico of a kind associated with Greek temples. Other circular shrines are found with groups of rectangular buildings. In this way 'selected architectural features of Greek religious tradition were included in local sacred places, whether the associated cult contained Greek elements or traditional practices' (Hodos 2006: 129). The significance of this development is illustrated by models of circular temples.

The Iron Age of Sicily illustrates three themes in the transition from circular to rectilinear buildings. The first was the way in which native communities resisted the influence of the colonists by adhering to their traditions of domestic architecture. That was made easier because the indigenous inhabitants had moved their settlements away from the areas that were settled from overseas. For a while, at least two architectural traditions coexisted despite

Montagnoli

Sabucina

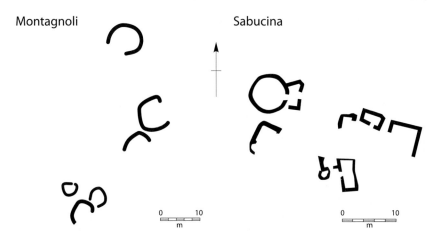

Figure 66 The forms of stone buildings in Iron Age Sicily showing the interplay between circular and rectangular forms.

increasing contacts between the different populations. Leighton (1999) has even suggested that colonial architecture was modified as a result of these connections.

A second stage in the archaeological sequence is marked by the adoption of rectilinear buildings across most parts of the island. It may have happened through a process of emulation of the kind documented by Lyons (1996), but, when it occurred, circular structures also changed their forms and associations. To an increasing extent they were employed as shrines or temples where offerings were made. On one level their characteristic architecture provided an obvious reference to the past and, in these terms, it might be considered as resistance to colonization. On another level, there is evidence that the circular form played an important role in relationships between people and the supernatural. That is evident from the models of temples. It raises the possibility that, long before the first colonies were established on the island, the distinctive form of the roundhouse had possessed a special significance. It could have been spiritual or cosmological references of the kind discussed in Chapter 2 that were most difficult to abandon. Such questions were hardly considered at the conference in Rome.

ROUNDHOUSES IN BRITANNIA

From Huts to Houses includes articles on Mediterranean archaeology, but there are none on Roman Britain, even though strikingly similar architectural developments took place there.

Again, they can be misinterpreted. Mattingly (2006) has made the point that specialists on the Roman period have overemphasized the pervasiveness of rectilinear architecture at the expense of a long-established tradition of circular houses. Whilst both forms did exist before the Conquest, rectangular buildings were rare and may have been confined to high status settlements whose occupants had contacts in the Roman world. Roundhouses, however, were the norm during the Bronze and Iron Ages and remained important for a long time afterwards. The problem is created by the assumptions that scholars have brought to the discussion. Mattingly distinguishes between studies that have treated the province of Britannia in isolation and a comparative perspective that considers its place within the Roman empire:

> A clear trend in many areas of Britain was the innate conservatism of vernacular architecture. If 'Roman Britain' was the land of the villa, then 'Britain in the Roman empire' was characterised overall by the roundhouse. Although increasingly supplemented in some regions by rectangular house forms, it was equally enduring in others. One explanation, of course, is that the issue of whether to embrace new styles of rural building was more pertinent to the upper echelons of late Iron Age society than to the bulk of the populace. A more fundamental objection is that even among the British elite groups we should not assume an unerring desire to adopt Roman architecture, manners and graces (2006: 367).

Although there are some sites where a roundhouse was replaced by a villa, Mattingly makes the point that there are many more places where both architectural forms were used together. Circular buildings did occur infrequently in the early levels of towns where some examples occupied peripheral locations. In most cases these buildings date from the first and second centuries AD. Far more roundhouses were situated in rural areas (Fulford and Holbrook 2011: 337). They had a longer history than their urban counterparts and were particularly common at enclosed settlements. Not all these circular structures were made of wood; from the late second century onwards some were masonry buildings. In certain cases villas were established on the same sites in the third and fourth centuries AD and, where those two kinds of structures were associated with one another, the circular examples seem to have served a variety of functions. They were used as domestic dwellings, agricultural buildings, and industrial workshops.

These developments recall a number of themes that have already featured here. The first point is that rectangular buildings replaced circular examples only gradually, and, when it happened, the change was never complete. The first rectilinear dwellings were built during the Iron Age and may have been inspired by Roman prototypes, but it was not for another two centuries that the process had its greatest impact. Before that time it was more apparent in towns than in the countryside. If new styles of architecture were adopted to emphasize social status—an idea that Mattingly treats with scepticism—that process was as protracted as it had been in Iron Age Sicily and it certainly did not happen everywhere in Roman Britain. It was different from the more rapid changes documented in Cameroon.

In fact, the change from circular to rectilinear buildings was mainly a feature of lowland England and did not extend to other regions towards, or beyond, the frontier zone. There is evidence of stone roundhouses in Northern and Western Britain, some of them of considerable proportions. Their inhabitants had contacts in the Roman world and even used imported artefacts, but only rarely did the forms of their dwellings deviate from the traditional design. Indeed, there are cases in which it was deployed on such a monumental scale that it may have acted as an assertion of political independence. Writing of the massive tower houses of southern and eastern Scotland, Mattingly says:

[They] do not appear to date earlier than the first century [AD] and to some extent may reflect a reaction to the Roman invasions of those areas, not because they offered better defence against the Roman army (they did not), but because they symbolised high status and a particular sort of defiance (2006: 434).

Two other processes identified by Mattingly recall the African and Sicilian examples. The first is the gradual loss of status of circular buildings in the later Roman period in lowland Britain. It may not have happened everywhere—the clearest evidence comes from sites where they are associated with masonry villas. In some cases they may have assumed specialized roles. Their use as farm buildings and workshops recalls the way in which Wandala roundhouses lost their status when rectilinear buildings became popular. In that case they were used as kitchens and animal pens.

The second case is very different. It recalls the evidence from Iron Age Sicily where the last circular buildings were temples rather than dwellings, although their architecture obviously drew on a domestic prototype. Chapter 7 considered the circular temples and shrines that were built in Britain from the Late Iron Age onwards. It seems likely that one source of their architecture was the traditional structure of domestic dwellings; there were also octagonal buildings (Figure 67). What is new is the recognition that such temples became more common as the frequency of roundhouses decreased (Lewis 1966). Again, it seems possible that this was a conscious reference to the past at a time when traditional ideas seemed to be under threat. It may also explain why some of these Late Roman shrines were on sites that had previously been used in the Iron Age. The choice of this architectural style could have carried a subtle message.

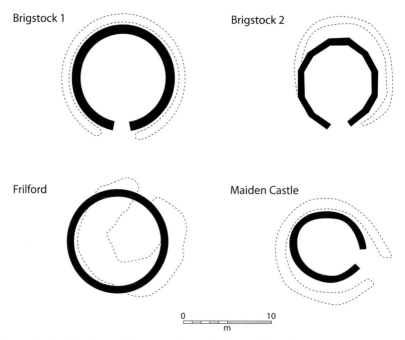

Figure 67 Outline plans of four circular and polygonal temples in Roman Britain.

TWO EXAMPLES

Two excavated sites, at opposite ends of Roman Britain, illustrate a number of these points. In the south there was the Roman town of Silchester, which replaced the capital of the Iron Age Atrebates (Clarke et al. 2007). In the north was the Roman villa at Holme House, Piercebridge, which was located only 50 kilometres south of Hadrian's Wall (Cool and Mason 2008; for a different interpretation, not followed here, see Willis 2010).

Silchester

Here, the evidence takes a distinctive form. Current excavations have recorded the remains of a range of timber structures which followed a different align-ment from most of the other buildings and may have conformed to the prevailing orientation of the Iron Age *oppidum* on the same site (Clarke et al. 2007). That has yet to be established, but it is clear that two rectilinear buildings, containing a total of six separate rooms, were laid out on an axis extending at an angle to the Roman street grid. They appear to be aligned on the midsummer sunrise. They do not belong to the earliest phase of Roman occupation and are dated between AD 70–80 and AD 125–150.

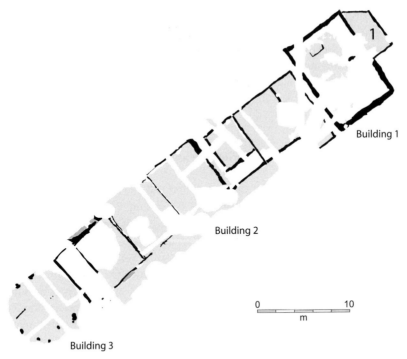

Figure 68 The relationship between a roundhouse (Building 3) and a range of rectangular buildings (Buildings 1 and 2) inside the Roman town at Silchester, England.

At one end of this alignment was a timber roundhouse (Figure 68). It is not clear whether it was a freestanding structure or whether it was screened by a rectilinear veranda or portico. It had a central hearth, but also contained a series of distinctive deposits. They focused on the south and south-east sides of the building, as well as its outer boundary, and included the burial of a baby, the cremated remains of sheep or goats, two intact pottery vessels, and several finds of brooches, which are interpreted as offerings. Similar deposits are frequently associated with pre-Roman sites, and the obvious emphasis on the south side of the structure has been recorded in other places. What is remarkable is that the example at Silchester is directly associated with a range of rectangular buildings and that it dates from a period when the Roman town was already well established.

In this case the evidence recalls some of the points made earlier. The building may have been inhabited, but it provided the focus for a series of votive deposits. The use of this structure was obviously governed by certain conventions concerning the character and locations of these offerings and it seems possible that the roundhouse was intended to play a specialized role. That would be particularly apparent if it had been concealed behind a screen that continued the alignment of the adjacent buildings. At the same time it is possible that the orientation of these structures referred to the way in which the town had been organized before it was reordered by the imposition of a grid. Was the construction of a circular building so long after the Roman Conquest intended as a deliberate reference to the past? The same could apply to the distinctive deposits that were associated with this structure.

Piercebridge

Piercebridge is located on the River Tees and was the site of a Roman fort, its civilian settlement, and a masonry villa which was one of the most northerly in Britain (Cool and Mason 2008). In addition, a series of votive offerings, mainly of coins and metalwork, was deposited in the river itself. They had a quite different character from the finds from excavation on dry land.

Not all these features originated at the same time. The site of the villa was first occupied by a timber roundhouse located at the centre of a square enclosure (Figure 69). The earliest coins and brooches found in the Tees may date from the same time, the Late Iron Age, or early Roman period. Towards the end of the first century AD a rectangular stone building, consisting of four rooms, was erected, and in the later second century it was enlarged by the addition of baths and a dining room. The villa was abandoned after a comparatively short period of use at about the time of the earliest military occupation on the opposite bank of the river.

The relationship between the villa and the roundhouse is of particular interest here. The circular building was in a middle of the earthwork

Piercebridge

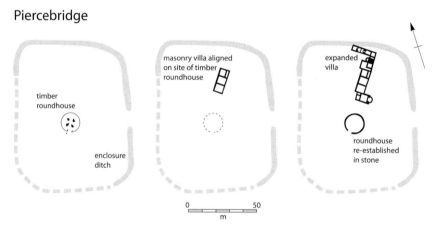

Figure 69 The structural sequence suggested by Cool and Mason (2008) at the Iron Age and Roman site of Piercebridge, England.

compound, although their entrances faced in different directions. The villa was aligned on the position of the timber structure, but it did not share the orientation of the enclosure itself. At first, the two structures do not seem to have been used together. The wooden roundhouse had been modified on several occasions but appears to have gone out of use when the villa was first constructed, for two water channels supplying the new building cut across the site of the older dwelling. When the villa was enlarged, however, it was equipped with a different water supply and at this stage the roundhouse was reinstated in its original position. This time it was constructed of stone. By that stage the earthwork enclosure had gone out of use, as one of the rooms added to the original design extended across the ditch.

Two features seem to be especially important. In this case the interplay between circular and rectangular structures took place well away from the core of the Roman province. There were other villas in north-east England, but this example was on the outer edge of the distribution of this kind of building. It was an appropriate place for Roman and indigenous styles of architecture to be combined. The artefacts deposited in the Tees illustrate the same mixture of native and non-local elements.

At the same time, when new rooms were added to that villa, the position of the roundhouse was re-established after a period of disuse. At this point the structure was rebuilt in stone. There seems to have been a conscious effort to recall, and even to monumentalize, the position of the earliest dwelling on the site. Now it was no longer isolated at the centre of a larger enclosure. The rectangular and circular structures formed a single architectural design not unlike that at Silchester.

THE END OF AN ARCHETYPE: THE CASTRO CULTURE IN PORTUGAL AND SPAIN

Such examples are intriguing, but, at present, it is difficult to tell how far they conform to a more general pattern. It is important to explore the same topic at a larger geographical scale. In order to do so the discussion turns to the relationship between rectilinear architecture and circular buildings in the Castro Culture of Portugal and Spain (Da Silva 1986; Gónzalez-Ruibal 2007; Ayán Vila 2008)

The term *castro* applies to the hillforts in the north-west of the Iberian Peninsula. Although most examples are found in Galicia and Northern Portugal, similar monuments occurred over an even wider area. For the most part they take the form of small defended enclosures, which are often circular in plan and contain a number of roundhouses. They have been studied for many years and it is unfortunate that so much of the research has been confined within national boundaries so that the Portuguese and Spanish examples are sometimes considered separately. It only adds to the confusion created by genuine regional distinctions among these remarkable monuments.

Even this simple definition needs qualification, for the nature of castros varied across time and space, and it is these distinctions that are especially relevant here. Their character undoubtedly changed between the Late Bronze Age and the early Roman period. These developments are most apparent from contrasts among the internal buildings and the ways in which they were organized (Ayán 2008). At the same time, some hillforts were very much larger than the others and have been interpreted as small towns. That is particularly true of a few Portuguese sites (Da Silva 1986).

Castros were only one expression of a tradition of circular domestic buildings that had begun by the Late Neolithic period. Although there are few well preserved settlements in this part of Iberia, nearly all the domestic dwellings that have been excavated can be identified as round or oval houses. The majority were built of wood, but they may be the local equivalent of the stone structures found on Copper Age defended sites further to the south and south-east (Jorge 1998; Ayán Vila 2008).

The use of hilltop locations for settlements in north-west Iberia is a feature of the Atlantic Late Bronze Age, and from the tenth and ninth centuries BC some of the sites were enclosed by earthworks or palisades. They have been described as '*proto-castros*' and produce distinctive artefact assemblages, including evidence of metalworking. Another characteristic is that they contain wooden roundhouses. They were succeeded by more monumental structures which were well established by the fifth century BC, although some were built significantly earlier. They were usually of stone, which applies not only to construction of defences which became such a striking feature of these places, but also to the domestic buildings inside them. They are the enclosures whose distinctive architecture is the defining characteristic of the Castro Culture (Gónzalez-Ruibal 2007; Ayán Vila 2008).

These monuments have two main characteristics. Although there are regional variations, the enclosures themselves are often circular and occupy prominent positions, often on hills (Figure 70). Those which are nearer to the coast enclose a number of roundhouses, but in many cases there is little to suggest that these buildings were grouped into compounds or that their spacing conformed to any overall design. Instead, it seems as if the dwellings were set apart from one another. They were all about the same size and there is nothing to indicate major social divisions among the inhabitants. The emphasis on circular constructions is so pervasive that Ayán Vila (2008) has suggested that the castro provided a model of the surrounding world.

Just as certain hilltop settlements had been drawn into the network of long distance contacts in the Late Bronze Age, north-west Iberia occupied a pivotal

Cividade de Terroso

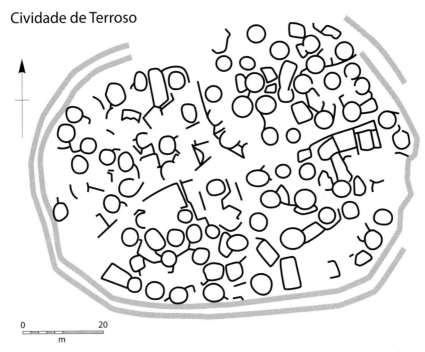

0   20

m

Figure 70 Plan of the Castro at Cividade de Terroso, Portugal, showing the curvilinear layout of the defences and the mixture of round and rectangular buildings in its interior.

position in the Iron Age. It was connected by sea not only with areas further up the Atlantic coast, but also with the West Mediterranean (Gónzalez-Ruibal 2004). That was especially important at a time that saw the expansion of Roman and Punic trade networks. Until recently, it was thought that castros retained their original character until the region came under Roman domination, but now it seems more likely that the nature of these monuments was already changing as a result of these contacts (Gónzalez-Ruibal 2007).

Certain hillforts in north-west Iberia illustrate two new developments. The first was the piecemeal adoption of rectilinear buildings. They took two different forms. The simplest examples were square and it was easy to fit them in between existing roundhouses on the same site. Others were larger rectangular structures. What both types share in common is that that were built in the midst of a group of circular structures and that these separate elements could be connected by straight sections of wall. They might also be grouped inside a small enclosure (Ayán Vila 2008). It is clear that the separate buildings fulfilled a variety of roles, from domestic dwellings to craft workshops, food stores, and animal pens. There was more than one of these compounds or 'courtyard houses' within a single hillfort. This way of organizing the internal space was very different from the dispersed distribution of roundhouses identified in the previous phase. In rare instances there is evidence that the reorganization of hillfort interiors went even further, and it seems as if these structures were linked to one another by streets. Ayán Vila (2008) suggests that the new layout was influenced by styles of building that were well established in the Mediterranean. This way of organizing the interior also allowed the construction of buildings which may have served the entire community.

Even if some of the inhabitants of the castros expressed their new allegiances through their use of an exotic style of architecture, the extent of this change should not be exaggerated. The creation of separate compounds within the hillforts must have reflected local social organization and so did the new patterns of communication within the settlement. Only the use of rectilinear structures was novel. Even then their adoption was selective. The compounds included roundhouses, as well as rectangular buildings, and the ways in which they were arranged suggest that, in some cases, the new structures respected the integrity of any circular dwellings that were already there. Space may have been reorganized on a limited scale, but there is little to suggest that roundhouses were being replaced at this stage. Instead, they were supplemented by another kind of structure. One reason for emphasizing the importance of traditional forms is that some of the buildings were decorated during this phase—the images focused on the position of the entrance. What is striking is that the new designs placed a special emphasis on *curvilinear* motifs (Ayán Vila 2008; Alves in press).

It was from the end of the second century BC that the change from round to rectilinear architecture reached its fullest extent. After that, many of the defended sites were abandoned. The most important development is seen at large 'proto-urban' sites in the north of Portugal, although the dating evidence provided by early excavations has its limitations. At enclosed settlements like Sanfins and Citânia de Briteiros the interior was arranged around a street grid which may have been inspired by the forms of settlements in Southern Europe (Da Silva 1986; Gónzalez-Ruibal 2007; Ayán Vila 2008; Figure 71). Rectangular buildings were established but roundhouses were also used. Again, there were communal buildings. Different kinds of structure were juxtaposed, but there seems to have been a formal subdivision of space within the defences. Perhaps different areas were allocated to particular households and their dependents. Sanfins provides persuasive evidence of this scheme.

At the same time, it is evident that the distribution of roundhouses inside certain enclosures does not conform to the new arrangement. These buildings are often at odds with the placing of rectilinear structures and their sites are poorly integrated into the overall configuration of boundary walls and streets. It is possible that the distinctive plan of such settlements results from an attempt to incorporate an existing network of roundhouses into a new, more

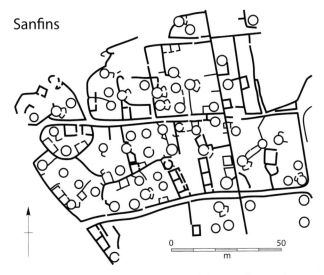

Sanfins

0   50
m

Figure 71 An area of circular and rectangular buildings and an embryonic street grid inside the Castro at Sanfins, Portugal.

rigid design. If that is true, then, once again, the change from one style of architecture to another did not go unopposed. It may be no accident that in the succeeding phase such places went out of use. After the Flavian period, which ended in AD 96, some of these sites were replaced in other locations by towns and villas whose layout could be agreed from the outset (Gónzalez-Ruibal 2007; Ayán Vila 2008).

In this case there were obvious tensions between the desire to reorder the forms of enclosed settlements and the way in which some of the occupants adhered to a traditional form of architecture. It is all too easy to suppose that it happened because the population was growing and space was at a premium, but it also involved ideas of order that were of fundamental importance to the people who lived there. Again, the interplay between rectilinear and circular architecture took on a political dimension.

THE END OF AN ARCHETYPE: EARLY MEDIEVAL IRELAND

Circular structures were equally common in Early Medieval Ireland and had an even longer history then the buildings in Portugal and Spain. In fact, they probably originated at about the same time, around 3000 BC when chambered tombs and domestic dwellings in all three countries shared this distinctive plan. In both these regions of Europe settlement sites are comparatively rare until the later Bronze Age. It was then that communities living along the Atlantic seaboard engaged in long distance exchange (Ruiz-Gálvez Priego 1998), but after that time the Irish sequence took a distinctive course. The settlements of the Iron Age have been difficult to find, perhaps because their inhabitants did not use pottery (Becker 2009). Enough is known to show that circular houses and curvilinear enclosures still remained important. This is demonstrated by another source of information, for it was during this phase that the royal centres discussed in Chapter 6 were established. They retained their significance into the Early Middle Ages. This period is considered here.

The clearest evidence comes from excavated monuments, most of which date from about AD 600 to 900, although their chronology may have been rather more extended. During this time the most prominent earthwork settlements are known as *raths* or *ringforts* and the commonest domestic structure was the roundhouse. Many examples of both types have been excavated. The sites are not uniformly distributed across the island and survive in greater numbers in the north-east and west, although it is known that others have been destroyed by modern agriculture (Stout 1997: Chapter 6). The main distinction between individual sites is created by the earthwork perimeter. In most cases it consists of a single bank and ditch, but there are a small number of sites with several concentric circuits. The entrances were usually towards the east and may reflect the position of the sunrise. A variant of the ringfort is the *cashel*, which is enclosed by a stone wall.

The term ringfort is a little misleading. They seem to have been self contained farms and, at best, their earthworks might have provided protection against a raid. These settlements played an important part in a pastoral economy at a time when the size of cattle herds was one way of measuring wealth. Inside the enclosures there were timber buildings, the earliest of which were circular and located towards the centre (Figure 72). They are usually interpreted as houses and were occasionally supplemented by the underground cellars known as souterrains. The number of roundhouses varied from site to site and, to a certain extent, the same is true of their sizes. It is likely that some of the structures were domestic dwellings, whilst others played an ancillary role. Even so, the emphasis on the circle remained important.

The earliest Irish laws shed some light on the ways in which the ringforts were used. It seems that two important measures of social position were the size of the enclosure and that of the principal dwelling. The *Crith Gablach*, which dates from the eighth century AD, specifies the relationship between status and the form of the earthwork perimeter:

> What is the due of a king...: ? Seven score feet...: are the measure of his stockade on every side. Seven feet are the thickness of its earthwork, and twelve

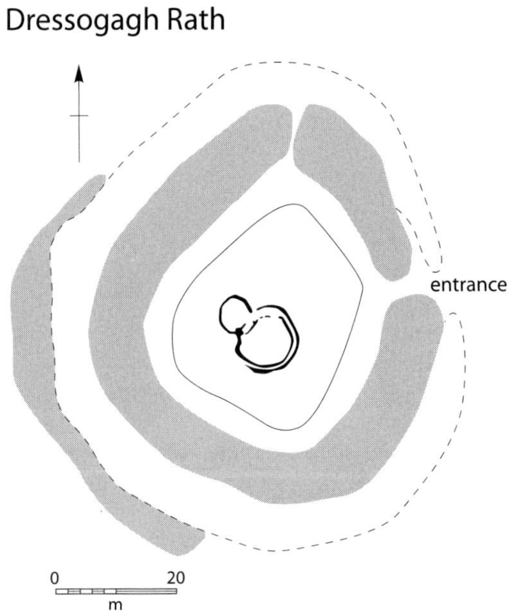

Dressogagh Rath

Figure 72 Simplified plan of the excavated ringfort of Dressogagh Rath, Ireland, showing the positions of two conjoined circular buildings.

feet its depth . . . : What is the rampart of vassalage? Twelve feet are the breadth of its opening and its depth and its measure towards the stockade. Thirty feet are its measure outwardly (Stout 1997: 113).

Stout observes that surviving earthworks often reflect this division. He also suggests that they can be divided into five distinct 'clusters' on the basis of their siting and morphology. The most striking differences concern the extent of the enclosures and the character of the earthworks that surround them. For the most part his classification is reflected by the finds from excavated sites (Comber 2008). Edwards takes a similar approach in her book *The Archaeology of Early Medieval Ireland*. She considers that:

Many larger and better defended sites, particularly multivallate ringforts, fulfilled a more complex role [than the others] . . . : Richer artefacts demonstrate the importation of luxury articles, and specialist craft pursuits suggest considerable wealth and higher status (1990: 33; see also Dowling 2011).

Even if the legal texts represent an ideal rather than the reality, it is clear that the construction and use of circular monuments followed certain conventions.

So did the use of roundhouses. Again, the *Crith Gablach* provides some information. Their diameters ranged from about five metres, which was the normal size of dwelling for an *ócaire* ('young lord') to buildings that were over eleven metres in diameter. They were considered suitable for kings. The smaller dwellings identified in this document resemble those most often found in excavation (Stout 1997: 118–19).

It is clear that the earthworks and houses referred to in the *Crith Gablach* were circular. So were a number of other structures in Ireland. It was certainly true of the royal centres, which may have reused the sites of older monuments, but it also applied to a significant number of enclosed graveyards. Perhaps more surprisingly, the same pattern extended to early Christian sites. Despite the presence of rectangular churches inside these enclosures, the boundary or *vallum* may have described a circle. Edwards reflects on this point:

> To the archaeologist many of the enclosures surrounding early ecclesiastical sites appear comparable with those encompassing secular ringforts ...: But, in addition, [they] seem to have been invested with the spiritual properties of sanctuary and divine protection. In this way the enclosures of the major church sites were not only similar to their secular counterparts, but also mirrored the Old Testament cities of refuge, and the concept of a 'holy of holies' in the centre ...: Surrounding areas of sanctuary ...: decreased in importance the further they were from the centre (1990: 106).

The early churches were rectangular buildings, but it does not seem that similar structures were particularly common. At the island hermitage of Illaunloughan in County Kerry, for instance, a stone oratory and a shrine were roughly square, but all four dwellings were roundhouses (White Marshall and Walsh 1998). Where there is evidence from other kinds of site, rectilinear structures replaced the circular buildings only gradually and there are defended settlements where both styles of architecture coexisted for some time. It is not clear why the change occurred, but in some areas the evidence for the continued use of ringforts and circular houses does not extend far beyond AD 900.

Several sources of inspiration have been suggested, but it is unlikely that the new developments were suggested by Roman architecture. Apart from a roughly square structure inside the Rath of the Synods at Tara (Grogan 2008), most of the rectilinear buildings were built too late to support this hypothesis. A second source may have been the Christian church, whilst a third might be Norse settlement in Ireland, which began as early as the ninth century AD (Doherty 1998; Ó Floinn 1998). What is striking is that, once it commenced, the change was not confined to domestic buildings, for circular earthwork enclosures became less frequent after that time. These developments only intensified after the Anglo-Norman invasion in the twelfth century.

This simple sequence is questioned in a recent study by O'Conor (1998), who points out that it is based on the results of excavations which have focused on only part of the island. He suggests that the use of ringforts and round-houses may well have continued in Gaelic-speaking areas, which were less susceptible to influence from outside. In fact, there is pictorial evidence to support his argument that circular architecture retained its importance in these regions. It may have been important to adhere to traditional norms as a way of asserting a local identity. An important clue is provided by FitzPatrick's study of royal inauguration sites during the Middle Ages. Some may have been ancient monuments, such as prehistoric barrows, and others were located amidst the remains of older earthworks, but there is no reason to doubt that many of them were newly built (FitzPatrick 2004). Her study considers the period between AD 1100 and 1600. It provides striking evidence that *round mounds* were deliberately selected for this purpose. For that reason, it seems possible that circular constructions kept their original significance for a longer period in Gaelic Ireland. It is a question that should be addressed by fieldwork.

The Irish case is informative for several reasons. Not only were circular monuments important throughout the island, they could be located amidst much older constructions that adhered to a similar plan. That is as true of Iron Age royal capitals as it is of the inauguration mounds that were built in the Middle Ages. At the same time, the circular archetype was represented in several different media. In the first millennium AD it extended from centres of Christian worship to the plans of enclosed farms, and from roundhouses to the decorated metalwork discussed in Chapter 3. The organization of different kinds of ringfort was regulated by early laws and so were the sizes of the roundhouses and the kinds of people who were permitted to live in them. It does not matter that these rules provided an ideal model that may not have been followed in reality. The fact that these circular structures were graded according to social rank is the revealing feature.

Most authors suppose that these norms broke down rapidly under outside influences, whether they came from Viking settlers or from the Anglo-Norman invaders. That may well be true, but it need not have happened everywhere. Again, it seems possible that traditional conceptions of space were kept alive for longer in places where local communities resisted outside pressures. In that respect, it may be that the Irish sequence, which seems to begin and end so abruptly, was as complex as that in any other region studied in this chapter.

Only one feature distinguishes this evidence from the remaining archaeological examples. Circular architecture pervaded every aspect of life in Early Medieval Ireland and yet this was a time when it had disappeared in most other parts of Europe. Here, it lasted longer than anywhere else, but in the end it lost its power. Perhaps that is why Giraldus Cambrensis, writing his *Topography of Ireland* not long after the Anglo-Norman conquest, was so confused by what he saw:

'To this day, as remains and traces of ancient times, you will find here *many trenches, very high and round* . . . : as well as walled forts which are still standing, although now empty and abandoned . . . : The people of Ireland have no use for castles' (Stout 1997: 115; my emphasis).

Part IV

Summing Up

10

From Centre to Circumference

DIALOGUES BETWEEN DESIGNS

This book began with one site in Ireland and closes with another.

The Loughcrew Hills in County Meath include at least twenty-five megalithic tombs, located on three summits along a prominent ridge. Many of them were investigated in the nineteenth century when Neolithic artefacts were found there. More recent work has been less extensive but features an analysis of the carved decoration inside these monuments, for the Loughcrew complex is one of the main concentrations of megalithic art in Europe (Shee Twohig 1981: 205–20).

Early excavation in the westernmost group of monuments had an unexpected result, for Cairn H contained a remarkable collection of artefacts which must have been deposited three thousand years after the tomb was built. They included bronze and iron rings, glass beads, and over four thousand bone flakes (Conwell 1873). A new excavation took place in 1943, but its results only added to the confusion and, perhaps for that reason, they were not published for more than six decades (Raftery 2009). They seemed to show that the artefacts, which obviously date from the Iron Age, were directly associated with the construction of the monument; today it seems more likely that they were a secondary deposit. When they were introduced to the site, the tomb may have been rebuilt. One reason why the bone flakes attracted so much attention is that a small number of them—about a hundred and fifty in all—were decorated in the same style as Iron Age metalwork. Most of the patterns are curvilinear and show the special emphasis on circles and arcs that characterize 'Celtic' art (Raftery 1984: 251–63).

This discovery illustrates a problem in Irish archaeology. A few stone tombs in other regions were decorated in a style that has been identified as either Neolithic or Iron Age (Shee Twohig 1981: 235–6), but in the case of the flakes from Loughcrew there is no such ambiguity. Not only do the incised patterns compare closely with those on metalwork, the decorated artefacts were associated with beads and rings dating to the end of the first millennium BC. Even so, two problems remain. Why were they deposited in such an unusual location? And why was the monument reconstructed when that happened? If the deposition of these objects had a special significance, might the same be true of their decoration?

It may be no coincidence that Cairn H contains a series of carved stones which can still be recognized today. So does its neighbour, Cairn L, where a few more bone flakes were found. These designs date from the Neolithic period, but, again, they are curvilinear. Cairn H includes six surfaces decorated with concentric circles, spirals, and arcs. Only one of the panels carries an angular design. The same is true at Cairn L where there are at least thirteen groups of curvilinear images on the stones and only three other panels (Shee Twohig 1981: 208–9, 211–13).

In each case the Neolithic motifs would have been recognizable to later visitors to the tomb and it seems much more than a coincidence that some of the Iron Age artefacts deposited there were decorated with curvilinear designs. They were not *copies* of the Neolithic panels, nor did they depart from the repertoire of La Tène art, but both groups of images shared the same predilection for circles and arcs. They were created in a specialized medium and executed at a distinctive location.

The circle was the common element and obviously was significant during the Neolithic and Iron Age phases at Loughcrew (Figure 73). For that reason the carved panels might have seemed comprehensible long after they were made. There was no attempt to change the patterns on the walls, even though there was a tradition of stone carving in Iron Age Ireland (Raftery 1994: 162, 181–2). The creation of new designs on the bone flakes did not involve the *rejection* of the older decoration. Instead, there was a kind of *dialogue* between both groups of images.

The same was true in the Castro Culture of north-west Iberia, although the evidence is less compelling. A number of these Iron Age hillforts were located on, or very close to, prehistoric rock carvings (Rey Castiñeira and Soto-Barreiro 2001). Although the date of these images is controversial—the oldest may originate in the Late Neolithic period, the Chalcolithic, or the Early Bronze Age (Peña and Rey 2001; Santos Estévez 2005)—it is clear that they were of considerable antiquity when the fortified settlements were established. In certain cases it seems likely that the petroglyphs were left exposed and were respected when their sites were occupied. There are two reasons for suggesting that the relationship between them was significant. The carved motifs were predominantly circular, just as many castros were circular, and most of the dwellings inside the earthworks were roundhouses. At the same time, these buildings were associated with a new style of decoration that was predominantly curvilinear (Ayán Vila 2008; Alves in press); it featured briefly in Chapter 9. The relationship between the two traditions of stone carving may have gone even further, for in north-west Iberia there are groups of decorated

Loughcrew

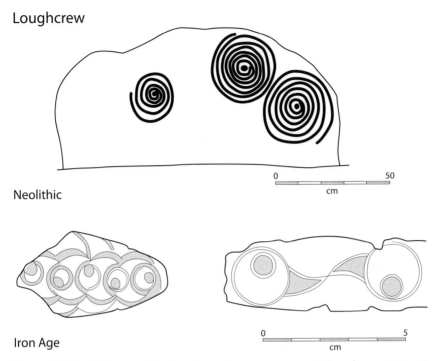

Neolithic

Iron Age

Figure 73 Neolithic carved designs from the passage grave at Loughcrew Cairn H, Ireland, and details of the decoration on two of the Iron Age bone flakes from the same monument.

outcrops with images in both styles (Santos Estévez 2008). At present, it seems likely that their periods of use were separated by a significant interval.

In this case, two possibilities arise. The visual culture of the Iron Age might have been suggested by the remains surviving from the past. An alternative is the interpretation favoured at Loughcrew. The oldest images may have been respected or even renewed because they included elements that seemed important to people in a later period. In this case it was the special importance of the circle (Alves in press). Similar concerns were expressed by the distinctive architecture of the late first millennium BC.

HISTORIES OF THE CIRCLE

The Iberian example combined circular designs and circular monuments. Both have featured in separate chapters of this book. Now it is time to draw these patterns together.

The previous section commented on two cases in which ancient art exerted an influence long after it had been created. To some extent that may have happened because it was visible and easy to recognize, but it seems just as likely that the later designs were intended as a conscious reference to the past. In each case the link was made because the societies involved placed such an emphasis on circular designs. At the same time, connections of this kind extend into other media, even in the same parts of Europe. Thus, the Irish royal centres discussed in Chapter 6 developed around a series of ancient monuments, in particular passage tombs which shared their circular outline. In fact, a Neolithic tomb amongst the earthworks on the Hill of Tara is decorated with a curvilinear design (O'Sullivan 2005). Similarly, the distribution of castros extended across a region of Iberia with a large number of circular mounds and cairns. They had gone out of use long before the first hillforts were built. In this case there is less evidence for a direct relationship between these structures, but their presence in the same parts of Portugal and Spain cannot have gone unnoticed.

In fact, there is evidence that the circular ordering of space was not only recognizable among these ancient monuments, it retained its power even when it was expressed in other media. The common link was usually the experience of living in a roundhouse, for it inculcated a particular idea of order among prehistoric communities. Because it formed such a fundamental part of daily life, it would have had a more immediate impact than the curvilinear images on metalwork that was displayed on special occasions. Once it had been established both in Ireland and Iberia, the architecture of the roundhouse proved to be extremely long lived. The same was true in Britain and across parts of the West Mediterranean.

One reason why this might have happened is that circular dwellings frequently provided the prototypes for large public monuments, whether they were timber circles or stone circles like those in the British Isles, the passage graves distributed along the Atlantic coastline from Portugal to Ireland, or more specialized structures like Sardinian nuraghi. The forms of many of these buildings referred to the conventions of domestic architecture, but they did so on a gigantic scale. That distinctive relationship can be identified in many different phases, from the chambered tombs built at the start of the Neolithic period to the royal centres of Early Medieval Ireland.

Rectangular buildings, however, had a smaller influence. Although there was a direct relationship between the last Neolithic longhouses and the first long mounds, it had few parallels during later periods of prehistory. The main exceptions are some massive buildings in the Late Neolithic of Western France, the Bronze Age cult houses of Scandinavia, and the so-called 'long barrows' which date from the Bronze Age and Iron Age in the Low Countries; the structures in Northern Europe were associated with cemeteries and were never built on an extravagant scale. Here, it was the longhouses themselves that became more elaborate (Herschend 2001). It happened in the Early Bronze Age and again in the first millennium AD. In fact, the main differences between the feasting halls of Late Iron Age Scandinavia and the domestic dwellings of the same period are their size and internal organization.

The second chapter discussed the interplay between two ways of interpreting circular dwellings. The first considered the lifespan of these buildings and the difficulties of enlarging them, whilst the other placed more emphasis on the symbolic significance of the roundhouse. Those approaches were not necessarily incompatible, but the weight placed on these separate factors has changed during the history of archaeology. Whatever the practicalities of living in a circular dwelling, people must have been aware of its distinctive ground plan and its relationship to the land and the sky. The alignment of the doorway as the principal source of light would have been an important consideration. Where some communities adopted another style of building—and no doubt invested it with a similar weight of symbolism—others adhered to traditional norms and reinforced them by constructing monuments which expressed the same concerns through public architecture. The more they identified the layout of the house with a wider system of belief, the more difficult it would have been to adopt an unfamiliar form of dwelling. Their distinctive shape must have been significant, for there are very few instances in which circular *monuments* were replaced by rectangular examples. At the same time where round *houses* were finally relinquished under social or political pressures, as happened in Iron Age Sicily and again in Roman Britain, their basic form remained important but was used for temples. Even if mobile communities had practical reasons for occupying circular buildings, those structures took on added connotations until they became more difficult to abandon. In their final manifestation they could be sacred monuments, far removed from their original roles.

The protracted history of the roundhouse is also a story of resistance to outside influence. The functional models put forward in the 1960s and 1970s considered the advantages of changing from an inefficient circular dwelling to a more adaptable rectangular house. The combination of increasing sedentism and growing community size made this development appear inevitable, yet it did not happen everywhere. There were communities who had made the change from hunting and gathering to farming but were slow to alter the shapes of their domestic buildings, and others again who elected not to do so. The practical advantages of rectangular architecture seem obvious, but some people in the past were unwilling to follow the trend, and it was those communities and their descendents who enshrined the circular form in monumental structures directed to the dead and the supernatural. The link between specialized monuments and domestic buildings would have made it even harder to envisage other conceptions of space. Of course, there were specialized round or oval structures at an early date—the most famous example is Göbekli Tepe (Schmidt 2006)—but, as monumental architecture became more widely distributed in Southern and Western Europe, the circular archetype took on a greater significance.

So far this account has emphasized the increasingly close relationship between circular houses and monumental buildings. After the Neolithic period there were few monuments whose forms were inspired by rectilinear dwellings, but that did not preclude the development of circular structures in areas characterized by longhouses. In most cases they were quite short lived. Examples include the Central European roundels considered in Chapter 7. They were impressive earthworks and must have been built by large numbers of people, but they were established in a world where longhouses were firmly established. The same applies to the first causewayed enclosures in continental Europe. It is equally true of domestic buildings, as round-houses were constructed in the Middle Neolithic period in the north of France. Again, they were not used over a lengthy period (Laporte and Tinévez 2004). Perhaps local communities had become too accustomed to life in rectangular dwellings.

There is an important exception to the trend, and it proves very revealing. Many parts of Northern and Western Europe contain circular mounds and cairns, the oldest of which are associated with Neolithic dolmens and passage graves. Long after most of the circular enclosures had gone out of use, round barrows and round cairns were still being built. Their distribution changed over time, but in many cases their history extends well into the first millennium AD. This tradition of mound building was extraordinarily long lived, but in Northern and Central Europe it ran in parallel, not with circular dwellings, but with the use of longhouses. The contrast between rectilinear and circular forms remained important for up to two thousand years.

Chapter 3 raised the possibility that the same distinction between rectangles and circles extended into other media and could be recognized from such varied sources as house decoration and the treatment of artefacts. Although there were obvious exceptions, it identified cases in which the people who lived in roundhouses employed linear designs on their pottery and metalwork. Conversely, there were instances in which the occupants of longhouses made bronze and gold objects embellished with curvilinear designs. The contexts in which they have been found include graves and votive deposits. On one level it suggests that these pieces may have been appropriate offerings to the dead or the supernatural. On another, it raises the possibility that the same idea might apply to the circular shape of the round barrow. Of course, this idea will come as no surprise to people who believe that the circle has mystical properties—a fashionable idea that actually goes back to Pythagoras (Ingold 2011)—but here the argument depends on purely archaeological evidence. In many parts of prehistoric Europe the distinction between the dead and the living, the sacred and the profane, may have been expressed by the use of these basic forms. In other areas structures of all kinds conformed to a circular template. It seems possible that, over the course of time, it took on so many connotations that it became increasingly difficult for communities to envisage any other way of ordering space.

GEOGRAPHIES OF THE CIRCLE

It is obvious that the use of space followed very different trajectories from one part of Europe to another. The adoption of new kinds of architecture was influenced by differences of environment, settlement pattern, and economy, but it was also affected by broader patterns of communication. For example, curvilinear architecture, extending from the forms of houses to those of public monuments, was most apparent in regions which were connected by sea. That does not imply that all those links were maintained over long periods or that some of them might not have been severed at different times in the past. Circular buildings are a significant feature of parts of the West Mediterranean, especially islands such as Sardinia and Corsica, and are equally important along the Atlantic coastline from Spain and Portugal as far north as Orkney. There are a few examples on the French side of the Channel. It would be wrong to suppose that such places were cut off from wider contacts. Rather, there were times when some, or all, of them were closely linked to one another (Cunliffe 2001). They include the Neolithic period, which saw the building of megalithic tombs, and the Chalcolithic phase, which witnessed the adoption of metallurgy and Beaker ceramics. Even the distribution of metalwork associated with the 'Atlantic' Late Bronze Age extends to the Mediterranean. Some of the same regions were linked by seaborne trade in the late pre-Roman Iron Age and areas along the western limits of Europe formed new connections during the early post-Roman period. That is when there is evidence for small-scale migration between Britain, Ireland, Brittany, and Galicia.

Compare this with the situation in Central and Northern Europe. Again, there were some connections by sea, but even more extended over land. In one direction, they included the North Atlantic, the English Channel, and the Baltic, and, in the other, they reached southwards along major rivers like the Rhine (Kristiansen 1998). For the purpose of this discussion all these regions shared important characteristics. Their inhabitants occupied rectangular buildings, often, but not always, longhouses, and the monument type with the most extended history was the round barrow. The distribution of these mounds changed over the course of time, but they were most common along the Channel coast, in the Low Countries, Germany, and south Scandinavia.

The lengthy history of these earthworks is illustrated by the way in which older structures were reused at different times between the Late Bronze Age and the Viking period. This practice has been investigated in Germany (Sopp 1999), Denmark (Pedersen 2006), Sweden, and Norway (Thäte 2007). There was considerable diversity, but all these studies show that round mounds were selected for new burials in preference to rectilinear monuments.

Thus, there was a clear division between one zone in which circular structures predominate and another with rectilinear houses and round mounds. That duality is encapsulated by the title of Cunliffe's recent book *Europe between the Oceans* (Cunliffe 2008). The distinction was partly a product of geography, but it was a legacy of history, too.

The clearest demonstration of this point comes from the Neolithic period. It seems clear that large areas of the continent were colonized by farming communities. In an early phase, settlements in south-east Europe contained groups of small rectangular buildings that sometimes developed into mounds. The occupation of new areas to the north and west saw the development of the longhouse. It is only when the process of expansion was checked in the fifth millennium BC that there is much evidence of monuments. Although they included earthwork enclosures with a variety of different plans, the most striking structures were rectangular mounds and cairns built in the image of a domestic dwelling. They were still constructed after the pattern of settlement had changed. Although the Linear Pottery Culture shows some local variations, there was also a basic continuity, and people seem to have acknowledged that their ancestors shared the same area of origin. That is suggested by the introduction of *spondylus* shells from Southern Europe and possibly by the orientations of their domestic buildings (Bradley 2002a: 26–9).

There was less uniformity along the other main axis in Neolithic Europe, which extended from the West Mediterranean along the Atlantic coastline, perhaps because indigenous communities played a greater role in the adoption of agriculture. It was in this zone that a series of circular tombs was established. It is a moot point how far they were conceived as copies of round-houses, but they certainly provided a point of departure for the invention of other kinds of monument. In this case people may not have thought that their communities shared a common origin, but there is good evidence of long distance exchange along the western margin of Europe (Klassen et al. 2011). The basic outline seems clear despite the fact that both the zones described here overlapped between Western France and Scandinavia.

During later periods contacts along both axes waxed and waned. There were times of comparative isolation, like the Late Neolithic period on either side of the Channel, and there were other phases when long distance connections resumed. Obvious examples include the adoption of Bell Beakers or the links that developed between the Nordic Bronze Age and Central Europe

(Kristiansen and Larsson 2005). What is striking is how often the new connections extended across the same regions as the first introduction of agriculture. Just as Neolithic Europe has been divided between the Linear Pottery Culture, on the one hand, and the various styles of Impressed Ware on the other, by the first millennium BC a similar division had emerged between the Urnfield Culture and the Atlantic Bronze Age (Figure 74). Although domestic architecture plays little part in the identification of these traditions, the distinction between local building styles is obvious.

That is important, as the character of the built environment would have played a part in determining how different communities perceived the world. It would also affect their dealings with other people whose settlements and monuments would have appeared more, or less, familiar to them. There is reason to suppose that people who have been brought up in settlements of circular buildings feel uncomfortable when they are faced with rectangular structures (Segall et al. 1966; Lawrence and Low 1990). Conversely, the inhabitants of longhouses might have been perplexed by the existence of roundhouses, especially if their experience of circular constructions was restricted to burial mounds. Where the forms of public architecture were influenced by domestic prototypes, as clearly happened in parts of Atlantic Europe, they would have had a particular impact. How would travellers who lived in a settlement of rectangular buildings have reacted to houses and hillforts where the circle was the dominant form? That would pose a special problem if the remains of older monuments conformed to the same organization of space.

It is obvious that such distinctions became increasingly evident over time as fewer communities adhered to traditional practices and beliefs. That may make it easier to understand the growing contrast between Southern and Western Europe and regions further to the north and east. Perhaps the distinctions between these zones originated largely by accident as agriculture was adopted from different sources and by different groups of people. In the course of time those divisions reinforced one another. Is it possible that the inhabitants of particular regions came to recognize their isolation? This might have encouraged them to develop links with other communities. Economic factors were very important, but they may not have been the only reason for forming new alliances.

By the first millennium BC a number of societies along the western edge of Europe would have shared the same perception of space and a process that had started almost by chance could have assumed a political dimension. Through the construction of monumental architecture, communities from Ireland to Iberia acquired a keener awareness of their own identities. It was only when their lands were taken over by Roman, Saxon, Viking, or Norman invaders that the situation changed. Until that happened, they remained the last inhabitants of a circular world.

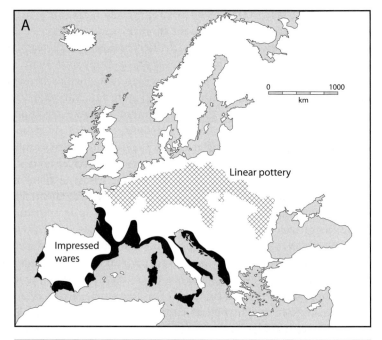

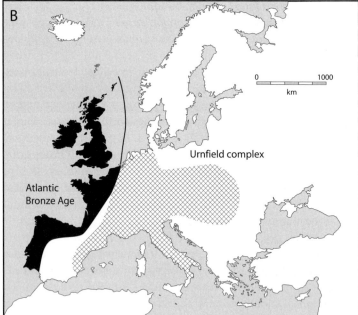

Figure 74 The dual character of prehistoric Europe during the Neolithic period and the Late Bronze Age, emphasizing the important division between east and west in both phases.

EPILOGUE: THE VIEW FROM LOUGHCREW

The best way of characterizing the distinctiveness of that world is by considering one of its latest manifestations. Circular forms maintained their importance in Ireland for longer than anywhere else. They were first expressed by the distinctive architecture of Neolithic tombs and their ultimate expression was probably the Early Medieval ringfort. In ancient Ireland nearly every building was circular and the same applies to stone and earthwork enclosures. Barrows and cairns shared a similar outline. Even the visual culture of both the Neolithic period and the Iron Age placed a special emphasis on curvilinear designs. To some extent the same applies to the art style described as 'Ultimate La Tène'. The landscape around Loughcrew illustrates nearly all these elements.

The introduction to this chapter mentioned the juxtaposition of Neolithic and Iron Age designs inside Cairn H, but there is more to say about Loughcrew. All twenty-five tombs on the high ground share a circular ground plan and no fewer than fourteen of them were decorated with pecked designs, among which both circles and spirals feature prominently (Shee Twohig 1981: 205–20). Other circular designs were made on natural surfaces in the surrounding landscape, most likely during the same period. A further example of the same style of rock art is a decorated cist associated with a Bronze Age round barrow. In this case the decorated surface is covered with concentric rings (Shee 1972).

It was not the only prehistoric monument on the lower ground below the passage tombs at Loughcrew. There were two stone circles in the area and a number of freestanding monoliths. In addition to the barrow with the decorated cist slab, there was also a round cairn attributed to the Early Bronze Age. Other structures were associated with the dead, for an inventory of the ancient monuments (Moore 1987) records three ring barrows and a ring cairn in the vicinity. The one linear monument in the entire area is an earthwork cursus (Newman 1999: 141–3); it has never been excavated and its age is unknown. The only other element which departs from a circular outline is a rectangular enclosure.

The area beyond the megalithic cemetery includes a large number of monuments which are likely to be of Early Medieval origin. There are no fewer than fourteen ringforts. As many as four examples have more than one circuit of earthworks and are likely to have been of higher status than the others. There is also a stone enclosure described as a cashel. Little is known about the features inside them, but three souterrains have been identified. In addition, the inventory records another five circular enclosures whose dates and functions are unknown. More examples have been found by remote sensing (Shell 2005). Several contain features which may mark the positions of roundhouses. It is not clear whether there are so many circular monuments because of the proximity of the Neolithic tombs, but most of the classes of monument discussed in earlier parts of the book are represented in this small area.

Like the royal centre at Uisneach with which Chapter 1 began, the chambered tombs at Loughcrew overlook an exceptionally wide area. No fewer than eighteen counties can be recognized between the hilltop and the horizon. Were such locations chosen because they conformed to a particular idea of order? Were special structures built there because they epitomized a circular conception of space? It is not possible to tell, but it is right to ask the question.

References

Akkermans, P. and Schwartz, G. (2003), *The Archaeology of Syria*. Cambridge: Cambridge University Press.

Almagro Basch, A. and Arribas, A. (1963), *El poblado y la necropolis megaliticos de Los Millares*. Madrid: Consejo Superior de Investigaciones Científicas.

Alves, L. B. (in press), 'The circle, the cross and the limits of abstraction and figuration in north-western Iberian rock art'. In: A. Cochrane and A. Jones (eds) *Visualising the Neolithic: Abstraction, Figuration, Performance, Representation*. Oxford: Oxbow.

Andersen, N. (1997), *The Sarup Enclosures, volume 1*. Moesgaard: Jutland Archaeological Society.

Andersen, N. (2009), 'Sarupområdet på Sydvestfyn i slutningen af 4. årtusinde f. Kr'. In: A. Schülke (ed.) *Plads og rum i tragtbaegerkulturen*, pp. 25–44. Copenhagen: Kongelige Nordiske Oldskriftselskab.

Andrén, A. (2004), 'I skuggan av Yggdrasil. Trädet mellan idé och realitet i nordisk tradition'. In: A. Andrén, K. Jennbert and C. Raudvere (eds) *Ordning mot kaos— studier av nordisk förkristen kosmologi*: 389–430. Lund: Nordic Academic Press.

Andrén, A. (2006), 'A world of stone. Warrior culture, hybridity, and Old Norse cosmology'. In: A. Andrén, K. Jennbert and C. Raudvere (eds) *Old Norse Religion in Long-term Perspectives*, pp. 33–8. Lund: Nordic Academic Press.

Aner, E. and Kersten, K. (1973), *Die Funde der älteren Bronzezeit des nordischen Kreises in Dänemark, Schleswig-Holstein und Niedersachsen, 1*. Copenhagen: National Museum.

Aner, E. and Kersten, K. (1978), *Die Funde der älteren Bronzezeit des nordischen Kreises in Dänemark, Schleswig-Holstein und Niedersachsen, 4*. Copenhagen: National Museum.

Anthony, D. (2010), *The Lost World of Old Europe. The Danube Valley, 5000–3500 BC*. Princeton: Princeton University Press.

Armit, I. (2003), *Towers in the North: the Brochs of Scotland*. Stroud: Tempus.

Arnoldussen, S. (2008), *A Living Landscape. Bronze Age Settlement Sites in the Dutch River Area c. 2000–800 BC*. Leiden: Sidestone Press.

Artursson, M., Linderoth, T., Nilsson, M.-L. and Svensson, M. (2003), 'Biggnadskultur I södra & mellersta Skandinavien'. In: M. Artursson (ed.) *I det neolitiska rummet*, pp. 40–171. Lund: Riksantikvarieämbetet.

Ashbee, P. (1960), *The Bronze Age Round Barrow in Britain*. London: Phoenix House.

Ashmore, P. (1999), 'Radiocarbon dating: avoiding errors by avoiding mixed samples', *Antiquity*, 73: 124–30.

Ayán Vila, X. (2008), 'A round Iron Age: the circular house in the hillforts of the Northwestern Iberian Peninsula', *e-Keltoi* 6: 903–1003.

Bailey, D. (2000), *Balkan Prehistory. Exclusion, Incorporation and Identity*. London: Routledge.

Bailey, D., Cochrane, A. and Zambelli, J. (2010), *Unearthed: A Comparative Study of Jomon Dogu and Neolithic Figurines*. Norwich: Sainsbury Centre for Visual Art.

Banck-Burgess, J. (1999), *Hochdorf IV. Die Textilfunde aus dem späthallstattzeitlichen Fürstengrab*. Stuttgart: Theiss.

Banning, E. (2011), 'So fair a house: Göbekli Tepe and the identification of temples in the Pre-pottery Neolithic of the Near East', *Current Anthropology*, 52: 619–60.

Bartoloni, G., Bursanelli, F., D'Atri, V. and De Santis, A. (1987), *Le urne a capanne rivenute in Italia*. Rome: Bretschneider.

Bastide, T.A. (2000), *Les structures d'habitat rural protohistorique dans le sud-ouest de l'Angleterre et le nord-ouest de la France*. Oxford: British Archaeological Reports.

Becker, K. (2009), 'Iron Age Ireland—finding an invisible people'. In: G. Cooney, K. Becker, J. Coles, M. Ryan and S. Sievers (eds.) *Relics of Old Decency. Archaeological Studies in Later Prehistory*, pp. 351–61. Dublin: Wordwell.

Behrens, H. (1981), 'The first "Woodhenge" in Middle Europe', *Antiquity*, 55: 172–8.

Benítez de Lugo Enrich, L. (2010), *Las motillas y el Bronce de La Mancha*. Ciudad Real: Anthropos.

Bertemes, F. and Spatzier, A. (2008), 'Pömmelte—ein Mitteldeutsches Henge-Monument aus Holz', *Archäologie in Deutschland*, 2008: 6–11.

Beskow Sjöberg, M. (1987), *Ölands järnålders gravfält, volume 1*. Kalmar: Högskolan Kalmar.

Besse, M. and Desideria, J. (2005), 'Bell Beaker diversity: Settlements, burials and ceramics'. In: M. Rojo-Guerra, R. Garrido-Pena and I. García-Martínez de Lagrán (eds) *El Campaniforme en la Península Ibérica y su contexto europeo*, pp. 89–105. Valladolid: Universidad de Valladolid.

Biehl, P. (2007), 'Enclosing places: a contextual approach to cult and religion in Neolithic Central Europe'. In: D. Barraclough and C. Malone (eds) *Cult in Context*, pp. 173–82. Oxford: Oxbow.

Biehl, P. (2010), 'Measuring time in the European Neolithic? The function and meaning of Central European circular enclosures'. In: I. Morley and C. Renfrew (eds) *The Archaeology of Measurement. Comprehending Heaven, Earth and Time in Ancient Societies*, pp. 229–43. Cambridge: Cambridge University Press.

Bietti Sestieri, A. (2010), *L'italia nell'età del bronce e del ferro: dalle palafitte a Romolo (2200–700 A.C.)*. Rome: Carocci.

Binford, L. (2001), *Constructing Frames of Reference: an Analytical Method for Archaeological Theory Building among Hunter Gatherer and Environmental Data Sets*. Berkeley: University of California Press.

Bittel, K. (1998), *Die keltischen Viereckschanzen*. Stuttgart: Theiss.

Bittel, K., Schiek, S. and Müller, D. (1990), *Die keltischen Viereckschanzen*. Stuttgart: Theiss.

Blair, J. (1995), 'Anglo-Saxon pagan shrines and their prototypes', *Anglo-Saxon Studies in Archaeology and History*, 8: 1–28.

Blake, E. (1999), 'Sardinia's nuraghi: four millennia of becoming', *World Archaeology*, 30: 59–71.

Blake, E. (2001), 'Constructing a Nuragic locale. The spatial relationship between tombs and towers in Bronze Age Sardinia', *American Journal of Archaeology*, 105: 145–62

Blanton, R. (1994), *Houses and Households: a Comparative Study*. New York: Plenum Press.

Bloch, M. and Parry, J. (1982), 'Introduction: death and the regeneration of life'. In: M. Bloch and J. Parry (eds) *Death and the Regeneration of Life*, pp. 1–44. Cambridge: Cambridge University Press.

Borg, K., Näsman, U. and Wegraeus, E. (1976), *Eketorp. Fortifications and Settlement on Öland, Sweden. The Monument.* Stockholm: Royal Academy of Letters, History and Antiquities.

Borges, J.L. (1965), *Fictions.* London: Calder.

Borić, D. (2003), '"Deep time", metaphor, mnemonic and apotropaic practices at Lepenski Vir', *Journal of Social Archaeology*, 3: 41–75.

Bourdieu, P. (1990), *The Logic of Practice.* Cambridge: Polity Press.

Bourgeois, J. (1998), 'La nécropole laténienne et Gallo-Romaine d'Ursel-Rozenstraat (Flandre oriental, Belgique)', *Revue Archéologique de Picardie*, 1: 111–25.

Bourgeois, Q. and Fontijn, D. (2008), 'Bronze Age houses and barrows in the Low Countries: an overview'. In: S. Arnoldussen and H. Fokkens (eds) *Bronze Age Settlements in the Low Countries*, pp. 41–57. Oxford: Oxbow.

Bradley, R. (1998), *The Significance of Monuments.* London: Routledge.

Bradley, R. (2000a), *An Archaeology of Natural Places.* London: Routledge.

Bradley, R. (2000b), *The Good Stones. A New Investigation of the Clava Cairns.* Edinburgh: Society of Antiquaries of Scotland.

Bradley, R. (2002a), *The Past in Prehistoric Societies.* London: Routledge.

Bradley, R. (2002b), 'Death and the regeneration of life: a new interpretation of house urns in Northern Europe', *Antiquity*, 76: 372–7.

Bradley, R. (2005a), *The Moon and the Bonfire. An Investigation of three Stone Circles in North-east Scotland.* Edinburgh: Society of Antiquaries of Scotland.

Bradley, R. (2005b), *Ritual and Domestic Life in Prehistoric Europe.* Abingdon: Routledge.

Bradley, R. (2007), *The Prehistory of Britain and Ireland.* Cambridge, Cambridge University Press.

Bradley, R. (2009), *Image and Audience. Rethinking Prehistoric Art.* Oxford: Oxford University Press.

Bradley, R. (2011), *Stages and Screens. An Investigation of Four Henge Monuments in Northern and North-eastern Scotland.* Edinburgh: Society of Antiquaries of Scotland.

Bradley, R. and Fraser, E. (2011), 'Round barrows and the boundary between the living and the dead'. In: D. Mullin (ed.) *Places In Between: The Archaeology of Social, Cultural and Geographical Borders and Borderlands*, pp. 40–7. Oxford: Oxbow.

Bradley, R. and Phillips, T (2008), 'Display, disclosure and concealment: the organisation of raw materials in the chambered tombs of Bohuslän', *Oxford Journal of Archaeology*, 27: 1–13.

Bradley, R., Phillips, T., Richards, C. and Webb, M. (2001), 'Decorating the houses of the dead: incised and pecked motifs in Orkney chambered tombs', *Cambridge Archaeological Journal*, 11: 45–67.

Bradley, R. and Widholm, D. (2007), 'Bronze Age cosmology in the South-west Baltic: a framework for research'. In: D. Widholm (ed.) *Stone Ships. The Sea and the Heavenly Journey*, pp. 13–48. Kalmar: Kalmar University.

Brandt, J. and Karlsson, L. (2001), *From Huts to Houses; Transformations of Ancient Societies*. Stockholm: Paul Aströms Forlag.

Breuil, H. (1936), 'Presidential address', *Proceedings of the Prehistoric Society of East Anglia*, 7: 289–322.

Brinkkemper, O. and van Wijngarden-Bakker, L. (2005), 'All round farming. Food production in the Bronze Age and Iron Age'. In: L. Louwe Kooijmans, P. van den Broeke, H. Fokkens and A. van Gijn (eds) *The Prehistory of the Netherlands, volume 2*, pp. 491–512. Amsterdam: Amsterdam University Press.

Brunaux, J-L. (1991), *Les sanctuaires celtiques et leur rapport avec le monde méditerranéen*. Paris: Errance.

Brunaux, J-L. (2009), *Les temples du sanctuaire gallo-romain de Ribermont-sur-Ancre*. Saint-Germain-en-Laye: Éditions Commios.

Brunaux, J-L., Meniel, P. and Poplin, F. (1985), *Gournay 1. Fouilles sur le sanctuaire et l'oppidum*. Révue archéologique de Picardie, numéro spécial.

Buchenschutz, O., Olivier, L. and Ailliéres, A-M. (1989), *Les Viereckschanzen et les enceintes quadrilaterales en Europe celtique*. Paris: Errance.

Bueno Ramirez, P. and de Balbín Behrmann, R. (2002), 'L'art mégalithique péninsulaire et l' art mégalithique de la façade atlantique: un modèle de capillarité appliqué à l'art post-paléolithique européen', *L'anthropologie*, 106: 603–46.

Burl, A., (1993), *From Carnac to Callanish; the Prehistoric Stone Rows and Avenues of Britain, Ireland and Brittany*. New Haven: Yale University Press.

Burl, A. (2000), *The Stone Circles of Britain, Ireland and Brittany*. New Haven: Yale University Press.

Burrow, S. (2010), 'Bryn Celli Ddu passage grave, Anglesey: alignment, construction, date and ritual', *Proceedings of the Prehistoric Society*, 76: 249–70.

Calado, M. (2002), 'Standing stones and natural outcrops: the role of ritual monuments in the Neolithic transition of the Central Alentejo'. In: C. Scarre (ed.) *Monuments and Landscape in Atlantic Europe*, pp. 17–35. London: Routledge.

Cámara Serrano, J., Alfonso Marrero, J. and Spanedda, L. (2010), *Links Between Megalithism and Hypogeism in Western Mediterranean Europe*. Oxford: British Archaeological Reports.

Carandini, A. and Capelli, R. (2007), *Roma: Romolo, Remo e la fondazioni della città*. Milan: Eleta.

Card, N. (2010), 'Neolithic temples of the Northern Isles', *Current Archaeology*, 31.1: 12–19.

Carsten, J. and Hugh-Jones, S. (1995), 'Introduction'. In: J. Carsten and S. Hugh-Jones (eds) *About the House. Lévi-Strauss and Beyond*, pp. 1–46. Cambridge: Cambridge University Press.

Carver, M. (2005), *Sutton Hoo: a Seventh-century Princely Burial Ground and its Context*. London: British Museum Press.

Cassen, S. (2000), 'Stelae reused in the passage graves of western France: history of research and sexualisation of the carvings'. In: A. Ritchie (ed.) *Neolithic Orkney in its European Context*, pp. 233–46. Cambridge: McDonald Institute for Archaeological Research.

Cassen, S. (2009), *Exercice de stèle*. Paris: Errance.

Cassen, S., Audren, C., Hinguant, S., Lannuzel, G. and Marchand, G. (1998), 'L'habitat Villeneuve-St-Germain du Haut-Mée', *Bulletin de la Société préhistorique française*, 95: 41–75.

Cassen, S., Boujot, C., Errera, M., Menier, D., Pétrequin, P., Marguerie, D., Veyrat, E., Vigier, E., Poirier, S., Dagneau, C., et al. (2010), 'Un dépôt sous-marin de lames polies néolithiques en jadeite et sillimanite, et un ouvrage de stèles submergé sur la plage dite du Petit Rohu près Saint-Pierre-Quiberon, (Morbihan)', *Bulletin de la Société préhistorique française*, 107: 53–84.

Cauvin, J. (2000), *The Birth of the Gods and the Origins of Agriculture*. Cambridge: Cambridge University Press.

Chapman, J. and Gaydarska, B. (2006), 'Does enclosure make a difference? A view from the Balkans'. In: A. Harding, S. Sievers and N. Venclová (eds) *Enclosing the Past: Inside and Outside in Prehistory*, pp. 20–43. Sheffield: J.R. Collis Publications.

Chapman, R. (2008), 'Producing inequalities: regional sequences in later prehistoric Southern Spain', *Journal of World Prehistory*, 21: 195–260.

Childe, V.G. (1949), 'The origin of Neolithic culture in Northern Europe', *Antiquity*, 23: 129–35.

Childe, V.G. (1958), *The Prehistory of European Society*. Harmondsworth: Penguin.

Clarke, A., Fulford, M., Rains, M. and Tootell, K. (2007), 'Silchester Roman town Insula IX: the development of an urban property c. AD 440–50 – c. AD 250', *Internet Archaeology*, 21.

Cleal, R., Walker, K. and Montague, R. (1995), *Stonehenge in its Landscape. Twentieth Century Excavations*. London: English Heritage.

Cole, H. (2000), 'The Western Sudan'. In: M. Blackmun Visoná, R. Poynor, H. Cole and M. Harris (eds) *A History of Art in Africa*. London: Thames and Hudson.

Collins, A.E.P. (1966), 'Excavations at Dressogagh rath, Co. Armagh', *Ulster Journal of Archaeology*, 29: 117–29.

Comber, M. (2008), *The Economy of the Ringfort and Contemporary Settlement in Ireland*. Oxford: British Archaeological Reports.

Conwell, E. A. (1873), *Discovery of the Tomb of Ollamh Foodhla*. Dublin: McGlashen and Gill.

Cool, H. and Mason, D. (2008), *Roman Piercebridge*. Durham: Architectural and Archaeological Society of Durham and Northumberland.

Costa, L.J. (2004), *Corse préhistorique*. Paris: Errance.

Coudart, A. (1998), *Architecture et société néolithique: l'unité et la variance de la maison danubienne*. Paris: Maison des sciences de l'homme.

Coularou, J. (2008), *Boussargues: une enceinte chalcolithique des garrigues du Sud de la France*. Toulouse: Musée du Pic Saint Loup.

Coupry, M. (1977), 'Circonscription d'Acquitaine', *Gallia*, 35: 449–72.

Cummings, V. (2002), 'Experiencing texture and transformation in the British Neolithic', *Oxford Journal of Archaeology*, 21: 249–61.

Cunliffe, B. (2001), *Facing the Ocean. The Atlantic and its Peoples 8000 BC – AD 1500*. Oxford: Oxford University Press.

Cunliffe, B. (2008), *Europe Between the Oceans*. New Haven: Yale University Press.

Daniel, G. (1941), 'The dual nature of the megalithic colonisation of prehistoric Europe', *Proceedings of the Prehistoric Society*, 7: 1–49.

Daniel, G. (1958), *The Megalith Builders of Western Europe*. London: Hutchinson.

Darvill, T. (2002), 'White on blond. Quartz pebbles and the use of quartz in Neolithic monuments in the Isle of Man and beyond'. In: A. Jones and G. McGregor (eds) *Colouring the Past*, pp. 73–93. Oxford: Berg.

Darvill, T. (2010), *Prehistoric Britain*, 2nd edition. Abingdon: Routledge.

Da Silva, A. (1986), *A Cultura Castreja*. Paços de Ferreira: Museu Arquéologico da Citânia de Sanfins.

Davidson, J. and Henshall, A. (1989), *The Chambered Cairns of Orkney*. Edinburgh: Edinburgh University Press.

DeBoer, W, (1997), 'Ceremonial centres from the Cayapas (Ecuador) to Chillicothe (Ohio, USA)', *Cambridge Archaeological Journal*, 7: 225–53.

De Lanfranchini, F. and Weiss, M.-C. (1997*), L'aventure humaine préhistorique en Corse*. Ajaccio: Éditions Abiana.

Demartis, G. (1984), 'Alcune osservazioni sulle 'domus de janas' riproducenti il tetto della casa dei vivi', *Nuovo Bolletino Archeologico Sardo*, 1: 9–19.

Deregowski, J. (1973), 'Illusion and culture'. In: R. Gregory and E. Gombrich (eds) *Illusion in Nature and Art*, pp. 160–91. London: Duckworth.

De Saulieu, G. (2004), *Art rupestre et statues-menhirs dans les Alpes*. Paris: Errance.

Dettori Campus, L. (1989), *La Cultura di Ozieri*. Ozieri: Edizioni il Torchetto.

Dikaios, P. and Stewart, J. (1962), *The Stone Age and Early Bronze Age in Cyprus*. Lund: Swedish Cyprus Expedition.

Doherty, C. (1998), 'The Vikings in Ireland: a review'. In: H. Clarke, M. Ní Mhaonaigh and R. Ó Floinn (eds) *Ireland and Scandinavia in the Early Viking Age*, pp. 288–330. Dublin: Four Courts Press.

Doneus, M. (2001), *Die Keramik der mittelneolithischen Kreisgrabenanlage von Kamegg, Niederösterreich*. Vienna: Verlag der Österreichischen Akademie der Wissenschaften.

Douglas, M. (1972), 'Symbolic orders in the use of domestic space'. In: P. Ucko, R. Tringham and G. Dimbleby (eds) *Man, Settlement and Urbanism*, pp. 513–21. London: Duckworth.

Dowling, G. (2011), 'The architecture of power: an exploration of the origins of closely spaced multivallate monuments in Ireland'. In: R. Schot, C. Newman and E. Bhreathnach (eds) *Landscapes of Cult and Kingship*, pp. 213–31. Dublin: Four Courts Press.

Edwards, N. (1990), *The Archaeology of Early Medieval Ireland*. London: Routledge.

Eliade, M. (1954), *The Myth of the Eternal Return*. New York: Pantheon Books.

Ellison, A. (1987), 'The Bronze Age settlement at Thorny Down: pots, post-holes and patterning', *Proceedings of the Prehistoric Society*, 53: 385–92.

Eogan, G. (1986), *Knowth and the Passage-tombs of Ireland*. London: Thames and Hudson.

Eogan, G. (1990), 'Irish megalithic tombs and Iberian comparisons and contrasts'. In: *Probleme der Megalithgräberforschung*, pp. 113–38. Madrid: Deutsches archäologisches Institut.

Eogan, G. (1998), 'Knowth before Knowth', *Antiquity*, 7: 162–72.

Evans, C. (1989), 'Perishable and worldly goods—artefact decoration and classification in the light of wetland research', *Oxford Journal of Archaeology*, 8: 179–201.

Evans, C. and Hodder, I. (2006), *Marshland Communities and Cultural Landscapes. The Haddenham Project, volume 2*. Cambridge: McDonald Institute for Archaeological Research.

Evans, C. and Lucy, S. (in press), *Mucking: Excavations by Margaret and Tom Jones 1965–1978: Prehistory, Context and Summary*.

Evans, J.D. (1971), 'Neolithic Knossos: the growth of a settlement', *Proceedings of the Prehistoric Society*, 37.2: 95–117.

Fabech, C. (1998), 'Kult og Samfund i yngre jernalder—Ravlunda som eksampel'. In: L. Larsson and B. Hårdh (eds) *Centrala platser, central Frågor. Samhällsstrukturen under järnåldern*. Lund: Almqvist and Wiksell.

Fabech, C. (2006), 'Centrality in Old Norse mental landscapes. A dialogue between arranged and natural places?' In: A. Andrén, K. Jennbert and C. Raudvere (eds) *Old Norse Religion in Long-term Perspectives*, pp. 26–32. Lund: Nordic Academic Press.

Faudet, I. (1993), *Atlas des sanctuaires romano-celtiques de Gaule*. Paris: Errance.

Fenwick, J. (1997), 'A panoramic view from the Hill of Tara, Co. Meath', *Ríocht na Midhe*, 9.3: 1–11.

Fernández-Posse, M., Gilman, A., Martín, C. and Brodsky, M. (2000), *Las comunidades agrarias de la Edad del Bronce en La Mancha oriental*. Madrid: Consejo Superior de Investigaciones Cientificas.

Field, D. (2008), *The Use of Land in Central Southern England during the Neolithic and Early Bronze Age*. Oxford: British Archaeological Reports.

FitzPatrick, E. (2004), *Royal Inauguration in Gaelic Ireland c. 1100–1600*. Woodbridge: Boydell Press.

Flannery, K. (1972), 'The origins of the village as a settlement type in Mesoamerica and the Near East: a comparative study'. In: P. Ucko, R. Tringham and G. Dimbleby (eds) *Man, Settlement and Urbanism*, pp. 23–53. London: Duckworth.

Fletcher, R. (1977), 'Settlement studies (micro and semi-micro)'. In: D. Clarke (ed.) *Spatial Archaeology*, pp. 47–162. London: Academic Press.

Fokkens, H. and Jansen, R. (2004), *Het vorstengraf van Oss*. Utrecht: Stichting Matrijs.

Fulford, M. and Holbrook, N. (2011), 'Assessing the contribution of commercial archaeology to the study of the Roman period in England, 1990–2004', *Antiquaries Journal*, 91: 323–45.

Garrow, D., Gosden, C., Hill, J.D. and Bronk Ramsay, C. (2009), 'Dating Celtic Art: a major radiocarbon dating programme of Iron Age and Early Roman metalwork in Britain', *Archaeological Journal*, 166: 79–123.

Garwood, P. (2005), 'Before the hills in order stood: chronology, time and history in the interpretation of Early Bronze Age round barrows'. In: J. Last (ed.) *Beyond the Grave. New Perspectives on Barrows*, pp. 30–52. Oxford: Oxbow.

Gasull, P., Lull, V. and Sanahuja, M. (1984), *Son Fornés: la fase Talayótica*. Oxford: British Archaeological Reports.

Gell, A. (1995), 'The language of the forest: landscape and phonological iconism in Umeda'. In: E. Hirsch and M. O'Hanlon (eds) *The Anthropology of Landscape: Perspectives on Place and Space*, pp. 232–54. Oxford: Clarendon Press.

van Gennep, A. (1909), *Les rites de passage*. Paris: Nourry.

Gerdin, A-L. (1999), 'Rösen—uttryck för makt eller platser där himmel och jord möts i det kosmiska rummet'. In: M. Olausson (ed.) *Spiralens öga. Tjugo artiklar kring aktuell bronsåldersforskning*, pp. 47–74. Stockholm: Riksantikvarieämbetet.

Gerritsen, F. (1999), 'To build or to abandon. The cultural biography of late prehistoric houses and farmsteads in the southern Netherlands', *Archaeological Dialogues*, 6.2: 78–114.

Gianotti, C., Mañana Borrazás, P., Criado Boado, F. and López-Romero, E. (2011), 'Deconstructing Neolithic monumental space: the Montenegro enclosure in Galicia (Northwest Iberia)', *Cambridge Archaeological Journal*, 21: 391–406.

Giardino, C. (1992), 'Nuragic Sardinia and the Mediterranean: metallurgy and maritime traffic'. In: R. Tykot and T. Andrews (eds) *Sardinia in the Mediterranean: A Footprint in the Sea*, pp. 304–16. Sheffield: Sheffield Academic Press.

Gibson, A. (1982), *Beaker Domestic Sites*. Oxford: British Archaeological Reports.

Gibson, A. (1995), 'The dating of timber circles: new thoughts in the light of recent Irish and British discoveries'. In: J. Waddell and E. Shee Twohig (eds) *Ireland in the Bronze Age*, pp. 87–9. Dublin: Stationery Office.

Gibson, A. (2000), 'Circles and henges: reincarnation of past traditions?' *Archaeology Ireland*, 14.1: 11–14.

Gibson, A. (2010), 'Excavations and surveys at Dyffryn Land henge complex, Powys, and a reconsideration of the dating of henges', *Proceedings of the Prehistoric Society*, 76: 213–48.

Gili, S., Lull, V., Micó, R., Rihuete, C. and Risch, R. (2006), 'An island decides: megalithic burial rites on Menorca', *Antiquity*, 80: 829–42.

Goldhahn, J. (2007), *Dödens hand—en essä om brons-och hällsmed*. Gothenburg: Gothenburg University.

González Ruibal, A. (2004), 'Facing two seas: Mediterranean and Atlantic contacts in the north-west of Iberia in the first millennium BC', *Oxford Journal of Archaeology*, 23: 287–317.

González Ruibal, A. (2007), *Poder y comunidad en el Noroeste de la Península Ibérica, 1200 a. C. – 50 d.C.* La Coruña: Brigantium 18.

Goody, J. (1958), *The Developmental Cycle in Domestic Groups*. Cambridge: Cambridge University Press.

Goring-Morris, N. and Belfer-Cohen, A. (2010), 'Different ways of being, different ways of seeing... Changing worldviews in the Near East'. In: B Finlayson and G. Warren (eds) *Landscapes in Transition*, pp. 9–22. Oxford: Oxbow.

Gosden, C. (2004), 'Grid and group. An interview with Mary Douglas', *Journal of Social Archaeology*, 4: 275–87.

Gräslund, B. (1994), 'Prehistoric soul beliefs in Northern Europe', *Proceedings of the Prehistoric Society*, 60: 15–26.

Gregory, R. (1998), *Eye and Brain. The Psychology of Seeing*, 5th edition. Oxford: Oxford University Press.

Gregory, T. (1991), *Excavations at Thetford 1980–1982. Fisons Way*. Norwich: East Anglian Archaeology 53.

Griffin-Pierce, T. (1992), *Earth is my Mother, Sky is my Father*. Albuquerque: University of New Mexico Press.

Grinsell, L. (1976), *Folklore of Prehistoric Sites in Britain*. Newton Abbot: David and Charles.

Groenman-Van-Waateringe, W. and Robinson, M. (1988), *Man-made Soils*. Oxford: British Archaeological Reports.

Grogan, E. (2008), *The Rath of the Synods, Tara, Co. Meath*. Dublin: Wordwell.

Grøn, O. (1995), *The Maglemose Culture. The Reconstruction of the Social Organisation of a Mesolithic Culture in Northern Europe*. Oxford: British Archaeological Reports.

Hagberg, U.E., Besbow-Sjöberg, M. and Boessneck, J. (1977), *The Archaeology of Skedemosse*. Stockholm: Almqvist and Wiksell.

Hamerow, H. (2010), 'The development of Anglo-Saxon rural settlement forms', *Landscape History*, 31: 5–22.

Harding, D. (2007), *The Archaeology of Celtic Art*. Abingdon: Routledge.

Harding D. (2009), *The Iron Age Round-house*. Oxford: Oxford University Press.

Häusler, A. (1977), 'Die Bestattungssitten der frühen Bronzezeit zwischen Rhein und oberer Wolga, ihre Voraussetzungen und ihre Beziehungen', *Zeitschrift für Archäologie*, 11: 13–48.

Hauzeur, A. (2006), *Le Rubané au Luxembourg: contribution à l'étude du Rubané du Nord-Ouest européen*. Luxembourg: Musée national d'histoire et d'art.

Hayden, C. (1999), 'Houses and monuments: two aspects of settlements in Neolithic and Copper Age Sardinia'. In: J. Brück and M. Goodman (eds) *Making Places in the Prehistoric World*, pp. 112–28. London: UCL Press.

Hedeager, L. (2011), *Iron Age Myth and Materiality. An Archaeology of Scandinavia AD 400–1000*. Abingdon: Routledge.

Henderson, J. (2007), *The Atlantic Iron Age. Settlement and Identity in the First Millennium BC*. Abingdon: Routledge.

Henry, F. (1965), *Irish Art in the Early Christian Period (to 800 AD)*. London: Methuen.

Henshall, A. (1972), *The Chambered Tombs of Scotland, Volume 2*. Edinburgh: Edinburgh University Press.

Herschend, F. (2001), *Journey of Civilization. The Late Iron Age View of the Human World*. Uppsala: Uppsala University Department of Archaeology and Ancient History.

Herva, V.-P. (2009), 'Buildings as persons: relationality and the life of buildings in a northern periphery of early modern Sweden', *Antiquity*, 84: 44–52.

Hobsbawm, E. and Ranger, T. (1983), *The Invention of Tradition*. Cambridge: Cambridge University Press.

Hodder, I. (1982), *Symbols in Action. Ethnoarchaeological Studies of Material Culture*. Cambridge: Cambridge University Press.

Hodder, I. (1984), 'Burials, houses, women and men in the European Neolithic'. In: D. Miller and C. Tilley (eds) *Ideology, Power and Prehistory*, pp. 51–68. Cambridge: Cambridge University Press.

Hodos, T. (2006), *Local Responses to Colonization in the Iron Age Mediterranean*. Abingdon: Routledge.

Hodson, R. (1964), 'Cultural groups within the British pre-Roman Iron Age', *Proceedings of the Prehistoric Society*, 30: 99–110.

Horne, P. and King, A. (1980), 'Romano-Celtic temples in Continental Europe: a gazetteer of those with known plans'. In: W. Rodwell (ed.) *Temples, Churches and Religion: Recent Research in Roman Britain*, pp. 369–555. Oxford: British Archaeological Reports.

Hoskin, M. (2001), *Tombs, Temples and their Orientation. A New Perspective on Mediterranean Prehistory*. Bognor Regis: Ocarina Books.

Hugh-Jones, C. (1979), *From the Milk River. Spatial and Temporal Processes in Northwest Amazonia*. Cambridge: Cambridge University Press.

Hunter, F. (2008), 'Celtic Art in Roman Britain'. In: D. Garrow, C. Gosden and J.D. Hill (eds) *Rethinking Celtic Art*, pp. 129–45. Oxford: Oxbow.

Hunter-Anderson, R. (1977), 'A theoretical approach to the study of house form'. In: L. Binford (ed.) *For Theory Building in Archaeology*, pp. 287–315. London: Academic Press.

Hyenstrand, Å (1969), 'Gravformer och symboltecken under yngre bronsålder', *Fornvännen*, 63: 185–9.

Ingold, T. (2000), 'Stop, look and listen! Vision, hearing and human movement'. In: T. Ingold, *The Perception of the Environment. Essays in Livelihood, Dwelling and Skill*, pp. 243–87. London: Routledge.

Ingold, T. (2007), *Lines. A Brief History*. Abingdon: Routledge.

Ingold, T. (2011), 'The shape of the earth'. In: T. Ingold (ed.) *Being Alive. Essays on Movement, Knowledge and Description*, pp. 99–114. Abingdon: Routledge.

Jacobsthal, P. (1944), *Early Celtic Art*. Oxford: Clarendon Press.

Jahier, I., Besnard-Vauterin, C., Le Paulier, H., Paris, P., Renault, V., San Juan, G., Dron, J.-L., Hincker, V. and Forfait, N. (2000), 'Les bâtiments des habitats de l'âge du fer en Basse-Normandie: panorama des découvertes'. In: S. Marion and G. Blancquaert (eds) *Les installations agricoles de l'age du fer en France septentrionale*, pp. 339–57. Paris: Éditions d'Ulm.

Jensen, J. (2006a), *Danmarks Oltid. Stenalder 13,000–2,000 f. Kr.* Copenhagen: Gyldendal.

Jensen, J. (2006b), *Danmarks Oltid. Bronsealder 2000–500 f. Kr.* Copenhagen: Gyldendal.

Johansen, K., Laursen, S. and Holst, M. (2004), 'Spatial patterns of social organisation in the Early Bronze Age of South Scandinavia', *Journal of Anthropological Archaeology*, 23: 33–55.

Johns, C. and Potter, T. (1983), *The Thetford Treasure: Roman Jewellery and Silver*. London: British Museum Publications.

Johnston, S., Campana, D. and Crabtree, P. (2009), 'A geophysical survey at Dún Ailinne, County Kildare, Ireland', *Journal of Field Archaeology*, 34: 385–402.

Johnston, S. and Wailes, B. (2007), *Dún Ailinne. Excavations at an Irish Royal Site, 1968–1975*. Philadelphia: University of Pennsylvania Museum of Archaeology and Anthropology.

Jope, E.M. (2000), *Early Celtic Art in the British Isles*. Oxford: Clarendon Press.

Jorge, S.O. (1998), 'Colónias, fortificações, lugares monumentalizados. Trajectória das concepções sobre un tema do Calcólitico peninsular'. In: S.O. Jorge and V.O. Jorge (eds) *Arqueologia. Percursos e interrogações*, pp. 69–150. Porto: Associação para o Desenvolvimento da Cooperação em Arqueologia Peninsular.

Joussaume, R. (1985), *Des Dolmens pour les morts*. Paris: Hachette.

Joussaume, R., Laporte, L. and Scarre, C. (2006), *Origine et développement du mégalithisme de l'ouest de l'Europe*. Bougon: Musée des Tumulus de Bougon.

Jung, C. (1980), *The Archetypes and the Collective Unconscious*. London: Routledge.

Kaul, F. (2004), *Bronzealders religion: studier af den nordiska bronsealders ikonografi*. Copenhagen: Kongelide Nordiska Oldskirftselskab.

Kent, S. (1990), 'A cross-cultural study of segmentation, architecture and the use of space'. In: S. Kent (ed.) *Domestic Architecture and the Use of Space*, pp. 127–52. Cambridge: Cambridge University Press.

Klassen, L., Pétrequin, P and Cassen, S. (2011), 'The power of attraction... Zur Akkumulation sozial wertbesetzer alpiner Artefakte im Morbihan und im westlichen Ostseeraum im 5 und 4 Jahrtausend v. Chr.'. In: S. Hansen and J. Müller (eds) *Sozialarchäologische Perspektiven: Gesellschaftlicher Wandel 5000–1500 v. Chr. Zwischen Atlantik und Kaukasus*, pp. 13–40. Kiel: Archäologie in Eurasien 24.

Kolb, M. (1997), 'Labour, ethnohistory and the archaeology of community in Hawai'i', *Journal of Archaeological Method and Theory*, 4: 265–86.

Kolb, M. (2005), 'The genesis of monuments among Mediterranean islands'. In: E. Blake and A.B. Knapp (eds) *The Archaeology of Mediterranean Prehistory*, pp. 156–78. Oxford: Blackwell.

Kossack, G. (1954), *Studien zum Symbolgut der Urnenfelder und Hallstattzeit Mitteleuropas*. Berlin: De Gruyter.

Kristiansen, K. (1984), 'Ideology and material culture: an archaeological perspective'. In: M. Spriggs (ed.) *Marxist Perspectives in Archaeology*, pp. 72–100. Cambridge: Cambridge University Press.

Kristiansen, K. (1990), 'Ard marks under barrows: a response to Peter Rowley-Conwy', *Antiquity*, 64: 322–7.

Kristiansen, K. (1998), *Europe Before History*. Cambridge: Cambridge University Press.

Kristiansen, K. and Larsson, T. (2005), *The Rise of Bronze Age Society. Travels, Transmissions and Transformation*. Cambridge: Cambridge University Press.

Kuijt, I. (2000), 'People and space in early agricultural villages: exploring daily lives, community size and architecture in later Pre-pottery Neolithic A period mortuary practices', *Journal of Anthropological Archaeology*, 19: 75–101.

Kuijt, I. and Goring-Morris, N. (2002), 'Foraging, farming and social complexity in the Pre-Pottery Neolithic of the Southern Levant: a review and synthesis', *Journal of World Prehistory*, 16: 361–440.

Kunst, M. (2001), 'Invasion? Fashion? Social rank? Considerations concerning the Bell Beaker phenomenon in Copper Age fortifications of the Iberian Peninsula'. In: F. Nicolis (ed.) *Bell Beakers Today*, pp. 81–90. Trento: Provincia Autonoma di Trento.

Kunst, M. (2006), 'Zambujal and the enclosures of the Iberian Peninsula'. In: A. Harding, S. Sievers and N. Venclová (eds) *Enclosing the Past. Inside and Outside in Prehistory*, pp. 76–96. Sheffield: J.R. Collis Publications.

Laing, L. (2005), 'The Roman origins of Celtic Christian art', *Archaeological Journal*, 162: 146–76.

Laing, L. and Longley, D. (2006), *The Mote of Mark: a Dark Age Hillfort in South-west Scotland*. Oxford: Oxbow.

Lane, A. and Campbell, E. (2000), *Dunadd. An Early Dalriadic Capital*. Oxford: Oxbow.

Laporte, L. and Tinévez, J. Y. (2004), 'Neolithic houses and chambered tombs of Western France', *Cambridge Archaeological Journal*, 14: 217–34.

Larsson, L. (1993), 'Relationer till ett röse—några aspekter på Kiviksgraven'. In: L. Larsson (ed.) *Bronsålderns Gravhögar*, pp. 135–50. Lund: Lund University Institute of Archaeology.

Lawrence, D. and Low, S (1990), 'The built environment and spatial form', *Annual Review of Anthropology*, 19: 453–505.

Laws, R. (1886), *Women's work in Heathen Lands*. Paisley: Parlane.

Layton, R. (1991), *The Anthropology of Art*, 2nd edition. Cambridge: Cambridge University Press.

Lecerf, Y. (1999), *Les pierres droites: réflexions autour des menhirs*. Rennes: Documents archéologiques de l'Ouest.

Leighton, R. (1999), *Sicily Before History: an Archaeological Survey from the Palaeolithic to the Iron Age*. London: Duckworth.

Leroi-Gourhan, A. (1982), *The Dawn of European Art*. Cambridge: Cambridge University Press.

Lewis, M. (1966), *Temples in Roman Britain*. Cambridge: Cambridge University Press.

Lewthwaite, J. (1985), 'Colonialism and nuraghismus'. In: C. Malone and S. Stoddart (eds) *Papers in Italian Archaeology, IV, Part ii*, pp. 220–51. Oxford: British Archaeological Reports.

L'Helgouach, J. (1996), 'De la lumière aux ténèbres'. In: J. L'Helgouach, C-T. Le Roux and J. Lecornec (eds) *Art et symboles du mégalithisme européen*, pp. 107–23. Rennes, *Revue archéologique de l'Ouest, Supplément 8*.

L'Helgouach, J. and Cassen, S. (2010), *Autour de la table: explorations archéologiques et discours savants sur des architectures néolithiques à Locmariaquer (Table de Marchands et Grand Menhir)*. Nantes: Université de Nantes.

Lilliu, G. (1988), *La civiltà dei Sardi: Del Palaeolitico all'età dei nuraghi*. Turin: Nuova Eri.

Lloyd Morgan, C. (1887), 'The stones of Stanton Drew. Their source and origin', *Proceedings of the Somerset Archaeological Society*, 33: 37–50.

Lo Schiavo, F. (2007), 'Votive swords in Gallura: an example of Nuraghic weapon worship'. In: C. Burgess, P. Topping and F. Lynch (eds) *Beyond Stonehenge*, pp. 225–36. Oxford: Oxbow.

Lynch, F. (1998), 'Colour in prehistoric architecture'. In: A. Gibson and D. Simpson (eds) *Prehistoric Ritual and Religion*, pp. 62–7. Stroud: Sutton.

Lyons, D. (1996), 'The politics of house shape: round versus rectangular in Déla compounds, northern Cameroon', *Antiquity*, 70: 351–67.

Macalister, R. and Praeger, R. (1928), 'Report on the excavation of Uisneach', *Proceedings of the Royal Irish Academy*, 38C: 69–12.

Madsen, T. (1979), 'Earthen long barrows and timber structures: aspects of Early Neolithic mortuary practice in Denmark', *Proceedings of the Prehistoric Society*, 45: 301–20.

Mallory, J. (2000), 'Excavation of the Navan ditch', *Emainia*, 18: 21–35.

Malone, C. (2003), 'The Italian Neolithic: a synthesis of research', *Journal of World Prehistory*, 17: 235–312.

Manby, T. (2007), 'Continuity of monumental tradition into the late Bronze Age. Henges to ring-forts, and shrines'. In: C. Burgess, P. Topping and F. Lynch (eds) *Beyond Stonehenge. Essays on the Bronze Age in Honour of Colin Burgess*, pp. 403–24. Oxford: Oxbow.

Masset, C. and Soulier, P. (1995), *Allées couvertes et autres monuments funéraires du néolithique dans la France du Nord-Ouest*. Paris: Errance.

Mattingly, D. (2006), *An Imperial Possession. Britain in the Roman Empire*. London: Allen Lane.

McGarry, T. (2009), 'Irish late prehistoric burial ring-ditches'. In: G. Cooney, K. Becker, J. Coles, M. Ryan and S. Sievers (eds) *Relics of Old Decency. Archaeological Studies in Later Prehistory*, pp. 413–23. Dublin: Wordwell.

McGuire, R. and Schiffer, M. (1983), 'A theory of architectural design', *Journal of Anthropological Archaeology*, 2: 277–303.

Megaw, R. and Megaw, V. (2001), *Celtic Art. From its Beginning to the Book of Kells*. London: Thames and Hudson.

Meijlink, B. (2008), 'The Bronze Age cultural landscape of De Bogen', In: S. Arnoldussen and H. Fokkens (eds) *Bronze Age Settlements in the Low Countries*, pp. 137–50. Oxford: Oxbow.

Meller, H. (2004), *Der geschmiedete Himmel: die weite Welt im Herzen Europas vor 3600 Jahren*. Stuttgart: Theiss.

Mezzena, F. (1998), 'Le stele antropomorfe nell'area megalitica di Aosta'. In: F. Mezzena (ed.) *Dei di pietra*, pp. 91–121. Skira: Regione autonoma Valle d'Aosta.

Midgley, M. (2005), *The Monumental Cemeteries of Prehistoric Europe*. Stroud: Tempus.

Midgley, M. (2008), *The Megaliths of Northern Europe*. Abingdon: Routledge.

Mohen, J.-P. and Scarre, C. (2002), *Les tumulus de Bougon*. Paris: Errance.

Moore, H. (1986), *Space, Text and Gender. An Anthropological Study of the Marakwet of Kenya*. Cambridge: Cambridge University Press.

Moore, M. (1987), *Archaeological Inventory of County Meath*. Dublin: Stationery Office.

Mordant, C. (1998), 'Emergence d'une architecture funéraire monumentale (vallée de la Seine et de l'Yonne)'. In: J. Guilaine (ed.) *Sépultures d'Occident et genèses des mégalithismes*, pp. 73–88. Paris: Errance.

Musson, C. (1970), 'House-plans and prehistory', *Current Archaeology*, 2: 267–75.

Näsman, U. and Wegraeus, E. (1976), *Eketorp. Fortifications and Settlement on Öland, Sweden. The Setting*. Stockholm: Royal Academy of Letters, History and Antiquities.

Naumov, G. (2007), 'Housing the dead: burials inside houses and vessels in the Neolithic Balkans'. In: D. Barraclough and C. Malone (eds) *Cult in Context. Reconsidering Ritual in Archaeology*, pp. 257–68. Oxford: Oxbow.

Naumov, G. (2009), *Pottery and Corporality: Neolithic Visual Culture from the Republic of Macedonia*. Oxford: British Archaeological Reports.

Needham, S. (2005), 'Transforming Beaker culture in North-West Europe. Processes of fusion and fission', *Proceedings of the Prehistoric Society*, 71: 171–217.

Newman, C. (1997), *Tara: An Archaeological Survey*. Dublin: Royal Irish Academy.

Newman, C. (1998), 'Reflections on the making of a "royal site" in early Ireland', *World Archaeology*, 30: 127–41.

Newman, C. (1999), 'Notes on four cursus-like monuments in County Meath, Ireland'. In: A. Barclay and J. Harding (eds), *Pathways and Ceremonies. The Cursus Monuments of Britain and Ireland*, pp. 141–7. Oxford: Oxbow.

Nieke, M. (1993), 'Penannular and related brooches: secular ornament or symbol in action?'. In: R. Spearman and J. Higgitt (eds) *Age of Migrating Ideas: Early Medieval Art in Northern Britain and Ireland*, pp. 128–34. Edinburgh: National Museums Scotland.

Nielsen, B. and Beck, J-K. (2004), 'Bronzealderens kulthuse i Thy. Anlaeg med relation til gravkulten', *Kuml*: 129–59.

Noble, G. (2006), *Neolithic Scotland. Timber, Stone, Earth and Fire*. Edinburgh: Edinburgh University Press.

O'Connell, A. (2009), *Report on the Archaeological Excavation of Lismullin 1, Co. Meath*, http://www.m3motorway.ie/Archaeology/Section2/Lismullin1/file,16727

O'Conor, K. (1998), *The Archaeology of Medieval Rural Settlement in Ireland*. Dublin: Royal Irish Academy.

Oestigaard, T. and Goldhahn, J. (2006), 'From the dead to the living: death as transactions and re-negotiations', *Norwegian Archaeological Review*, 39: 27–48.

Ó Floinn, R. (1998), 'The archaeology of the Early Viking Age in Ireland'. In: H. Clarke, M. Ní Mhaonaigh and R. Ó Floinn (eds) *Ireland and Scandinavia in the Early Viking Age*: 131–65. Dublin: Four Courts Press.

O'Kelly, M. (1982), *Newgrange. Archaeology, Art and Legend*. London: Thames and Hudson.

Olausson, M. (1995), *Det inneslutna rummet*. Stockholm: Riksantikvarieämbetet.

O'Sullivan, M. (1996), 'Megalithic art in Ireland and Brittany: divergence or convergence?' In: J. L'Helgouach, C-T. Le Roux and J. Lecornec (eds) *Art et symboles du mégalithisme européen*, pp. 81–96. Rennes: *Revue archéologique de l'Ouest, Supplément 8*.

O'Sullivan, M. (2005), *Duma na nGaill. The Mound of the Hostages, Tara*. Bray: Wordwell.

Parker Pearson, M. (2007), 'The Stonehenge Riverside Project: excavations at the east entrance of Durrington Walls'. In: M. Larsson and M. Parker Pearson (eds) *From Stonehenge to the Baltic. Living with Cultural Diversity in the Third Millennium BC*, pp. 125–44. Oxford: British Archaeological Reports.

Parker Pearson, M., Chamberlain, A., Jay, M., Marshall, P., Pollard, J., Richards, C., Thomas, J., Tilley, C. and Welham, K. (2009), 'Who was buried at Stonehenge?', *Antiquity*, 83: 23–39.

Parker Pearson, M. and Ramilsonina (1998), 'Stonehenge for the ancestors. The stones pass on the message', *Antiquity*, 72: 308–26.

Pászter, J., Barna, J. and Roslund, C. (2008), 'The orientation of rondels of the Neolithic Lengyel Culture in Central Europe', *Antiquity*, 82: 910–24.

Patton, M. (1996), *Islands in Time: Island Sociogeography and Mediterranean Prehistory*. London: Routledge.

Pätzold, J. (1960), 'Rituelles Pflügen beim vorgeschichtlichen Totenkult', *Prähistorische Zeitschrift*, 38: 189–239.

Pedersen, A. (2006), 'Ancient mounds for new graves. An aspect of Viking Age burial customs in southern Scandinavia'. In: A. Andrén, K. Jennbert and C. Raudvere (eds) *Old Norse Religion in Long-term Perspectives*, pp. 346–53. Lund: Nordic Academic Press.

Peña Santos, A. and Rey García, J.M. (2001), *Petroglifos de Galicia*. La Coruña: Vía Láctea Editorial.

Petrasch, J. (1990), 'Mittelneolithische Kreisgrabenanlagen in Mitteleuropa', *Bericht der Römisch-Germanischen Kommission*, 71: 407–564.

Pétrequin, P. Pinigre, J.-F. (1976), 'Les sépultures collectives mégalithiques en Franche-Comté', *Gallia Préhistoire*, 19: 287–394.

Piggott, S. (1956), 'Excavations in passage graves and ring cairns of the Clava group, 1952–1953', *Proceedings of the Society of Antiquaries of Scotland*, 88: 173–207.

Piggott, S. (1965), *Ancient Europe from the Beginnings of Agriculture to Classical Antiquity*. Edinburgh: Edinburgh University Press.

Pirovano, C.. (1985), *Civilta Nuragica*. Milan: Electa.

Pollard, J. and Robinson, D. (2007), 'A return to Woodhenge: the results and implications of the 2006 excavation'. In: M. Larsson and M. Parker Pearson (eds) *From Stonehenge to the Baltic. Living with Cultural Diversity in the Third Millennium BC*: 159–68. Oxford: British Archaeological Reports.

Pospieszny, L. (2010), 'Living with ancestors: Neolithic burial mounds of the Polish lowlands'. In: Kiel Graduate School 'Human Development in Landscapes' (ed) *Landscapes and Human Development: The Contribution of European Archaeology*, pp. 143–57. Bonn: Habelt.

Raczky, P. and Anders, A. (2008), 'Late Neolithic spatial differentiation at Polgá-Csöszhalom, eastern Hungary'. In: D. Bailey, A. Whittle and D. Hofmann (eds) *Living Well Together? Settlement and Materiality in the Neolithic of South-East and Central Europe*, pp. 35–53. Oxford: Oxbow.

Raftery, B. (1984), *La Tène in Ireland: Problems of Origin and Chronology*. Marburg: Vorgeschichtlichen Seminars Marburg.

Raftery, B. (1994), *Pagan Celtic Ireland*. London: Thames and Hudson.

Raftery, J. (2009), 'Newtown, Loughcrew, Oldcastle, County Meath. Cairn H, August 5–November 10, 1943'. In: G. Cooney, K. Becker, J. Coles, M. Ryan and S. Sievers (eds) *Relics of Old Decency. Archaeological Studies in Later Prehistory*, pp. 531–42. Dublin: Wordwell.

Randsborg, K. (2006), 'Opening the oak coffins. New dates, new perspectives', *Acta Archaeologica*, 7: 1–162.

Randsborg, K. and Nybo, C. (1984), 'The coffin and the sun: demography and ideology in Scandinavian prehistory', *Acta Archaeologica*, 55: 161–84.

Rapaport, A. (1969), *House Form and Culture*. Englewood Cliffs: Prentice Hall.

Rasmussen, M. (1993), 'Gravhøje og bopladser. En foreløbig undersøgelse af lokalisering og sammenhaenge'. In: L. Larsson (ed.) *Bronsålders gravhögar*, pp. 171–85. Lund: Institute of Archaeology.

Rees, A. and Rees, B. (1961), *Celtic Heritage. Ancient Tradition in Ireland and Wales*. London: Thames and Hudson

Rey Castiñeira, J. and Soto-Barreiro, M.J. (2001), 'El arte rupestre de Crastoeiro (Mondim-de-Basto, Portugal) y la problemática de los petroglifos en castros'. In: A. Pereira Dinis (ed.) *O povoado da Idade do Ferro do Crastoeiro, Norte de Portugal*, pp. 159–200. Braga: Universidade do Minho.

Richards, C. (2004), 'A choreography of construction—monuments, mobilisation and social change in Neolithic Orkney'. In: J. Cherry, C. Scarre, and S. Shennan (eds) *Explaining Social Change*, pp. 103–13. Cambridge: McDonald Institute for Archaeological Research.

Richards, C. (2005), *Dwelling Among the Monuments: The Neolithic Village of Barnhouse, Maeshowe Passage Grave and Surrounding Monuments at Stenness, Orkney*. Cambridge: McDonald Institute for Archaeological Research.

Robbins, M. (1966), 'House types and settlement patterns: an application of ethnology to archaeological inference', *Minnesota Archaeologist*, 28: 3–26.

Robin, G. (2009), *L'architecture des signes. L'art pariétal des tombeaux néolithiques autour de la Mer d'Ireland*. Rennes: Presses Universitaires de Rennes.

Roughley, C. (2004), 'The Neolithic landscape of the Carnac region, Brittany: new insights from digital approaches', *Proceedings of the Prehistoric Society*, 70: 153–72.

Rowan, Y. and Golden, J. (2009), 'The Chalcolithic period of the Southern Levant: a synthetic review', *Journal of World Prehistory*, 22: 1–92.

Rowley-Conwy, P. (1987), 'The interpretation of ard marks', *Antiquity*, 61: 263–6.

Roymans, N. and Kortlang, F. (1999), 'Urnfield symbolism, ancestors and the land in the Lower Rhine Region'. In: F. Theuws and N. Roymans (eds) *Land and Ancestors, Cultural Dynamics in the Urnfield Period and the Middle Ages in the Southern Netherlands*, pp. 33–61. Amsterdam: Amsterdam University Press.

Rück, O. (2009), 'New aspects and models for Bandkeramik settlement research'. In: D. Hofmann and P. Bickle (eds) *Creating Communities. New Advances in Central European Neolithic Research*, pp. 159–85. Oxford: Oxbow.

Ruggles, C. (1999), *Astronomy in Prehistoric Britain and Ireland*. New Haven: Yale University Press.

Ruiz-Gálvez Priego, M. (1998), *La Europa Atlántica en la Edad del Bronce*. Barcelona: Crítica.

Rykwert, J. (1976), *The Idea of a Town. The Anthropology of Urban Form in Rome, Italy, and the Ancient World*. Princeton: Princeton University Press.

Sabatini, S. (2007), *House Urns. A European Late Bronze Age Trans-cultural Phenomenon*. Gothenburg: Gothenburg University.

Saidel, B. (1993), 'Round house or square? Architectural form and socio-economic organisation in the PPNB', *Journal of Mediterranean Archaeology*, 6: 23–53.

Santos Estévez, M. (2005), *Arte rupestre: estilo y construcción social del espacio en el Noroeste de la Península Ibérica*. Santiago de Compostela: Universidade de Santiago de Compostela.

Santos Estévez, M. (2008), *Petroglifos y paisaje en la prehistoria reciente del noroeste de la Península Ibérica*. Santiago de Compostela: Consejo Superior de Investigaciones Científicas.

Scarre, C. (2004a), 'Contexts of monumentalism: regional diversity at the Neolithic transition in north-west France', *Oxford Journal of Archaeology*, 21: 23–61.

Scarre, C. (2004b), 'Displaying the stones. The materiality of 'megalithic' monuments'. In: E. DeMarrais, C. Gosden and C. Renfrew (eds) *Rethinking Materiality*, pp. 141–52. Cambridge: McDonald Institute for Archaeological Research.

Scarre, C. (2010), 'Rocks of ages: tempo and time in megalithic monuments', *European Journal of Archaeology*, 13: 175–93.

Scarre, C. (2011), *Landscapes of Neolithic Brittany*. Oxford: Oxford University Press.

Schier, W. (2008), 'Uivar: a late Neolithic–early Eneolithic fortified tell site in Western Romania'. In: D. Bailey, A. Whittle and D. Hofmann (eds) *Living Well Together? Settlement and Materiality in the Neolithic of South-East and Central Europe*, pp. 54–67. Oxford: Oxbow.

Schmidt, K. (2006), *Sie bauten die ersten Tempel: das rätselhafte Heiligtum der Steinzeitjäger—Entdeckung am Göbekli Tepe*. Munich: Beck.

Scholz, N. (1986), 'Joseph Beuys – 7000 Oaks in Kassel', *Anthos*, 3: 32.

Schot, R. (2006), 'Uisneach Midi a medón Érenn: a prehistoric 'cult' centre and 'royal site' in Co. Westmeath', *Journal of Irish Archaeology*, 15: 39–71.

Schot, R. (2011), 'From cult centre to royal centre: monuments, myths and other revelations at Uisneach'. In: R. Schot, C. Newman and E. Bhreathnach (eds) *Landscapes of Cult and Kingship*, pp. 87–113. Dublin: Four Courts Press.

Schot, R., Newman, C. and Bhreathnach, E. (2011), *Landscapes of Cult and Kingship*. Dublin: Four Courts Press.

Schultz Paulsson, B. (2010), 'Scandinavian models: Radiocarbon dates and the origin and spreading of passage graves in Sweden and Denmark', *Radiocarbon*, 52: 1002–17.

Segall, M., Campbell, D. and Herskovit, M. (1966), *The Influence of Culture on Visual Perception*. Indianapolis: Bobbs-Merrill.

Senna-Martinez, J.-C. and Quintà Ventura, J.-M. (2008), 'Neoliticão e megalitismo na plataforma de Mondego: algunhas reflexões sobre a transicão Neolítico antigo/ Neolítico médio'. In: M. Hernández Pérez and J. Soler Díaz (eds), *IV Congresso del Neolítico Peninsular, tomo 2*, pp. 77–84. Alicante: Museo Arqueológico de Alicante.

Sharples, N. (2010), *Social Relations in Later Prehistory. Wessex in the First Millennium BC*. Oxford: Oxford University Press.

Shee, E. (1972), 'Three decorated stones from Loughcrew, Co. Meath', *Journal of the Royal Society of Antiquaries of Ireland*, 102: 224–33.

Shee Twohig, E. (1981), *The Megalithic Art of Western Europe*. Oxford: Clarendon Press.

Shell, C. (2005), 'The Loughcrew Landscape Project', *Past*, 51: 1–3.

Sheridan, A. and Higham, T. (2006), 'The re-dating of some Scottish specimens by the Oxford Radiocarbon Accelerator Unit', *Discovery and Excavation in Scotland*, 7: 296–314.

Sievers, S. (1991), 'Armes et sanctuaires à Manching'. In: J-L. Brunaux (ed.) *Les sanctuaires celtiques et leur rapport avec le monde méditerranéen*, pp. 146–55. Paris: Errance.

Sigvallius, B. (2005), 'Sailing towards the afterlife'. In: T. Artelius and F. Svanberg (eds) *Dealing with the Dead*, pp. 159–71. Stockholm: Riksantikvarieämbetet.

Sopp, M. (1999), *Die Wiederaufnahme älteres Bestattungsplätze in den nachfolgenden vor- und frühgeschichtlichen Perioden in Norddeutschland*. Bonn: Habelt.

Stamper, J. (2005), *The Architecture of Roman Temples*. Cambridge: Cambridge University Press.

Stead, I. (1979), *The Arras Culture*. York: Yorkshire Philosophical Society.

Steel, L. (2004), *Cyprus Before History. From the Earliest Settlers to the End of the Bronze Age*. London: Duckworth.

Stepanovic, M. (1997), 'The age of clay. The social dynamics of house destruction', *Journal of Anthropological Archaeology*, 16: 334–95.

Stöckli, W. (2005), 'Absolute und relative Chronologie der Bandkeramik und des Beginns des Mittelneolithikums im Rheinland und im Rhein-Main-Gebiet'. In: J. Lüning, C. Friedrich and A. Zimmerman (eds) *Die Bandkeramik im 21 Jahrhundert*, pp. 139–46. Rahden: Marie Leidorf.

Stone, J.F.S. (1941), 'The Deverel-Rimbury settlement on Thorny Down, Winterbourne Gunner, S. Wilts', *Proceedings of the Prehistoric Society*, 4: 114–35.

Stout, G. and Stout, M. (2008), *Newgrange*. Cork: Cork University Press.

Stout, M. (1997), *The Irish Ringfort*. Dublin: Four Courts Press.

Svanberg, F. (2005), 'House symbolism in aristocratic death rituals of the Bronze Age'. In: T. Artelius and F. Svanberg (eds) *Dealing with the Dead. Archaeological Perspectives on Prehistoric Scandinavian Burial Ritual*, pp. 73–98. Stockholm: Riksantikvarieämbetet.

Thäte, E. (2007), *Monuments and Minds. Monument Re-use in Scandinavia in the Second Half of the First Millennium AD*. Lund: Acta Archaeologica Lundensia.

Theunissen, L. (2009), *Midden-bronstijdsamenlevingen in het zuiden van de Lage Landen*. Leiden:, Sidestone Press.

Thomas, J. (1990), 'Monuments from the inside. The case of the Irish megalithic tombs', *World Archaeology*, 22: 168–78.

Thomas, J. (2007), 'The internal features at Durrington Walls: investigations in the Southern Circle and Western Enclosures, 2005–2006'. In: M. Larsson and M. Parker Pearson (eds) *From Stonehenge to the Baltic. Living with Cultural Diversity in the Third Millennium BC*, pp. 145–57. Oxford: British Archaeological Reports.

Thörn, R. (2007), *Det ideologiska landskapet*. Malmö: Malmökulturmiljö.

Topping, P. (1992), 'The Penrith henges. A survey by the Royal Commission on the Historical Monuments of England', *Proceedings of the Prehistoric Society*, 58: 249–64.

Trigger, B. (1981), 'Archaeology and the ethnographic present', *Anthropologica*, 23: 3–17.

Trnka, G. (1991), *Studien zu mittelneolithischen Kreisgrabenanlagen*. Vienna: Verlag der Österreichischen Akademie der Wissenschaften.

Turner, V. (1969), *The Ritual Process*. London: Routledge and Kegan Paul.

Valera, A.C. (in press), 'Fossos sinuosos na Pré-História Reciente do Sul do Portugal: ensaio do analise crítica', *Actas de VI Encontro de Arquelogia do Sudoeste Peninsular*.

Van Dyke, R. (2007), *The Chaco Experience. Landscape and Ideology at the Center Place*. Santa Fe: School for Advanced Research Press.

Verger, S. ed. (2000), *Rites et espaces en pays celte et méditerranéen*. Rome: École française de Rome.

Victor, H. (2001), 'Bronsålderns kulthus—ett möte mellan profant och sakralt'. In: H. Bolin, A. Kaliff and T. Zachrisson (eds) *Mellan sten och brons*, pp. 133–52. Stockholm: Stockholm Archaeological Reports.

Victor, H. (2002), *Med graven som granne. Om bronsålderns kulthus*. Uppsala: Department of Archaeology and Ancient History, Uppsala University.

Villes, A. (1997), 'Les figurations dans les sépultures collectives neolithiques dans la Marne, dans le contexte du Bassin Parisien', *Brigantium*, 10: 149–77.

Waddell, J. (1998), *The Prehistoric Archaeology of Ireland*. Galway: Galway University Press.

Waddell, J., Fenwick, J. and Barton, K. (2009), *Rathcroghan. Archaeological and Geophysical Survey in a Ritual Landscape*. Dublin: Wordwell.

Waldren, W. (1982), *Balearic Ecology and Culture*. Oxford: British Archaeological Reports.

Wangen, V. (1998), 'Gravfeltet på Gunnarstorp. Et monument over dødsriter og kultutøvelse'. In: E. Østmo (ed.), *Fra Østfolds oltid*, pp. 153–71. Oslo: Universitetets Olssakamlings Skrifter.

Warner, R. (2000), 'Keeping out the Otherworld. The internal ditch at Navan and other Iron Age 'hengiform enclosures', *Emainia*, 18: 39–44.

Waterman, D. (1997), *Excavations at Navan Fort 1961–71*. Belfast: The Stationery Office.

Watkins, T. (2004), 'Building houses, framing concepts, constructing worlds', *Paléorient*, 30: 5–24.

Watkins, T. (2008), 'Supra-regional networks in the Neolithic of Southwest Asia', *Journal of World Prehistory*, 21, 139–71.

Watkins, T. (2010), 'New light on the Neolithic revolution in south-west Asia', *Antiquity*, 84: 621–34.

Watson, A. (2001), 'Composing Avebury', *World Archaeology*, 33: 296–314.

Watson, A. (2004), 'Making space for monuments: notes on the representation of experience'. In: C. Renfrew, C. Gosden and E. DeMarrais (eds) *Substance, Memory, Display*, pp. 79–96. Cambridge: McDonald Institute for Archaeological Research.

Webster, G. (1996), *A Prehistory of Sardinia 2300–500 BC*. Sheffield: Sheffield Academic Press.

Wells, P. (2007), 'Weapons, ritual and commemoration in Late Iron Age Northern Europe'. In: C. Haselgrove and T. Moore (eds) *The Later Iron Age in Britain and Beyond*, pp. 468–77. Oxford: Oxbow.

Whitehouse, R. (1981), 'Megaliths of the Central Mediterranean'. In: J.D. Evans, B. Cunliffe and C. Renfrew (eds) *Antiquity and Man*, pp. 106–27. London: Thames and Hudson.

White Marshall, J. and Walsh, C. (1998), 'Illaunloughan, Co. Kerry: an island hermitage'. In: M. Monk and J. Sheehan (eds) *Early Medieval Munster. Archaeology, History and Society*, pp. 201–11. Cork: Cork University Press.

Whiting, J. and Ayres, B (1968), 'Inferences from the shape of dwellings'. In: K.C. Chang (ed) *Settlement Archaeology*, pp. 117–33. Palo Alto: National Press Books.

Widholm, D. (1998), *Rösen, ristningar och riter*. Lund: Acta Archaeologica Lundensia.

Widholm, D. and Regnell, M. (2001), 'Grave monuments and landscape in South-eastern Sweden', *Lund Archaeological Review*, 7: 29–49.

Wieland, G. (1999), *Keltische Viereckschanzen. Einem Rätsel auf der Spur*. Stuttgart: Theiss.

Wilhelmi, K. (1990), 'Ruinen und Nordhorn. Zwischen Ussel und Ems: besondere Rechteck- und Quadratgräben der Eisenzeit', *Helinium*, 30: 93–122.

Willis, S. (2010), 'Roman Piercebridge', *Archaeological Journal*, 167: 228–33.

Index

Aillevans, megalithic tomb 71–2, 89, 91
Allées couvertes 83
Andrén, A. 153–4, 155
Arbor Low, henge 109
Archetypes, definition of 9
Art styles 21, 48–9, 60–6, 212
Atlantic Bronze Age 17, 200, 215
Avebury, henge 100, 111
Avenues, timber 183
Axis mundi 38–9

Balloy, Neolithic cemetery 82
Balnuaran of Clava, cemetery 105, 107, 113
Barnhouse, settlement 85
Bell Beakers 56–9, 213, 214
Beltane 3, 5
Beuys, J. 93–4, 95
Binford, L. 27
Borges, J. L. 24
Bougon, cemetery 88–9
Boyne Valley 7, 55, 80, 96
Brochs 16
Broomend of Crichie, henge 109
Bryn Celli Ddu, passage grave 103,
    104, 107

Callanish stone circle 102, 103, 107
Carnac 99–100
Carrowkeel, cemetery 80
Castro Culture 23, 195–9
Castros 23, 195–9, 210
    imposition of a street grid 198–9
Causewayed enclosures 145–6, 212
Cauvin, J. 48–9, 64–6, 67–8
Celtic art 6, 60–61, 62–4, 65–6
Chaco Canyon 156–7
Christian art in Ireland 63–4, 66
Citânia de Briteiros 198
Clava Cairns 104–5
Comita, in Roman architecture 158
Corded Ware 56
Corlea, wooden road 135
Corrymony, passage grave 105
Cosmology 36, 42, 59
    and the shoreline 181
    and the sun 181–3
    Bronze Age 180–2
    Old Norse 154
Crith Gablach 200–2

Cult houses, Northern Europe 166, 167–8,
    181, 210

De Bogen, settlement and round
    barrows 163–4, 168, 169, 177
Developmental cycle of human groups 28
Domus de janas 72–3, 80, 89, 91, 116
Douglas, M. 25–7
Dunadd, royal centre 64
Durrington Walls, henge 128–30, 134
Dyffryn Lane, stone circle 109

Eketorp, ringfort 152–3, 154–5, 156, 159
Eliade, M. 9
Enclosed graveyards, Ireland 202
Ethnography 21, 25–6, 27, 33, 50–2, 185–6
Etruscans 17

Feasting 30, 128, 131–2, 134
Filitosa, torri 121–2
Fire cult 3, 5, 6, 7
Flannery, K. 25–7, 28, 30, 32, 41
'Flat' settlements, in Central Europe 140

Garton Slack, cemetery 147
Gender, and visual culture 48, 49, 52, 52, 67
Giraldus Cambrensis 203
Glastonbury, lake village 61
Göbekli Tepe, temple 43–4, 212
Goseck, roundel 143–5, 156
Gournay-sur-Aronde, sanctuary 146–7
Great Houses 22, 114, 115, 124, 125
Gregory, R. 161
Grooved Ware 53–6
Grydehoj, mortuary house 167–8

Haddenham, shrine 150–1
Hågahögen, barrow and cult house 168
Hallstatt, cemetery 66
Henges 22, 97
    and rites of passage 110–11
    and stone circles 107–12
    and timber circles 125, 128–30
    as containers of supernatural forces 109–10
    chronology of 108
    comparison with amphitheatres 108–9
    relationship to passage graves 102–7
Hodder, I. 26, 49, 66
Hogans 37–9, 40

Hopewell Culture 124, 128
House models 46–7, 48, 52, 188
House plans
    and the storage of wealth 30
    apsidal 13
    oval 13, 57
    symbolic significance of 33–9
House urns 47–8
Houses
    abandonment of 12, 74–5, 140, 141,
        142, 175
    as living creatures 73–4, 84–5
    as metaphor for the social group 73–4
    as prototypes for temples 43–3
    as prototypes for tombs 71–4, 75–6
    beneath round barrows 169–72
    burning of 12, 74–5, 140, 141, 142
    cross-cultural analysis of plans 27, 32, 33
    decorated 45–56
    enlargement of 28–30
    internal organization of 40–1
    repair of 28
    subterranean 43
Human Relations Area Files 27
Hunter gatherers, dwellings of 10–11, 27, 43
Hypogea, Mediterranean 72–3, 76

Illaunloughan, hermitage 202
Impressed Wares 13, 215
Inauguration mounds, Ireland 203
Inishkea 63
Ireland, ancient provinces of 4, 135–6
Ismantorp, ringfort 151–2, 154–6, 159

Jung, C. 9

Kassel, '7000 oaks' 93
Kivas 22
Kivik, cairn and cult houses 168
Knockaulin, royal centre 125–6, 134
Knocknarea, cemetery 80
Knossos, settlement 11
Knowth, cemetery 80

La Haute Mée, settlement 93
La Tène, art style 60–2
    river deposit at 60
    Ultimate La Tène art style in Ireland 62–4
Le Grand Menhir Brisé 98
Lepenski Vir, settlement 10–11
Linear Pottery Culture 13, 30, 53, 59, 74–5,
    81–2, 87, 214, 215
Lismullin, enclosure 134
Longhouses/rectangular houses 12–13, 21,
    53, 57, 75, 81–2, 161–2, 163, 169–72,
    175–7, 210–11

and circular monuments 163–4, 169–73,
    175–9
as prototypes for long mounds,
    Neolithic 71–2, 74–6, 81–4, 86–8
as prototypes for long mounds, Late Bronze
    Age/Iron Age 177
Long Meg and her Daughters, stone circle 100
Long mounds/long cairns 21, 71–2, 76–8,
    81–4
Los Millares, settlement and cemetery 14–15,
    79–80, 91
Loughcrew,
    Iron Age bone flakes 207–8
    megalithic art at 207
    megalithic cemetery at 207–8, 217–18
Lunulae 56

Manching, internal enclosure 146
Maeshowe, passage grave 85, 104, 107
Mayburgh, henge 111
Megalithic art 53–6, 65, 84, 91–2, 96
Megalithic tombs 71–2, 75–8, 116
    chronology of 76–8
    distribution of 76–8
    orientations of 85
    regional styles of 77–8
Metalwork, decorated 56–64
Midh 4, 135–6
Mobility and house forms 32
Monasteries, Ireland 202
Monte d'Accodi, monument 116–17
Monte Saraceno de Ravanusa, settlement 188
Moore, H. 26
Mote of Mark, royal centre 64
Motillas 15, 120–1, 123
Mortuary houses 167–8, 181
Mucking, ringwork 130–2
Mycenaeans 17, 119

Nankani, settlements of 51–2
Navajo, houses of 37–9
Navan Fort, royal centre 125–6, 132–5
Navetas 122
Neolithic Revolution 11
Ness of Brodgar, settlement 128
Newgrange, passage grave 97, 105, 107, 113
Nordic Bronze Age 214
North Cameroon, traditional housing 185–6
Nuba, settlements of 50–1
Nuraghi 16, 116–20, 210
    models of nuraghi 16, 118

Odensala Prästgård, hillfort 167
Orkney, Neolithic 53–6, 80, 82–3, 86,
    91, 101
Ozieri Culture 72–3

Passage graves 53–6, 75–8, 79–81, 210, 212
 and stone circles 102–7
 solar orientations of 104
Pastoralists, dwellings of 27, 33
Perigueux, Roman temple 148
Piercebridge, roundhouse and Roman
  villa 194–5
Pirá-piraná, longhouses of 36–9, 42, 85
Pit houses 12
Plaggen soils 173
Pléchâtel, timber buildings 84
Plough marks, under barrows 170–2
Polgár-Csöszhalom, settlement and tell 140,
  141–3, 156, 159
Pollution, concepts of 26
Pottery, decoration of 53–61
Pre-pottery Neolithic 11
Proto-castros 196
Proto-nuraghi 117

Rath of the Synods, royal centre 18–19, 202
Rathgall, hillfort 132
Rathnew, royal centre 5
Ring barrows, Ireland 180
Ringforts, Bronze Age 22, 125–6, 130–2
 in Ireland 200–203
 on Öland 151–6
Rock art
 in Britain and Ireland 55, 65
 in north-west Iberia 198, 208–9
Romano-Celtic temples 147–51
Rome 13
Round mounds/round cairns 8, 19–20, 23, 56,
  76–81, 83, 86–8, 90–2, 163–4, 164–6,
  167–8, 169–72, 212
 and roads 173–4
 on coast or offshore islands 174–5
 relationship to roundhouses 175–6, 177–80
 reuse of 214
 use of turves in 172–3
Roundels 22, 139–40, 142–6, 157–8
 orientations of 143, 144, 159
Roundhouses 7–8, 13, 14, 16, 17–18, 22,
  28–30, 32, 50–2, 53–7, 59–60, 126–7, 147,
  161–3, 175–6
 in Iron Age Sicily 188, 211
 in Roman Britain 189–91
 in the Castro Culture 192–4, 195, 196–9
 practicalities of construction and
  maintenance 27–32, 33–45, 211
 relationship to passage graves 72–3, 79–80,
  86–8, 89–92
 relationship to round barrows 161–3,
  175–6
 relationship to Roman villas in
  Britain 190–1

Romano-British 191–2, 211
 symbolism of 23–45, 211
Royal centres (Ireland) 4, 6, 22, 126, 132–5,
  210
 siting of 134

Sacred art 61, 64, 65–6, 212–13
Sacred wells 118–19
Sanctuaries, in Gaul 146–7
Sanfins, castro 198–9
Sant' Andrea Priu, tomb 73
Sarnowo, cemetery 82
Sarup, enclosure with nearby cemetery 87–8
Sesi 120
Settlements, internal organization of 30–2
Shap, stone avenue 100
Sicily, Iron Age 187–9
 changing house plans 188–9
Silchester, Roman town 192–4
Skedemosse, votive deposit 151
Son Fornés, talayot 122
Space, perceptions of 33–5, 40–2, 184–5,
  211–12, 215, 218
Specchie 120
Square barrows 147
Standing stones 21–2, 95–6
Stanton Drew, stone circles 107
Statue menhirs 95–6, 112, 117, 121
 distribution of 98,
Stone alignments 21–2, 98–102, 112
 distribution of 98
Stone circles 21–2, 97, 98–112
 and henges 107–112, 113
 and passage graves 102–7
 and stone avenues 100
 chronology of 102–7
 folklore of 97–8
 grading of monoliths 101
 orientations of 101
 sources of raw material 107
Stone, symbolic properties of 93–5, 97
Stonehenge 107, 111, 129–30
Stones of Stenness, henge 104, 108,
  111, 127
Stora Kalvö, island cemetery 164–6, 169, 174
Sutton Hoo, cemetery 64

Talayots 16, 120, 122
Tara, royal centre 4, 6, 18–19, 105, 132, 135,
  210
Tells 12, 140, 141–2, 145–6
Thetford, temple 148–9
Thorny Down, settlement 161–2, 177–8
Thwing, ringwork 130–2
Timber circles 125, 126, 128, 178–9
 orientations of 128

Tombi di giganti 117, 121–2
Torri 16, 120, 121–2
Traditions, invention of 6

Uivar, tell 140–1, 145, 156, 159
Uisneach, royal centre 3–7, 9, 109, 135–6, 218
Urnfield Complex 48, 215

Ursel-Rozenstraat, cemetery 149–50

Viereckschanzen 146
Vulci 47

Wood, symbolic properties of 93–5
Woodhenge, timber circle 128–30